CRANFORD PUBLIC LIBRARY N.J.

3 9520 00077 1859

Free Public Library
Cranford, N. J.

W9-DDX-066

The Mother Tongue

Books by the same author

Mathematics for the Million

Science for the Citizen

The Loom of Language (by Frederick Bodmer)
(edited and arranged by Lancelot Hogben)

From Cave Painting to Comic Strip

Essential World English

Mathematics in the Making

Free Public Library
Cranford, N. J.

The
Mother
Tongue

by

Lancelot Hogben

NEW YORK

W · W · NORTON & COMPANY · INC ·

Copyright © 1964 by Lancelot Hogben

First American Edition 1965

Library of Congress Catalog Card No. 64-18750

PRINTED IN THE UNITED STATES OF AMERICA

1 2 3 4 5 6 7 8 9 0

Contents

Quiz sections are to be found at the ends of Chapters

List of illustrations

Foreword

Throughout this book I have used the most modern Danish spelling convention which substitutes $\mathring{A}$, $\mathring{a}$ for *AA, aa,* thus bringing Danish orthography into line with Swedish and Norwegian. I have usually cited the ablative singular case form of a Latin noun because this tallies with the singular one of Italian, Portuguese and Spanish.

Before the invention of printing, individual scriveners (copyists) used different conventions of English spelling. These partly, but not wholly, reflect local dialect differences, and present the writer with a wide range of choice. Thus Wright's grammar of Old English cites *eom, eam* and *am* for our (*I*) *am,* and *eowic, eow* and *iow* for our *you.* In citing an O.E. word, what has commonly dictated my selection is whether the spelling most closely resembles that of a familiar contemporary descendant.

If I have sometimes labelled an exhibit as the English of Alfred the Great, the reader should therefore interpret this to refer to English as spoken in his time and not necessarily to the English (Wessex) dialect Alfred himself used.

Some who have read the proofs of this book have expressed disappointment at the fact that I have made so little use of the International Phonetic script. This is partly because it is impossible to convey the equivalent value of unfamiliar, more especially vowel, sounds without the free issue of a phonograph record. It is also because no rendering of Anglo-American vowel sounds could be commonly acceptable to Scotsmen and Kentish men, Virginians and Canadians, New Zealanders and Australians.

To critics disposed to accuse me of being too vowel shy, I would add that Jewish scholars equipped only with a consonantal alphabet laid the foundations of comparative linguistics by recognition of the Semitic family about a millennium before the work of Jones and Grimm on the affinities of the Indo-European languages.

I am deeply indebted to Maureen Cartwright, who prepared the final MS for press while I was in British Guiana. Joyce Sparer and Peter Simms kindly assisted her in preparation of the galleys.

Acknowledgments

The illustrations on pp. 90 and 131 are reproduced from *The Signs of Civilisation* by Lancelot Hogben, by courtesy of Rathbone Books Ltd.

Those on pp. 53, 84, 87, 93, 96, 97, 99, 103 and 104, and the illustrations of the Rosetta Stone reproduced from *The Loom of Language*, by Frederick Bodmer, appear by courtesy of George Allen and Unwin Ltd.

The illustrations of an Early Paper Mill, Playing Cards and a specimen of Caxton's books are reproduced from *Cave Painting to Comic Strip* by Professor Hogben, by courtesy of the Trustees of the British Museum.

The Trustees of the British Museum have also kindly given permission for reproduction of early Anglo-Saxon writings

The illustration of the Welsh Railway Station in Anglesey appears by courtesy of D. B. Hutton, Esq.

The Mother Tongue

The Argument

Being what this book is about

1 It is often said that those of us who have grown up as members of the largest literate speaking community in the world of today are notoriously bad linguists.

2 We have the excuse that most of us are not in everyday contact with frontiers and few of us live in bilingual or multilingual societies.

3 None the less, English-speaking adolescents have the advantage of being able to make a useful start by taking pen-friends speaking other tongues.

4 This great advantage arises from our hybrid heritage. From Low German settlers in Britain (subsequently occupied by Scandinavian conquerors and immigrants) we have inherited a broad basis of grammar and vocabulary as a passport to any of the contemporary Teutonic languages, in particular to Dutch, German, Swedish, Danish and Norwegian.

5 As a result of the Norman Conquest of England and of the long struggle of Norman-English kings to conquer France, we have also assimilated a considerable vocabulary which is basically a modern descendant of Latin, whence closely related not merely to French, but also to Italian, to Spanish and to Portuguese.

6 Through Church scholarship, the Law, and the present-day advance of science, the Anglo-American, more than any other, speech community has assimilated a vast vocabulary of ancestral Latin and of Greek terms.

7 Such then is the heritage which the historical sketch of Chapter 2 discloses. The aim of this book is to make the best use of it. That of our first chapter is to give a foretaste of how we can do so by making lively familiar associations to words we may meet in unfamiliar guise.

8 To accomplish our aim, we have to take stock of the way in which pronunciation has changed in the centuries which separate the English of Alfred the Great (O.E.) from the Anglo-American of Abraham Lincoln.

9   We can hope to make sense of such changes only if we start (Chapter 3) with a historical survey of the vagaries of English spelling and the rich mine of clues which its inconsistencies equip us to exploit as memory-aids. Against this background, a study (Chapter 4) of the way in which pronunciation changes discloses a programme for memorising, with the minimum of effort, a vocabulary for self-expression in more than a dozen European languages.

10   Two other chapters (5 and 6) deal with a difficulty different from that of assembling a vocabulary. The gap which separates the grammar of O.E. from that of Anglo-American is even greater than that which separates Anglo-American from German or from French and its Latin sisters; and we can intelligently sidestep some of the pitfalls of an alien grammar by learning a little about how that of the mother tongue has changed.

11   The writer hopes that English-speaking readers of this book will likewise wish to learn (Chapter 7) how the resources of their hybrid heritage furnish them with a passport to the international vocabulary of modern science based almost exclusively on classical Latin or (increasingly) on Greek roots.

12   This leaves us with one topic (Chapter 8) of much-neglected importance to an intellectually mature person who starts to learn any foreign language. Here we may leave it as an open question: what do we try to convey when we assert that a French or German word *means the same* as an English one (and *vice versa*)?

1

Our Hybrid Heritage

A contemporary adult or adolescent, reared within an English-speaking community, approaches the study of another language with an initial handicap and a considerable advantage. The handicap merits no more than a single paragraph; for one reason or another, it is sufficiently familiar. But the advantage which is the main theme of this book is one of which few highly-educated persons are well aware. One reason for this is that formal education does nothing, or next to nothing, to exploit it. Otherwise there would be no need to record what follows.

Many Europeans such as the Swiss, Alsatians and Belgians are bilingual by upbringing or dwell near frontiers on either side of which people speak different languages. If, as is true of the Scandinavians and the Dutch, they belong to relatively small speech communities, they cannot look forward to instruction through the written word at a high level in their mother tongues because printing costs are prohibitive, and some familiarity with at least one of the leading western European languages (English, Spanish, French and German) is almost a *sine qua non* of success in salesmanship or secretarial work in the world of trade. Thus very many Europeans have frequent opportunities for the use of a language foreign to the home; and many have a powerful incentive for studying one or more.

Contrariwise, most people who habitually use English as their medium of communication never mingle with people who speak any other language. Only the few who live along the Mexican border of the United States and along the frontiers of Quebec Province come into daily contact with sizeable speech communities other than their own. With large populations of Afro-Asians who use English as their medium of higher education, they enjoy the advantage of being able to purchase textbooks and translations of high quality at the lowest available price. For these or other reasons connected with the circumstance that contemporary English, henceforth referred to as Anglo-American, is the largest literate speech community in the world, its citizens have little direct incentive to study, and few opportunities to use, any language but their own. On the other side of the balance sheet, they enjoy the immense benefit of their *hybrid heritage*.

The meaning of the expression last used will not be wholly clear to many readers of *The Mother Tongue*, still less will its benefits be self-evident. To be sure, the overwhelming majority may know that the language of England for five centuries before the Norman Conquest (A.D. 1066) was a mixture of Teutonic dialects, and as such allied to Dutch, German and the Scandinavian tongues; that the language of the English ruling classes and of the law courts for three centuries afterwards was French; that French of that time, like Italian, Spanish, Catalan,

Portuguese and Roumanian, was a descendant of the provincial Latin of the Roman Empire; and that an enormous number of words based on the Latin of the Empire have been added to our vocabulary through the influence of the Church, of Law, and of advancing scientific knowledge. However, these considerations add up to little, unless we are alert to the peculiar difficulty which confronts an intelligent Anglo-American adolescent or adult intent on learning a foreign language.

Nothing can alter the fact that a beginner has to commit to memory a heavy load of words and rules before there is any appreciable reward for effort; but teachers of foreign languages pay little attention to how one can minimise the tedium of memorisation. None the less, it is a commonplace that we remember a new item of information most readily if we can relate it by lively association to what we already know or to what enlists our interest. Whence it should also be, but alas is not, a commonplace that the likelihood of investing with lively associations a word foreign to our own language habits is greater if its source is closely *related* to our language. Lucklessly, language relationship is to most learners a closed book and to most of their teachers at best a somewhat nebulous concept.

Before we scrutinise a few examples of the art of forming lively associations as an aid to language learning, let us first be clear about what we mean by language relationship, e.g. when we classify the major ingredients of our Anglo-American vocabulary as members either of the *Teutonic* clan or of the *Romance* (Latin) clan. Professional students of the science of comparative linguistics say that languages are related primarily when a large proportion of the words in two languages are *detectably* of common origin in the sense that members of the same pair have come to be different by changes of pronunciation over a long period of time in different regions of what was once a single speech community, e.g. Italy, Gaul and the Iberian Peninsula at the beginning of the Christian era. The number of such pairs which are detectably alike and the extent to which age has masked their resemblance is our criterion of whether two languages are more or less closely related.

If very closely related, as is English to Swedish by virtue of its Teutonic parentage, one needs few clues to make the distinction between what is detectable and what is not. For instance, many bright young children, having less prejudice than adults about the proprieties of spelling, would need only (at most) the clue that two Swedes were leaving the homestead, when one said to the other: SKALL VI GÅ NU? This example illustrates different ways in which age can mask clues to common ancestry. In Swedish spelling Å stands roughly for the sound of *aw* in *paw*. In the long story of the evolution of the Teutonic clan, we can confidently conclude that the *v*-sound, spelt V in Scandinavian, replaced what was once the *w*-sound in Anglo-American WE or WISH, and that the *sh* sound of *ship* has in many words replaced the *sk* of *skate*. In Swedish SK stands for both sounds, presumably because the shift occurred much later in Swedish than in English and never affected so large a proportion of words. The I of VI stands for its sound in *élite*.

Here, as elsewhere in this book, we shall restrict to the use of consonants our discussion of how pronunciation changes in the evolution of minor local dialects to languages not inter-communicable at any level—spoken or written. This is partly because we recognise on the printed page similarities of word-pairs of the sort under discussion mainly, if not wholly, by their consonants, partly because vowel values of inter-communicable dialects may be widely different and partly because the sound values of the vowel signs A, E, I, O, U, in closely related languages may be widely different. Indeed, French and English share no simple vowel values which are precisely alike, whence their use of the same signs cannot tally. Since nothing has brought comparative linguistics as an aid to learning into disrepute more than speculation about the evolutionary history of vowel sounds, we recommend at the outset the exercise (Quiz 1) at the end of this chapter.

The reader may next try out, as an exercise in detection, two other Quiz exhibits. The first (Quiz 2) illustrates the use of languages placed in one of three clans spoken at one time or another in the homeland of the Anglo-American speech community:

(a) the *Celtic* clan before and throughout the Roman occupation (*circa* 600 B.C. to A.D. 420);

(b) the *Teutonic* clan throughout the subsequent period which embraces the Scandinavian occupation and ends with the Norman Conquest;

(c) the *Latin* clan during 300 years when the Norman and Plantagenet nobility spoke French.

In Quiz 2, we have a sentence from the Lord's Prayer in Old English (*circa* A.D. 900) and in twelve modern European languages which an understanding of our hybrid heritage enormously reduces the tedium of learning.

Henceforth, we shall speak of any of the items included under (b) and (c) as our sister languages. Our third exhibit (Quiz 3) gives us a foretaste of their place in a wider speech community, the great *Indo-European* family which embraces (in addition to the foregoing clans) Greek, from which modern science has taken so many terms now in everyday Anglo-American usage, Russian and the other Slav languages, Persian, Hindu and Sanskrit, the ancestral language of North India and Pakistan in Homeric times.

To weave these strands into a fabric of lively associations, it should now be clear that we need to acquaint ourselves with: (i) how pronunciation changes in such a way as to generate different languages within a territory where the inhabitants could communicate at an earlier period without misunderstanding; (ii) how different uses of their writing signs reflect such changes. We also need to know a little about the way in which the meanings of words change. Such changes are on the agenda for the latter part of this chapter and in the final one.

Fig. 1.   Map of Roman Britain, A.D. 300.

At the outset, it is necessary to insert a few words about spelling. Otherwise we shall bog ourselves down in a mass of confusion between what the eye and the ear respectively recognise. All the sister languages of Anglo-American use the same Roman alphabet augmented by two Greek letters (Y and Z) and at least one arte-fact (J); but they do not use all the signs in the same way. Thus J may have four different values. In Spanish it stands for the *ch* of *loch* in Scots dialect and *auch* in German. In Italian, as in German, Dutch and the Scandinavian languages, it has the value of *y* in *yesterday*. In French it has a sound for which Anglo-American spelling makes no explicit provision, the one common to *measure, treasure, leisure, effusion, illusion, confusion, collusion*. All the foregoing uses are different from that of the English J in *jam*. Similarly, Z has widely different values. In German and Italian it stands for the sound of *ts* in *cats*. In Spanish it stands for that of *th* in *thin*. At the beginning of a Dutch word its value corresponds to the English *z* in *zebra*; but between two vowels it may commonly represent the *s* in *sin*.*

From these examples, it will be clear that we can side-step misunderstanding only if we enlist a convention to distinguish the written sign from the spoken sound. In this book, we shall use capitals for the *signs* as such and lower case (small) letters for the corresponding sounds. For instance, S in English may stand for the *s*-sound of *sin* and *this* or the *z*-sound of *zebra* in *his* and *muse*. Similarly, the English F may stand for the *f*-sound in *off* and for the *v*-sound in *of*.

Having completed this book, the reader should be able to mitigate the hard grind of learning about fifteen European languages. Many readers, perhaps most, will have at least a nodding acquaintance with French or German or both. To illustrate some of the requirements of a programme of language learning to lighten the load on the memory by exploiting our hybrid heritage, let us therefore select examples of German and French words. For memorising any of them, conventional methods of teaching rarely offer us a recipe for agreeable (or even painless) diges-tion, and if the immediate outcome is not manifest at first sight, they should give the receptive reader a foretaste of the many ways in which language learning could be fun.

Our discussion will presuppose the recognition of a threefold division of the Teutonic clan into North, East and West branches. Where we henceforth speak of

---

* Except in the Language Museum (pp. 155-160), we shall not elsewhere cite Portuguese with French, Italian and Spanish examples of words of like origin; but the following remarks on the consonant signs may be helpful: C and G each have two values equivalent to those of French, and J like the second G value is equivalent to the French J. The symbol Z may stand for *z* as in *zebra* or be equivalent to the French-Portuguese J. Portuguese S, like G, J and Z, may have this value, also, like S in English, either the pure *s* of *hiss* or the *z*-sound in *his*; and it can also have, like German S before certain consonants, the sound value of *sh* in *ship*. The couplets CH, LH, NH in native words are respectively like CH in *chef*, LL in *billiards* and NY in *Bunyan*.

Scandinavian (North Teutonic) we signify: (a) the very closely akin official languages of Sweden, Norway and Denmark themselves less far apart than the Buchan dialect of Aberdeen and the Somerset dialect of England; (b) Icelandic, which differs very little from the Old Norse of the Scandinavian conquerors of, and settlers in, Britain before the Norman Conquest. We shall also have occasion to mention the now extinct *Gothic* (East Teutonic) because by far the earliest available written record of a Teutonic language is a Gothic translation of the Gospels (*circa* A.D. 360) by a Byzantine bishop, Ulfilas. This is the so-called *Codex Argenteus* preserved in the museum of Uppsala in Sweden. Its antiquity, which places it nearest an as yet unknown ancestral Teutonic, confirms many inferences which comparative study of other sources compels us to make. To forestall misunderstanding in what follows, our third division of the Teutonic clan, West Teutonic or Germanic, calls for more detailed comment.

When one speaks of Old English before the coming of the Norsemen as a mixture of *Low German* dialects, one means dialects most closely allied to what are now severally called Dutch in Holland, Flemish in Belgium and *Platt-Deutsch* in the countryside of North Germany. What is now the official German of Germany (East or West), Austria and Switzerland is what philologists call *High German*, distinguished at an early date from Low German, Gothic and Scandinavian by some very characteristic changes of pronunciation, collectively known as the *Second Teutonic Sound Shift*. Throughout the rest of this chapter, we shall speak of modern Low German as Dutch and of modern High German as German. For brevity we shall refer to English before the Norman Conquest as O.E.

On this understanding, let us now see how much fun learning new words in a Teutonic and in a Romance language may be. We shall start with twenty-one German words.

1. AUGE shares the same ancestry with *augo* (Gothic), *oog* (Du.), *øje* (Dan.), *öga* (Swed.)* and the O.E. word EAGE. Before a front vowel† (*e* or *i*) the O.E. *g* gave place to the sound of *y* in *ye*, whence the later spelling *eye*. This change was probably complete before the Norman Conquest. Finally, the consonantal *y* faded out in the single diphthong syllable, as now pronounced. A parallel change took place in Swedish, but did not go so far; thus *öga* retains the hard *g* of *Auge*. In the Norwegian equivalent *øye*, spelling keeps in step with the sound change; but *y*

---

* We have seen that Swedish (like Norwegian and Danish) uses Å for a sound (till recently spelt AA in Danish) like AW in *paw*. Swedish uses Ö where Danish and Norwegian use ø for a sound roughly like U in *fur*, and Ä where Danish and Norwegian use Æ for either a short English E as in *men* or AI in *fair*. The Celtic alphabet of the Anglo-Saxon monks used Æ for a sound like A in *hat*.

† One speaks of vowels as *front* or *back* according to the position of the tip of the tongue.

itself retains its value as a consonant. In Danish G usually retains its hard (*g*) sound value: *øje* is a conspicuous exception.

2. BAUM, for which the Dutch equivalent is *boom*, recalls one of two synonyms of O.E., *viz.* TREO and BEAM. The former recalls the Scandinavian word for *tree*, i.e. *træ* (Dan.) and *träd* (Swed.) shortened to *trä* for *timber, wood*. *Beam* has now a more restricted use, dating from the time when whole tree trunks made up the structural framework of a domestic building. However, it retains its original meaning in compound folk names for some British trees, e.g. *whitebeam, hornbeam*.

3. BLUME, corresponding to *bloem* in Dutch, turns up in Chaucer's time as *bloom*. Here the Old Norse (*blomi*) for *flower* appears to have ousted O.E. BLOSTMA which is the ancestor of *blossom*, the latter reminiscent of *blomst* (Dan.) and *blomster* (Swed.) by an inversion not uncommon, e.g. English dialect *axed* for *asked*. Both *bloom* and *blossom* have largely given way to the Norman invader *flower*, which we recognise as equivalent to Modern French *fleur* in *fleur de lys*. The corresponding adjective *floral* illustrates the dual nature of the Latin part of our hybrid heritage. On the one hand, we inherit through the Norman Conquest a corrupt Latin of what had been the Roman province of Gaul, e.g. *père* and *mère*. On the other hand, scholarship has equipped us increasingly with a vocabulary of classical Latin, as illustrated by the corresponding adjectives *paternal* and *maternal*, likewise based on *pater* and *mater*. As we shall see more fully at a later stage (p. 42 and p. 151), both Anglo-American and Modern French have many couplets of which the members are traceable to different stages in the evolution of the same word, e.g. English *frail* and *fragile*, *royal* and *regal*, *loyal* and *legal*.

4. FEIND. This corresponds to FEOND in O.E., *fijands* (Gothic), *vijand* (Dutch), *fiende* (Swed.) and *fjende* (Dan.), the original meaning of which was displaced in English by recourse to the French word *ennemi*. It is akin to the primitive Teutonic verb for *hate*, in Gothic *fijan*. The O.E. equivalent of *enmity* is *feondscipe* (=fiendship), in Dutch *vijandschap*. We use its survivor in modern English, i.e. *fiend*, chiefly for celestial enemies (devils), whence people we dislike intensely; but we meet it in its earlier more general connotation in the Anglo-Saxon version of the parable of the tares in the cornfield (Matt. xiii, 25): *tha com his feonda sum and ofer-seow hit mid coccele on middan tham hwæte* (=then came some enemy of his and sowed it over with cockles in amid the wheat). We here render *coccele*, translated in the modern English Bible as *tares* (*Vicia* sp.), as *cockles*, a word which still survives in the folkname for a British wheat-field weed called the *corn cockle*. It is worthy of note that spelling here gives us no clue to the different origin of the name *cockle* for an edible British coastal clam, so called from French *coquille* (=shell, as in *shellfish*).

5. KNABE, unlike the preceding, may at first sight suggest nothing even to those of us who already know that the *b*-sound in German words commonly replaces the *v*-sound of an English word between two vowels. Of three O.E. words for *boy* (the last-named word, a late immigrant, possibly from the Frisian Islands) one was CNAFA. To make use of this fact, we need a little premedication about O.E. spelling and how words acquire sometimes a more exalted, sometimes a more derogatory, meaning. O.E. derived its alphabet from Celtic monks in the early Roman form, which lacks the Greek intruder K. Thus C had its hard value, as in *cat*. By the same token,* the alphabet of the monks had no symbol for the *v*-sound in *knave*. Thus F did service for both the *v*- and the *f*-sound as in *of* and *off*. At the beginning of a word its sound value was *f*. Usually between two vowels it had the *v* value in *of*. During the century of transition after the Norman Conquest, terminal A became E, just as terminal A (e.g. *öga* above) where retained in Swedish and Icelandic has given place to E in Danish (e.g. *øje*) and Norwegian (e.g. *øye*). We have thus reconstructed the descendant of CNAFA as *knave*, fully pronounced with initial K as two syllables in Chaucer's time. Even the original CNAFA could have a slightly discouraging meaning, on all fours with that of the *house-boy* of the Colonial *Herrenvolk*. Today we all associate it with the card-pack house-boy who stole the tarts, and its meaning is now wholly derogatory; but *Knabe* is the customary German equivalent of the contemporary word *boy* and as such has no essentially derogatory content. Side by side with CNAFA, two other words for *boy* were in use, one of which is the key to our next item. The other, CNAPA, is equivalent to the contemporary Dutch equivalent (*knaap*) for *boy*.

6. KNECHT is both the German and the Dutch word for a man-servant. Its ancestral equivalent in O.E. (CNIHT = *boy*) has no derogatory implication, and the descendant of the latter has an exalted significance. The initial CN calls for no further comment, but we need to know that H before T or at the end of a word in O.E. spelling has the guttural sound retained in Scots dialect and perpetuated by Scots comedians as in *a bra brecht munlicht necht* = *a fine* (Scandinavian *bra*) *bright moonlight night*. Tudor English employs GH where German and Dutch exhibit CH; and Anglo-American spelling retains it as a dummy. With this clue, we have arrived at *knight*. In the O.E. version of the New Testament Gospels, the disciples are LEORNING-CNIHTA, i.e. *learning boys*, and there was as yet no tie-up, as in the time of Chaucer, between knighthood and *chivalry*, a word of French origin related to *chevalier*, literally a *horseman*. It is no accident that the words for *knight* in the sister Teutonic languages, *Ritter* (Germ.), *ridder* (Du. and Dan.), *riddare* (Swed.), each

---

* In the Roman alphabet of Caesar U and V were different ways of writing the same sign on wax or stone. Each, like Welsh W, could have a consonantal value (the *w* of *woe*) before a vowel at the beginning of a word, elsewhere short like U in *full* or long like OO in *fool*.

recall *rider*. Like *chevalier*, these belong to an age when horsemanship was a preroga-
tive of nobility. *Chevalier* itself calls for further comment *en passant*. Before *a*, Latin
hard *c* acquired the *sh-* sound represented in French spelling by CH (as in *chef*).
Thus *chien* and *canine* are a couplet on all fours with *fleur* and *floral* mentioned above.
One Latin word for horse was *caballus*, whence the zoological (Linnaean) name for
the domestic horse, *Equus caballus*. The Spanish word for a gentleman is *caballero*,
being a person one can more confidently trust with horses than with women.
Between vowels, Latin *b* becomes *v* in Italian as in French. Thus the Italian word
for *horse* is *cavallo*, as in *cavalry* and *cavalier*.

7. REICH, like *rijk* (Du.), *rig-rige* (Dan.), *rik-rike* (Swed.), has a double meaning,
the most familiar of which is *realm* or *empire*; but it also means *rich*, the adjectival
value being traceable to an era when land ownership was the hallmark of opulence.
O.E. RICE has both meanings, one of which survives in *bishopric*, otherwise ousted
by French *realm* or by another O.E. word, CYNINGDOM, the ancestor of *kingdom*.
However, the O.E. version of the New Testament Gospels always refers to the
kingdom of heaven as *heofena rice*, never as *heofena cyningdom*. To recognise the connexion of RICE and Anglo-American *rich*, we need to know that the *k*-sound before
a *front* vowel (*e* or *i*) gradually gave way to the sound represented by CH as in *chat*.
Like the *g-y* sound shift already mentioned, this was largely complete (see p. 141)
by the time the Normans arrived. Where we now find SH at the beginning of a
word, we find SC in O.E. and SK in Swedish or Icelandic. This betokens a shift of
pronunciation which went on slowly *pari passu* with the *g-y* and *k-ch* changes in the
same situation, i.e. before a front vowel. SH (=*sh*) at the beginning of an Anglo-
American word is a signpost of native (i.e. Teutonic) origin. Contrariwise, SH
with the same sound value *sh* at the end of an Anglo-American verb (as in *finish*) is
an equally reliable signpost of French origin, unless the word is a monosyllable
(e.g. *fish*, *wish* or *wash*). Nearly all such words (e.g. *abolish*, *furnish*) belong to the
class of French verbs which have an augmented stem in the plural, e.g. *finir*, to
finish, *nous finissons*, we finish. The reader who has any acquaintance with French
may here ask how it happens that the French word *riche* is so much like the native
English *rich* with the same meaning. The answer is that it is a descendant of *riki*, one
of the words that the Teutonic Franks bequeathed to the country named after them.
Ricco in Italian and *rico* in Spanish with the same meaning are bequests of the
occupation of Italy and Spain by Teutonic Goths and Vandals. In Gothic, *reiks*
means both *mighty* and *prince* or *ruler*. This is clearly equivalent to Latin *rex* (stem
reg-) and Irish *ri* (stem *riog-*) for *king*. In Sanskrit, *raj* = *rule* (cf. *Raja*(*h*) = *king*) exhibits
the German *Reich* as part of the common stock of Indo-European words. Closely
related to Latin *rex* are *regale* (*regal*) and *regulare* (*regulate*) from which, through
French, English derives *royal* and *rule*(*r*).

8. SCHINKEN-BRÖTCHEN is none other than a *ham sandwich*; but we find ourselves in unexpected company if we digest it thoroughly. Let us start with the second part. German *Brötchen* is a diminutive of *Brot*, Dutch *brood*, Danish *brød*, Swedish *bröd* and O.E. BREAD (spelt now as before). In isolation one uses it for a roll, in combination for a sandwich. Like *skinke* (Dan.) and *skinka* (Swed.), *Schinken* is the German for English and Dutch *ham*, which is the proximal part of the hind leg of the *Schwein* (English *swine*). Its ancestry is the same as that of the O.E. word SCANCA for *leg*, as in the expression *Shanks's pony* or *Shanks's mare* (=one's own legs). German *Bein*, Dutch *been*, Scandinavian *ben*, mean *bone* (O.E. BAN) and *leg*. For *bone*, German has also *Knochen*, of which the diminutive form *Knöchel* is equivalent to the Modern English *knuckle*. The last-named also recalls *knokkel*, an alternative Danish word for *bone*. The English word *leg* comes from the Old Norse *leggr*, possibly related to the word for *body* or *members*, in Dutch *lichaam*, in Danish and Norwegian *legeme*.

9. SCHWARZ, like the foregoing, illustrates both the German spelling convention (also that of early Middle English) for the *sh*-sound of *ship*, and one of the most characteristic features of the German (i.e. High German) sound pattern in contradistinction to that of other Teutonic languages. This is the shift from the *t*-sound to *ts* (spelt Z) at the beginning (as in *Zinn* for *tin*) or at the end of a word and elsewhere to *s* (spelt SS as in *Wasser* for *water*). *Schwarz* is the common Teutonic word for *black*: *swarts* (Gothic), *zwart* (Du.), *svart* (Swed.), *sort* (Dan.). As such it is equivalent to O.E. SWEART, which survives in *swarthy*, otherwise supplanted by BLÆC.

10. SEE, like *sjö* (Swed.) and *sø* (Dan.), may mean *sea* or *lake*. In Dutch *zee*, and in O.E. SÆ, means the former. For an extensive sea or ocean, the German word is *Meer*. The Dutch word *meer*, like the O.E. MERE, signifies a *lake*. The O.E. word persists in poetry and English place-names (e.g. *Windermere*), but has otherwise given way to the French *lac*. Teutonic *meer* or *mere* is a word of great antiquity in the Indo-European family, equivalent to the Latin *mare* (whence *marine*) and its French descendant, *mer*. Our Modern English *ocean* is a Latin intruder.

11. TAL, equivalent to *dal* in Dutch, Swedish and Danish, illustrates the rule that *d* in other Teutonic words gives place to *t* in German. The O.E. DÆL persists as *dale* in English place-names and in poetry; but in common use it has succumbed to *valley*, from an Old French word (=*vallée* in Modern French).

12. TIER. Where we have *d*, at least at the beginning of a word, in other Teutonic languages, we find *t* in German (e.g. *Tochter* for *daughter*). Thus the equivalents are

dier (Du.), *dyr* (Dan.) and *djur* (Swed.). This has the same meaning as O.E. DEOR, displaced by *beast* from an Old French word based on the same Latin source as *bestial*, and by *animal*, which preserves the same form in French as in ancestral Latin. Needless to say, the modern descendant of DEOR is *deer*, with a far more restricted meaning, i.e. only for members of the zoological family *Cervidae*. For the animal species most dear to a Norman huntsman, O.E. had one word (DA=*doe*) not represented in Dutch, but four others which run true to form in terms of our Low German heritage:

	OLD ENGLISH	DUTCH
buck	BUCC	bok (cf. *Springbok*)
hind	HIND	hinde
hart	HEORT	hert
roe	RAHA	ree

13. VOGEL, common to German and Dutch, is equivalent to *fugl* (Dan.) and *fågel* (Swed.). The O.E. parent of our current word *fowl* is FUGEL. This might not suggest itself to you unless you already knew something about German-Dutch spelling conventions. Just as F does service both for the *f*- and for the *v*- sound in O.E. spelling, V has the same *f*-sound value in German-Dutch. Thus *Vater* (Germ.), *vader* (Du.), are equivalent to *father*, just as *vis* (Du.), *Fisch* (Germ.) are equivalent to our *fish*. We have already seen that the *g*-sound before a front vowel in O.E. was giving place to the consonant *y* as in GEOLU (Du. *geel*, Germ. *gelb*, Scand. *gul*) for *yellow* or GIST (Du. *gist*, Germ. *Gischt*, but *skum* in Norwegian) for *yeast*. Eventually (if not at the beginning of the word), it was due to disappear as such. What happened with EAGE happened also with FUGEL, the common Teutonic word exhibited above. However O.E. had a synonym which illustrates what philologists call *metathesis*, i.e. the switch-round of pronunciation illustrated by *axed* and *asked*. BRID (or BRIDD), now the *bird* in the hand, eventually displaced the *fowls of the air* in the King James Bible, and persists as such in Scots dialect. Many examples of such common Teutonic co-twins (cf. TREO and BEAM above) have left their remains, one in the Scandinavian and the other in the German-Dutch branch of the Teutonic family; but BRID-FUGEL is a couplet of which the first member is, at least today, peculiarly English. Another example on all fours is DOCGA-HUND. The second (our *hound*) is the word for *dog* in modern Swedish, Danish, Dutch (spelt *hond*) and German. Among several words for *horse*, O.E. had HORS and HENGEST, a couplet which sufficiently exposes the mythological nature of two suppositious Saxon conquerors (Hengist and Horsa) of Kent. In truncated guise, the second member of the couplet ties up with *hest* (Dan.) and *häst* (Swed.), Icelandic, however, retains *hross* equivalent to HORS. In Dutch *ros* and

German *Ross,* we have survivors from the same crib; but the current common words *paard* (Du.) and *Pferd* (Germ.) seem to be intruders alien to the Teutonic brotherhood.

14. WERWOLF is a word which the reader will almost certainly, and correctly, tie up with our word *were-wolf* (=*varulv* in Swed. and Dan.), meaning literally *man-wolf.* In English, the first component survives only in this compound, but in German in one other. In modern Teutonic languages the word *man* (Du.), *man* (Swed.), *Mann* (Germ.), *mand* (Dan.), has displaced one which existed side by side with the very Teutonic MANN of O.E. and *manna* in the earlier Gothic texts. In Gothic its partner was *wair.* In O.E. it was WER, and in the O.E. Gospel of St. Matthew, it was *tham wisan were, se his hus ofer stan ge-timbrode* (=the wise man who his house over stone timbered). Here we have a link with a very old past. Latin had more than one word for *man.* One (*homo*) has come into English in *homicide.* The other, *vir* (pronounced like English *were* in *werewolf,* cf. footnote on p. 24), has many derivative intruders such as *virile* and (no longer in its peculiarly Roman sense) *virtue.* In short, this exhibit gives us a glimpse into a past far more remote than days when werewolves were still credible.

15. WÜRZE prompts one to say something more about a spelling convention illustrated by our last item. The *v*-sound existed neither in the ancestral Latin of French, Italian, Spanish, etc., nor in the common ancestor of the Teutonic family. In all its descendants the *v*-sound (as in Danish *varulv*) replaces the *w*-sound in English *werewolf.* This shift occurred very early in the break-up of provincial Roman speech into its modern descendants. It also occurred very early in the Scandinavian branch of the Teutonic family, but not at all in English. It occurred somewhat late in German and in Dutch dialects; and we do not meet it in some contemporary German dialects. Hence in German, as in Dutch, the sign W, originally written as a double U (UU or VV) when U and V were alternative ways of writing the same Roman sound, usually has the sound value we have adopted as V under French and Italian influence, as in *valve* or *value.* To proceed further, we need to take stock of another spelling convention, and of another change of pronunciation already mentioned. In modern German (or, as scholars say, High German, in contradistinction to Dutch-Flemish Low German), we recall that:

(a) the *t*-sound gives place at the beginning of a word (cf. *Zunge* for *tongue*), and commonly at the end if as here followed by a neutral vowel, to the *ts*-sound (as in *hits* or *fits*) represented in German spelling by the Greek Z;

(b) elsewhere, *t* may give way to the pure *s* represented in German by SS as in *hiss,* whence we recognise *Wasser* as English and Dutch *water.*

In any event, we recognise Z in a German word as a signal to substitute T, and derive WURTE. With a very slight change of meaning, we are therefore ready to recognise its relation to the O.E. word WYRT, meaning *herb*. The word *herb* itself is of French origin (=*herbe*), the latter with a more restricted meaning, i.e. *grass* (from O.E. and Danish *græs*, Norwegian *gress*, Dutch and German *Gras*). The German word *Würze* now means *spices*, which is a modern and not unusual use of *herb*, as in *omelette aux fines herbes*; but the O.E. word still survives with its original meaning in many folk names for plants such as *figwort*, *stitchwort*, *St. John's wort*, *spleenwort*. Actually WYRT has a special significance which we may link with *root* crops. *Root* is the meaning of the German *Wurzel*, Dutch *wortel*. By metathesis, it may indeed share the same ancestry as *root* with Danish *rod*, Swedish *rot*, and with Latin *radix* as in *radish* and *Radical* (=one who goes to the root of the matter). Here we should take stock of a very early Church Latin intruder (*planta*) into all the main modern representatives of the Teutonic family: *plante* in O.E. and Danish, *planta* in Swedish and *Pflanze* in German. In O.E. PLANTE had much the same meaning as WYRT, as has *gras* in Icelandic. Though it is one of the few Latin words which entered our vocabulary before the Norman Conquest, it bears the unmistakable sign of its origin. Where words have an initial *p*-sound in other Indo-European languages, we find *f* in the Teutonic branch (cf. Latin *pisc-* and *pater* for *fish* and *father*). Thus *plante*, etc., cannot share with Latin a common ancestry *before* the Teutonic and Italic branches of the Indo-European family diverged. It is as alien to native English or Danish as is *riche* to native French.

16. ZIMMER, coming after what has gone before, may suggest *timber*. Its usual modern meaning is *room*, itself a good Teutonic word, being *rums* in Gothic, *rum* in Swedish, Danish and O.E., with a more extended meaning in German *Raum*, i.e. *space*. Now *Zimmer* can oddly mean the wood-prop chamber of a mine, and as such ties up with *zimmern* (O.E. TIMBRIAN), *to build*. Thus we are back with Swedish *timmer* and Danish *tømre* to modern English *timber*, and through *zimmern* (Swed. *timra*) to the wise man (Matt. vii. 24) who timbered his house above stone. Here the very unlikelihood of some of our journeyings should make it more dramatically easy to find a peg in the cloakroom for our mnemonic equipment.

17. ZUNGE, for which we have *tong* (Du.), *tunga* (Swed.) for O.E. TUNGE, should not be too difficult to spot after what we know of the value of Z as a signpost. It is, of course, the Anglo-American *tongue*. The Teutonic ancestry of most Anglo-American words for parts of the body is detectable. A noteworthy exception is *face*, which is French, with a more elderly adjectival partner *facial* (Lat. *faciale*—see footnote on case-forms below p. 31). In this connexion, as a parting shot, *knee* (CNEO in O.E., *knie* in German and Dutch, *knä* in Swedish and *knæ* in Danish) has an ancestry which antedates the divergence of the Teutonic brotherhood from more remote

relatives within the greater Indo-European family. It is of common parentage with the Latin and Greek roots which we have assimilated respectively in *genuflexion* (=knee-bending) and *hexagon* (=six-kneed figure).

The foregoing are nouns, our next three exhibits are verbs; and in passing we note that the dictionary form (so-called *infinitive*) of the West Germanic (including the O.E.) verb, unlike the Scandinavian, has the terminal -N.

18. NEHMEN corresponds to O.E. NIMAN and Dutch *nemen*, meaning *take*. The word is interesting both as an example of *strong* (p. 70) verbs which do not tally in Scandinavian and West Germanic and as an example of the suppression of the Low German verb by its Viking equivalent, *taka* in Icelandic, *taga* in Swedish, *tage* in Danish, as a result of the Norse conquests of, and settlements in, Britain during the two centuries before the Norman Conquest.

19. STERBEN corresponds to O.E. STEORFAN (F here pronounced as *v*) and Dutch *sterven* meaning *die*. This illustrates the High German shift from the *v*- to the *b*-sound. Its modern descendant is *starve* with a restricted meaning, i.e. *die for lack of food* or (in many British dialects) *die of cold*. Here again, the Viking word took root: in Icelandic *deyja*, Swedish *dö* and Danish *dø*. These are themselves descendants of a verb common to all the Teutonic languages in their earliest stages but surviving only as an adjectival derivative in West Germanic: DEAD in O.E., *dood* in Dutch, *tot* in German with the High German shift from the *d*- to the *t*- sound.

20. WERDEN, like O.E. WEORTHAN, Dutch *worden* and Icelandic *vertha*, literally means *become*, but each of the foregoing could form a passive construction with the past participle, e.g. (German) *was wird getan=what is being done*, (Dutch) *wat wordt gedaan*. This construction is obligatory in German and Dutch, but the mixed verb *be* could take its place in O.E. and alone does so in Anglo-American. The O.E. verb WEORTHAN lingered on into Shakespeare's time as the now archaic curse, *woe worth the day*.

21. WOHNEN is of the same ancestry as O.E. WUNIAN. Like Dutch *wonen*, it means *dwell*, for which Old Norse had *dvelja*, Swedish has *dväljas* and Danish *dvæle*. The O.E. verb DWELLAN had a more restricted meaning, *tarry*. GEWUNOD, the past participle of WUNIAN, meant *accustomed*. It had contracted to *wont* in the English of Shakespeare's time and still lingers on in the archaic expression, *it was his wont to do so*.

As we shall see more clearly at a later stage, pronunciation changes locally in many different ways which conspire to obscure the common ancestry of words current in different speech communities; and one of these, henceforth referred to as *sound-shift,* has cropped up again and again in the foregoing examples to show how we may make the dead bones of the dictionary live by forming lively associations to our word-list of items essential to communication in a foreign language. Incidentally, we have taken cognisance of the fact that the Latin contribution to our hybrid heritage came to us by two different routes: (a) indirectly through French, both as an immediate result of the Norman Conquest, and later through territory acquired through marriage or conquest by English kings of the Angevin and Lancastrian dynasties; (b) directly through ecclesiastical, legal and later, to an even greater extent, through scientific progress. As already stated, Modern French is itself a mixture of a native stock of words inherited from Roman Gaul and a large accretion of classical Latin introduced by scholars. To illustrate what is the most characteristic sound-shift in the genesis of native French from parental Latin, i.e. from C as in *cat* to CH as in *chivalry* or *chef,* we shall now set out side by side their native French and Latin parents together with English derivatives, where possible from both sources. This will be an aid to memorisation.

FRENCH	LATIN*	ENGLISH DERIVATIVES
chaîne	catena	chain—catenary
chair	carne (nom. caro)	charnel-house—carnal
chance	cadentia	chance—cadence
chandelle	candela	chandelier—candle
chanter	cantare	chant—cantata
char(iot)	carro	chariot—car
charité	caritate	charity—caress (indirectly)
charpentier	carpentario (=coach maker)	carpenter
charte	charta	chart—cartography
chaste	casto	chastity
chat	cato (vulg.)	cat
château	castello	chatelaine—castle
châtier	castigare	chastise—castigate
cher	caro	cherish—caress
cheval	caballo	chivalry—cavalry
cheveu	capillo	capillary
chèvre	capra	Capricorn
chien	cane	canine
chou	caule	cauliflower

* Except for *chair* (when the table cites the nominative as well), the Latin nouns and adjectives, as elsewhere in this book, are ablative singular case forms. The reason for this is that their terminals correspond closely with their descendants in Italian, Spanish and Portuguese.

When we have acquainted ourselves more fully with the grammatical peculiarities of the sister languages, we shall see that the foregoing table does not adequately illustrate the dissipation of final syllables of nouns and adjectives involved in the loss of separate case forms in the Romance languages, as in English and Dutch. Nor does it display a characteristic feature of phonetic erosion in French, which one speaks of as *elision*, meaning that one articulates the final consonant (like *t* in *dit* or *lait*) of many words only when the succeeding word begins with a vowel. Moreover, consonantal sounds which existed in the middle of a parental Latin word may have left no trace in French pronunciation, even if preserved in writing. Thus the French equivalent (*fils*) of Latin *filius* (=son, boy) retains the nominative case terminal in speech (pronounced *fees*); but the L exists only as a mark on paper.

The foregoing examples sufficiently illustrate what intriguing associations we can form if we acquaint ourselves with the different ways in which the pronunciation of words changes in different territories, with the way in which meanings may change *pari passu*, and with the diverse spelling conventions in use among different speech communities. None the less the reader may harbour doubts about whether the proportion of words which yield to such treatment justifies the effort of the attempt. So far as the issue concerns contemporary sister languages of Modern English—six Teutonic and six Romance—the answer is that we can rely on the procedure illustrated above to lighten the task of memorising at least 60 per cent. of the items on a list of words essential to self expression. If one has a large vocabulary of scientific, especially biological, terms, one also has at one's disposal 800 or more roots based on Greek words. The *Concise Oxford Dictionary* which cites the ancestry of an English word (if known) provides the reader with a means of verifying intelligent guess-work. For instance, it sufficiently discloses why French *pain* and Latin *panem* in the Lord's Prayer Quiz (p. 35) turn up in *pantry*, *pannier* and *marzipan*. Archaic or wholly obsolete words are of special interest. For instance, Chaucer's (now obsolete) *eke* (O.E. ÆC) for *also* is a pan-Teutonic word: *auk* (Goth.), *ook* (Du.), *auch* (Germ.). From the same source probably came the Swedish (*och*) and Danish (*og*) words for Old and Modern English *and* (Germ. *und*).

In the foregoing pages, there have been citations from different versions of the English Bible. The reader who perseveres will meet many more in subsequent chapters. The reason for this signifies no pretensions to piety on the part of the author. As mentioned, our earliest source of information about the Teutonic clan is the Gothic version of the Gospels, and our most voluminous prose composition of English before the Norman Conquest is also a translation from the same source. Word for word, we can compare the Anglo-Saxon Gospels with a version of the whole Bible in the English of Chaucer's time, with others about the time when Henry VIII severed the connexion of the English Church with Rome, with the so-called

Authorised version which the Pilgrim Fathers took with them to New England and with Anglo-American translations undertaken during the last century.

The writer's source for Biblical material to illustrate the evolution of the Mother Tongue is a volume which will give delight to many readers, if able to obtain it from a library. In 1865 J. Bosworth, Oxford Professor of Anglo-Saxon, assisted by G. Waring of Trinity College, Cambridge, issued a version of the New Testament gospels exhibiting in parallel columns the Anglo-Saxon, Wycliffe and Tyndale versions together with what remains of the Gothic. A second edition (Russell Smith, publishers, London) appeared in 1874.

QUIZ CORNER 1

Note: the reader can confirm his or her answers here, and with very few exceptions elsewhere, by consulting the Concise Oxford Dictionary, *which cites derivations and affinities of all words listed, if known.*

Quiz 1

Vowels and Consonants

1. Cover (2) below and study this:

..e .o..o.a... a.e ..e .a.. ..a.e.o.. o. ..i.. .e .e.y .o.. .o. .e.o..i.i..
.o... i. ..ee.. o. i. .ea.i..
   .ou .a. .i..o.e. ..i. .o. .ou..e.. i. .ou ..y .o .a.e .e..e ou. o. ...i.
e.e..i.e a..e. .i... ..yi.. .i..ou. .u..e.. .o .a.e .e..e o. ..e .a.e .e..e..e.
..e. .ou .a. .ee ..e .o.e. .i... o..y
   .e.e .e .a.e .e.o.e u. ..e .o..o.a.. .i... o..y .u. i. i. .o. .e.o.. .ou.
.o.e. .o .i.. i. ..e .a..
   ..e a...e. i. .e.o. ..i..e. u..i.e .o..

2. Now cover (1) and fill in the vowels to make sense:

Th. c.ns.n.nts .r. th. h.rd fr.m.w.rk .n wh.ch w. r.l. m.st f.r r.c.gn.s.ng
w.rds .n sp..ch .r .n r..d.ng.
   Y.. c.n d.sc.v.r th.s f.r y..rs.lf .f y.. tr. t. m.k. s.ns. ..t .f th.s .x.rc.s.
.ft.r f.rst tr..ng w.th..t s.cc.ss t. m.k. s.ns. .f th. s.m. s.nt.nc.s wh.n y..
c.n s.. th. v.w.l s.gns .nl.
   H.r. w. h.v. b.f.r. .s th. c.ns.n.nt s.gns .nl. b.t .t .s n.t b.y.nd y..r
p.w.r t. f.ll .n th. g.ps
   Th. .nsw.r .s b.l.w wr.tt.n .ps.d. d.wn

The answer is below written upside down.
to fill in the gaps.
Here we have before us the consonant signs only but it is not beyond your power
see the vowel signs only.
after first trying without success to make sense of the same sentences when you can
You can discover this for yourself if you try to make sense out of this exercise
words in speech or in reading.
The consonants are the hard framework on which we rely most for recognising

Quiz 2

The following sentence is from the Lord's Prayer in thirteen languages belonging to one or other of three groups.

Put them by number in each as below:

> **Teutonic** 7. ....
> **Latin** 9. ....
> **Celtic** .. ..

Give the reference in St. Matthew's Gospel, Chapter .... verse ....
    and/or
a translation of the sentence in Modern English:

....

1. Panem nostrum supersubstantialem da nobis hodie.
2. Urne dæghwamlican hlaf syle us to-dæg.*
3. Geef ons heden ons dagelijksch brood.
4. Dyro i ni heddiw ein bara beunyddiol.
5. O pão nosso de cada dia dai-nos hoje.
6. Dacci oggi il nostro pane cotidiano.
7. Unser täglich Brot gieb uns heute.
8. Giv os i Dag vort daglige Brød.
9. Danos hoy nuestro pan sobresubstancial.
10. Gef oss i dag vort daglegt brauð.
11. Tabhair dhuinn an diugh ar n-aran leitheil.
12. Giv oss i dag vårt dagliga bröd.
13. Donne-nous aujourd'hui notre pain quotidien.

After studying the Language Museum (pp. 155-160) and consulting the etymological entries of the *Concise Oxford Dictionary*, fill in by number:

German ...... **Dutch** ...... **Swedish** ...... **Icelandic** ......
Old English ...... **Danish** ...... **Latin** ...... **French** ...... **Portuguese**
...... **Spanish** ...... **Italian** ...... **Gaelic** ...... **Welsh** ......

---

* CLUE: *half a hlaf is better than what?*

Quiz 3

All the languages of the Lord's Prayer Quiz share some word material with one another, with Russian and its sister tongues (Polish, Czech, Bulgarian and the dialects of Yugoslavia), and also with Persian and with most of the languages spoken in India except in the south. These include Hindustani, Urdu, Bengali and Hindi. Of such languages of India known to us in writing, the oldest is Sanskrit which, like Latin, is now a dead language with many descendants. Here are two groups of words used by people who speak, or once spoke, languages which scholars place in the great INDO-EUROPEAN family.

A

	LATIN	GAELIC	RUSSIAN	PERSIAN	SANSKRIT
1.	PATER	ATHAIR	OTETS	PEDAR	PITA
2.	MATER	MATHAIR	MAHT	MADAR	MATA
3.	FRATER	BRATHAIR	BRAHT	BARADAR	BHRATR
4.	SOROR	PIUTHAR	SESTRAH	KHAHAR	SVASAR
5.	FILIUS	MAC	SYN	PESAR	SUNUS
6.	FILIA	NIGHEAN	DOCH	DOKHTAR	DUHITA

B

	LATIN	GREEK	RUSSIAN	PERSIAN	HINDUSTANI	SANSKRIT
a.	duo	duo	dvah	do	do	dvi
b.	tres	treis	tree	seh	tin	trayas
c.	quattuor	tessares	chetyre	chahar	char	catur
d.	quinque	pente	pyaht	panj	panch	pañca
e.	sex	hex	shest	shesh	chha	sas
f.	septem	hepta	sem	haft	sat	sapta
g.	octo	octo	vosem	hasht	ath	asta
h.	novem	ennea	devet	neuh	nau	nava
j.	decem	deca	deset	dah	das	dasa

FILL IN:

	1	2	3	4	5	6
A. **English**	......	......	......	......	......	......
Welsh	......	......	......	......	......	......

	a	b	c	d	e	f	g	h	j
B. **English**	......	......	......	......	......	......	......	......	......
Welsh	......	......	......	......	......	......	......	......	......

Quiz 4

The reader who wishes to get a close-up view of how the scholar fumbles his way to the reconstruction of a language hitherto undeciphered by taking advantage of bilingual (or trilingual) inscriptions such as the Rosetta Stone, may with profit try out the following exercise from a British (Northumberland No. 1.) intelligence test designed by Professor Godfrey Thomson:

"The sentences below are in a foreign language, and their meanings are given in English. In each English sentence a word is in bold type, and you have to underline the word which corresponds to it in the foreign sentence. You can do this by comparing the sentences with each other. *Notice that the foreign words are not always in the same order as the English words.*"

1. Kuchh malai.
   Kuchh puri leoge.
   Misri leoge.

   Some cream.
   Will you take some **cake?**
   Will you take sugar?

2. Ek piyala chae.
   Yih chae bahut achchhi hai.
   Chae bilkull taiyar hai.
   Kab taiyar karoge?
   Main bahut pyasa hun.
   Bahut achchhi hai.
   Yih mera rumal nahin hai.

   A cup of **tea**
   This **is** very good tea.
   Tea is **quite** ready.
   When will you make **ready?**
   I am **very** thirsty.
   It is very **good.**
   This is not my handkerchief.

Quiz 5

Common Words

The small words we use most commonly are nearly all Teutonic ones, although sometimes the meaning has changed slightly. In O.E. we often find MID where we should now use *with*. TIL means *till* or *to* and still means *to* in North Scottish dialect. You can check whether your guesses are right by looking up the solution in the *Concise Oxford Dictionary*.

	OLD ENGLISH	DUTCH	GERMAN	SWEDISH	DANISH
1.	AND	EN	UND	OCH	OG
2.	ÆFTER	NA	NACH	EFTER	EFTER
3.	ANDLANG	LANGS	LANGS	LÄNGS	LANGS
4.	BA	BEIDE	BEIDE	BÅDA	BÅDE
5.	BEFORAN *or* ÆR	VOOR	BEVOR *or* VOR	FÖRE	FØR
6.	BEHINDAN	ACHTER	HINTER	BAKOM	BAG
7.	BENEOTHAN	BENEDEN	UNTER	UNDER	UNDER
8.	BI	BIJ	NEBEN *or* BEI	VID	VED
9.	BUFAN	BOVEN	ÜBER	ÖVER	OVER
10.	EALL	AL	ALLE	ALLA	ALLE
11.	FOR	VOOR	FÜR	TILL *or* FÖR	TIL *or* FOR
12.	FRAM	VAN	VON	FRÅN	FRA
13.	HER	HIER	HIER	HÄR	HER
14.	HWA?	WIE?	WER?	VEM?	HVEM?
15.	HWÆT?	WAT?	WAS?	VAD?	HVAD?
16.	HWÆS?	VAN WIE?	WESSEN?	VEMS?	HVIS?
17.	HWAM?	WIE?	WEM *or* WEN?	VEM?	HVEM?
18.	HWÆR?	WAAR?	WO?	VAR?	HVOR?
19.	HWONNE?	WANN-EER?	WANN?	NÄR?	NÅR?
20.	HWY?	WAAROM?	WARUM?	VARFÖR?	HVOR-FOR?

	OLD ENGLISH	DUTCH	GERMAN	SWEDISH	DANISH
21.	HU?	HOE?	WIE?	HUR?	HVOR-DAN?
22.	IN	IN	IN	IN	I
23.	MID *or* WITH	MET	MIT	MED *or* VID	MED *or* VED
24.	NE	NIET	NICHT	INTE	IKKE
25.	NEAH	NABIJ	NEBEN	NÄRA	NÆR
26.	OF	VAN	VON	AV	AF
27.	OFER	OVER	ÜBER	ÖVER	OVER
28.	SWA	ZO	SO	SÅ	SÅ
29.	THÆT	DAT	DASS	DET	DET
30.	THES	DEZE	DIESE	DENNA	DENNE
31.	THA	ZIJ	SIE	DE	DE
32.	THÆM	ZE	SIE	DEM	DEM
33.	THÆRA	HUN	IHRER	DERAS	DERES
34.	THÆR	DAAR	DORT	DÄR	DER
35.	THONNE	DAN	DENN	DÅ	DA
36.	TIL	TOT	BIS	TILL	TIL
37.	TO	NAAR	ZU	TILL	TIL
38.	UNDER	ONDER	UNTER	UNDER	UNDER
39.	UPPAN	OP	AUF	PÅ	PÅ
40.	UTE *or* UTAN	BUITEN-ZIJDE	ÄUSSERE	UTE	UDE

Besides these, the following O.E. survivors are very common words:

41. ...... ÆT	45. ...... ON
42. ...... BEGEONDAN	46. ...... THURH
43. ...... BETWIX *or* BETWEONAN	47. ...... WITHINNAN
44. ...... GEMANG	48. ...... WITHUTAN

Quiz 6

Native Words

Study these three samples with the help of the *Concise Oxford Dictionary* to check on the origin of each word. In the first example native words have replaced 5 alien words in the English Bible of A.D. 1611 and in the second 13 have been replaced.

A. John. i. 1-14. (*Authorised Version* of A.D. 1611.)

In the beginning was the Word, and the Word was with God and the Word was God. The same was in the beginning with God. All things were made by Him, and without Him was not any thing made that was made. In Him was life, and the life was the light of men. And the light shineth in darkness; and the darkness understandeth it not. There was a man sent from God whose name was John. The same came for a witness, to bear witness of the light, that all men through him might believe. He was not that Light, but was sent to bear witness of that Light. That was the true Light which lighteth every man that cometh into the world. He was in the world, and the world was made by him, and the world knew him not. He came unto his own, and his own welcomed him not. But as many as welcomed him, to them gave he might to become the sons of God, even to them that believe on his name, which were born not of blood nor of the will of the flesh nor of the will of man, but of God. And the Word was made flesh and dwelt among us, and we beheld his brightness, the brightness as of the only begotten of the Father, full of kindness and truth.

B. Ps. xxiii. (*Authorised Version* of A.D. 1611.)

The Lord is my shepherd. I shall not want.
He maketh me to lie down in green meadows.
He leadeth me beside the still waters.
He healeth my soul. He leadeth me in the paths of righteousness for his name's sake.
Yea though I walk through the dale of the shadow of death I will fear no evil.
For thou art with me.
Thy rod and thy staff give heart to me.
Thou makest ready a board before me in front of my foes,
Thou bathest my head with sweet fat. My bowl runneth over.
Of a truth goodness and forgiveness shall follow me all the days of my life,
And I will dwell in the house of the Lord for ever.

C. Summary of a Mathematical Paper in a learned Journal.

Inadequacies are pointed out of some existent methods of setting fiducial limits to estimates of heritability where more than two components of variance are involved. Although anormality of distribution may preclude the possibility of setting precise fiducial limits, a method is presented by which estimates of sampling variance may be derived for all ratios involving such components. For a simplified classification the method gives a close approximation to Fisher's standard error of the intra-class correlation coefficient.

In the first 142 words of John i (verses 1-10) A.V., only one of them is not native. Which is it?

    1. ......

Among the first 230 (verses 1-14) there are four others. List as (a) the original and as (b) the native word which replaces it:

   2a. ...... 3a. ...... 4a. ...... 5a. ......
    b. ......   b. ......   b. ......   b. ......

What are the thirteen alien words in the English rendering of the Psalm as given in the translation of A.D. 1611?

   6. ......   7. ......   8. ......   9. ......
  10. ...... 11. ...... 12. ...... 13. ......
  14. ...... 15. ...... 16. ...... 17. ......
  18. ......

Our third exhibit is about as extreme an example of the use of alien words in scientific writing as it would be possible to find.

    19. How many words are there in all?   ......
    20. How many words are native?   ......
    21. How many *different* words are native? ......

Quiz 7

French and Latin Couplets

The same Latin word may come into English through French or directly from classical literature. As in French itself, we therefore meet many couplets, sometimes with a distinction of meanings.

LATIN WORD	MEANING	FROM FRENCH	FROM CLASSICAL LATIN
1.	......	amiable	amative
2.	......	approval	approbation
3.	......	benison	benediction
4.	......	caitiff	captive
5.	......	chain	catenary
6.	......	chastise	castigate
7.	......	crown	coronation
8.	......	delay	dilatory
9.	......	dispense	depend
10.	......	fashion	faction
11.	......	feat	fact
12.	......	forge	fabric
13.	......	frail	fragile
14.	......	hotel	hospital
15.	......	lesson	lecture
16.	......	nourishment	nutriment
17.	......	orison	oration
18.	......	parlance, parole	parable
19.	......	penance	penitence
20.	......	pity	piety
21.	......	poignant	pungent
22.	......	poison	potion
23.	......	pursue	persecute
24.	......	ransom	redemption
25.	......	reasonable	rational
26.	......	royal	regal
27.	......	sever	separate

LATIN WORD	MEANING	FROM FRENCH	FROM CLASSICAL LATIN
28.	......	sure	secure
29.	......	surface	superficial
30.	......	treason	tradition

Quiz 8

Latin and French Prefixes

The following Latin prefixes attach themselves to English verbs and/or nouns:
AB- (**away, from**), AD- (**to**), ANTE- (**before**), CIRCUM- (**around**), CONTRA-
(=COUNTER, **against**), CUM- (=COM-, CON-, COL-, COR-, CO-, **with**),
DE- (**away, from**), E(X)- (**out of**), EXTRA- (**outside**), IN- (**into** or **not**),
INTER- (**between**), INTRA- (**within**), INTRO- (**inwards**), JUXTA- (**beside**),
PER- (**through**), PRAE- (=PRE, **before**), PRAETER- (**beyond**), PRO- (**in
front of, forward**), RETRO- (**backwards**), SINE- (**without**), SUB- (**under**),
SUBTER- (**under**), SUPER- (**over, above**), TRANS- (**across**), ULTRA-
(**beyond**).

Now fill in a single English word synonymous with the following phrases (you can
find the first syllable of the word by comparing the word in bold type in each
phrase with the list above):

1. To choose one **out of** a group   ......
2. Talking **around** a subject   ......
3. To write one's name **under** a document   ......
4. To blow air **into** something   ......
5. Syllable fixed **before** a word   ......
6. To cease (i.e. stop **from**) doing something   ......
7. To sit **before**, at a meeting   ......
8. To come **between** two people   ......
9. Working **with** someone else   ......
10. **Not** strongly flavoured   ......
11. To bring (nation, etc.) **under** a yoke   ......

12. To walk **back** (opposite of PROGRESS)   ......
13. Very old, dating from **before** the flood   ......
14. To order **against** another order   ......
15. A job held **without** the necessity to do any work ......
16. To place one note **with** another   ......
17. Person equal **with** another in age   ......
18. To bore **through** something   ......
19. A bending **inwards**   ......
20. **Within** the walls (of a University, etc.)   ......
21. To carry sense **across** from one language to another ......
22. To shout news **in front of** everyone   ......
23. A secret understanding **with** opponents   ......
24. Glancing **over** the surface of a subject   ......
25. To assemble articles **with** others of the same kind ......
26. To put **out**, quench   ......
27. To give warning **to** a person   ......
28. **Above** earthly things   ......
29. A feature shared **with** others   ......
30. To look **into** a matter   ......
31. An escape **under** cover of an evasion   ......
32. To be in postal communication **with**   ......
33. **Beyond** what is natural   ......
34. Wandering **outside** reasonable bounds   ......
35. One whose thoughts are turned **inwards**   ......
36. To be of one mind **with** another   ......
37. To fit something **to** a particular purpose   ......
38. To deny a statement by (i.e. speak **against**) someone ......
39. To lead **away**, kidnap   ......
40. Tense expressing what has gone **beyond**   ......
41. To mark **with** wrinkles or ridges   ......
42. **Not** possessing life   ......
43. To strain something **through** a filter   ......
44. Breeding **between** different species   ......
45. To carry (people, etc.) **across** a distance   ......
46. To free **from** (*N.B.* B-V sound shift)   ......
47. A room entered **before** a second   ......
48. Able to be **overcome**   ......

49. To put **beside** ......
50. To differ **from** the usual ......
51. To draw a line **around** ......
52. Temporary union of one political party **with** another ......
53. To walk (or move) **forward** ......
54. **Outside** the ordinary ......
55. Thing which drives an aeroplane **forward** ......
56. To strive **with** another for a prize ......
57. Season when Jesus came **to** earth ......
58. To take the faults **from** (a book, etc.) ......
59. One who explains **between** two persons ......
60. **Above** the speed of sound ......

Quiz 9

Latin and French Suffixes

I. Latin *noun* suffixes carried over into English (often **via** Norman French) in **a** modified form include:

-ITIA (*or* -ITIUM)	= **-ise** *or* **-ice**	-ITAS	= **-ity**
-ICIUM	= **-ice**	-ENTIA	= **-ence**
-ULUS (*or* -ULUM)	= **-le** *or* **-ule**	-ANTIA	= **-ance**
-MENTUM	= **-ment**	-URA	= **-ure**
-TIO(NEM)	= **-tion**	-OR	= **-or**
-SIO(NEM)	= **-sion**		

All these suffixes are reliable as signs of Latin origin except -OR (**sailor**). Give the English nouns derived from the following Latin words:

1. SACRIFICIUM ......
2. CULTURA ......
3. ELEVATOR ......
4. FASCICULUS ......
5. IUSTITIA ......
6. EMOLUMENTUM ......
7. PETULANTIA ......
8. IUNCTURA ......
9. TRUCULENTIA ......
10. TRACTOR ......
11. EXCURSIO ......
12. EXERCITIUM ......
13. HOMUNCULUS ......
14. POTENTIA ......
15. OBLIGATIO ......
16. NEGATIO ......

17. SCRUPULUS	......	24. VARIATIO	......
18. REPUGNANTIA	......	25. ARTIFICIUM	......
19. HOSPITIUM	......	26. CARBUNCULUS	......
20. FISSIO	......	27. PERSEVERANTIA	......
21. INTELLEGENTIA	......	28. SESSIO	......
22. VITIUM	......	29. TESTAMENTUM	......
23. RETICULUM	......	30. TONSURA	......

II. Latin *adjective* suffixes surviving in English in a modified form are:

-OSUS =-ose *or* -ous	-LENTUS =-lent
-ILIS =-ile *or* -il	-IBILIS =-ible
-ARIUS =-ary	-ABILIS =-able
-ICUS =-ic	-ALIS =-al
-AX =-acious	

Of these, -OUS (**righteous**), -IC (**Byronic**) and -ABLE (**lovable**) are unreliable as a sign of Latin origin.

Give the English words derived from the following Latin adjectives:

1. MOBILIS	......	13. INVIDIOSUS	......
2. COMICUS	......	14. VENALIS	......
3. SOCIABILIS	......	15. EFFICAX	......
4. TURBULENTUS	......	16. CIVILIS	......
5. RUSTICUS	......	17. STIPENDIARIUS	......
6. OTIOSUS	......	18. CREDIBILIS	......
7. PECUNIARIUS	......	19. FRAUDULENTUS	......
8. UTENSILIS	......	20. SALARIUS	......
9. VERAX	......	21. HORRIBILIS	......
10. MUTABILIS	......	22. MOROSUS	......
11. DOCILIS	......	23. LETHARGICUS	......
12. LUMINOSUS	......	24. PASTORALIS	......

III. Two Latin and two French *verb* terminals have equivalents in English:

LATIN	FRENCH
-ARI =-ate	-ISER (Greek $\iota\zeta\omega$) =-ise
-ARE =-ate	-IR =-ish

All four suffixes are reliable indications of Romance origin. Give the English forms of the following Latin and French verbs:

1. POLIR	......	9. OSCULARI	......
2. MACULARE	......	10. MORALISER	......
3. DOMINARI	......	11. PERMEARE	......
4. HARMONISER	......	12. BLANDIR	......
5. IMPRECARI	......	13. SATIRISER	......
6. FOURNIR	......	14. ACCOMPLIR	......
7. AUTORISER	......	15. SEGREGARE	......
8. INTERROGARE	......	16. CALUMNIARI	......

Give one additional example of each group, checking their origins by reference to an etymological dictionary:

LATIN	FRENCH
17.	19. ......
18.	20. ......

Quiz 10

Common French Phrases

PHRASE	MEANING
1. Fin de siècle	....
2. Hors de combat	....
3. Nom de plume	....
4. Dieu et mon droit	....
5. Faute de mieux	....
6. Oyez	....
7. Honi soit qui mal y pense	....
8. En passant	....
9. Vingt-et-un	....
10. Le lapin agile	....
11. Entente cordiale	....
12. Chemin de fer	....

PHRASE	MEANING
13. Pâtisserie	....
14. Savoir faire	....
15. Beau geste	....
16. Le moulin rouge	....
17. Blasé	....
18. Chef d'œuvre	....
19. Canaille	....
20. Détente	....
21. Un soupçon	....
22. Canard	....
23. Tour de force	....
24. Sans souci	....
25. Nouveau riche	....
26. Bête noire	....
27. Faux pas	....
28. De bon marché	....
29. Idée fixe	....
30. Laissez faire	....
31. Ci-devant	....
32. Papier-mâché	....
33. Mal de mer	....
34. Enfant terrible	....
35. Au revoir	....
36. Entre nous	....
37. Comme il faut	....
38. Répondez s'il vous plaît	....
39. Poste restante	....
40. Par avion	....
41. Cherchez la femme	....
42. Cordon bleu	....
43. Embarras de richesses	....
44. Mot juste	....
45. Fait accompli	....
46. Par excellence	....
47. Tête-à-tête	....
48. A la carte	....

PHRASE	MEANING
49. Clair de lune	. . . .
50. Vive la guerre	. . . .
51. Vis-à-vis	. . . .
52. Embonpoint	. . . .
53. Coup de grâce	. . . .
54. Après moi, le déluge	. . . .
55. La ville lumière	. . . .
56. Eau de vie	. . . .
57. Broderie anglaise	. . . .
58. Noblesse oblige	. . . .
59. Nous avons changé tout cela	. . . .
60. Café au lait	. . . .
61. Café noir	. . . .
62. Vin ordinaire	. . . .
63. Vin rouge	. . . .
64. Mise en scène	. . . .
65. L'état, c'est moi	. . . .
66. Wagon-lit	. . . .
67. Fête champêtre	. . . .
68. Table d'hôte	. . . .
69. Vol-au-vent	. . . .
70. Chacun à son goût	. . . .
71. Le roi soleil	. . . .
72. Belles lettres	. . . .
73. Carte blanche	. . . .
74. Amour propre	. . . .
75. Faites vos jeux	. . . .
76. Touché	. . . .
77. Hors d'œuvre	. . . .
78. Entrée	. . . .
79. Bourgeois	. . . .
80. Cause célèbre	. . . .
81. La Comédie Française	. . . .
82. Agent provocateur	. . . .
83. De longue haleine	. . . .
84. Ile de France	. . . .

PHRASE	MEANING
85. Cœur de lion	. . . .
86. Sauve qui peut	. . . .
87. Pièce de résistance	. . . .
88. Finisterre	. . . .
89. Crème de menthe	. . . .
90. Rouge et noir	. . . .
91. Pâté de foie gras	. . . .
92. Soi-disant	. . . .
93. M'aidez (Mayday)	. . . .
94. Souvenir	. . . .
95. J'adoube	. . . .
96. Qui s'excuse, s'accuse	. . . .
97. Vers libre	. . . .
98. Polonaise	. . . .
99. Rapprochement	. . . .
100. A la recherche du temps perdu	. . . .

2
The Folk Background in the Homeland

During the past two and a half millennia, the homeland of the Anglo-American language has been the site of four linguistic upheavals, three of them associated with the migrations of European tribes speaking dialects of different clans of the same great *Indo-European* family, i.e. that in which we now assemble Persian, Hindustani, Urdu, Sanskrit, the ancient Hittite tongue, Greek, the Slavonic group (Russian, Polish, Bulgarian, etc.), the Celtic (Irish, Gaelic, and Welsh, etc.), Teutonic (German, Swedish, etc.), and Latin (French, Spanish, etc.). One of these upheavals signalises the coming of the Iron Age to an island whose people already had some knowledge of the use of metals; but we know nothing about the speech of the Bronze-Age builders of Stonehenge (*circa* 1500 B.C.) whose descendants were already trading their tin with Phoenician mariners little more than 500 years later. It seems that they were Mediterranean migrants, and the fact that Welsh has a large substratum of words which are alien to other Indo-European languages makes it unlikely that their speech was akin to that of their several successors.

The mists which enshroud the linguistic background of Britain do not begin to disperse till about four or five centuries before the beginning of the Christian era, when a great Celtic migration began. Possibly harassed by Teutonic warriors from the north, Celtic-speaking peoples with iron tools and weapons ranged far afield in the middle of the first millennium B.C. About 400 B.C., when Rome was a small city state, one horde descended into Italy and besieged Rome, which was saved from their fury, according to legend, by the sacred geese of Juno's temple. Others poured into Asia Minor where they founded the kingdom of Galatia. Others from Celtic-speaking Gaul (now France) and the Netherlands poured into Britain where the aborigines had as yet no knowledge of the use of iron. Some who crossed the Channel conquered and colonised England, Wales and Scotland. Others, somewhat later (350-300 B.C.), embarked from Southern Gaul to establish themselves as a ruling caste in Ireland. We may speak of the two groups last mentioned respectively as British (or Brythonic) and Irish (or Goidelic). Aside from place names and a few inscriptions, we know nothing about their speech, or about that of Gaul itself before it became a Latin-speaking Roman province in Caesar's time; but it is likely that Celts of all sorts then spoke intercommunicable dialects which had widely diverged when the written record began with the Christianisation of Britain and Ireland.

By then Brythonic, called P-Celtic for a reason divulged later (p. 151), and Goidelic (Q-Celtic) were sharply distinguishable. As descendants of the Brythonic of the Roman occupation (roughly A.D. 50 to 400) we distinguish three dialects:

Welsh, still spoken by nearly three-quarters of a million people in Wales; Cornish, usually said to have died out at the end of the eighteenth century, though it probably lingered into the first quarter of the nineteenth century among immigrants to the mines of South Wales; and Breton, now spoken by about a million peasants in the north-west corner of France. The last named has no direct relation to the language of Gaul before the Roman conquest. Those who speak it are descendants of Cornish legionaries who settled in Brittany when withdrawn by the departing Romans, *circa* A.D. 410. Of the descendants of Goidelic as spoken at the time of the Roman withdrawal from England, Erse (*Irish Gaelic*) is today the official language of Eire, from which so many Americans have come. From time to time, more especially during the first six centuries of the Christian era, the Irish made raids into the offshore islands of North Britain. One result of these was the occupation of the Isle of Man (off Liverpool) where a Gaelic dialect (*Manx*) could still boast 358 native speakers in 1951. Another, shortly after the Roman withdrawal, was the creation of the Scots* kingdom of Dalraida, embracing what we now call Argyllshire and the Western Isles of Scotland. There the *Scots Gaelic* dialect still survives, now with few more than 50,000 speakers.

The spread of the Celtic languages now spoken by less than two million people on the western fringe of Britain and of France was comparatively short-lived. When Celtic adventurers brought Iron-Age culture to Britain, Rome was a small city state, Latin was a minor Italic dialect and a considerable part of the population of what is now Italy (including Sicily) spoke Celtic or Greek dialects, Etruscan and Phoenician, the last two of which are not Indo-European languages. Four centuries later, for no simple reason other than a much higher level of literacy than that of all the above-mentioned speech communities except Greek, Latin had become the dominant language of all Italy, of the Iberian peninsula, and largely of what had been Celtic Gaul. By the end of the Western Empire, the Celtic of Gaul and North Italy, the aboriginal language or languages of the Iberian peninsula except in the Basque provinces, Etruscan and Italic dialects other than Latin itself were virtually extinct. In Britain, subjugated between A.D. 40 and A.D. 100 by the emperor Claudius and his successors, the Celtic nobility were doubtless familiar with Latin, from which

---

* To anyone who is not acquainted with the ups and downs of Scottish history, it is puzzling to learn that the original Scots—in contradistinction to the Picts of the Roman writers—were Irish, as indeed is now the major part of the population of Glasgow recruited more than a millennium later from the same source. What was the speech of the Picts who occupied all of Scotland north of the line between Edinburgh and Glasgow throughout the Roman occupation we can merely guess. From Roman sources we know that they retained a matrilineal clan organisation which was presumptively that of the Bronze-Age folk. Seemingly also, they could communicate with their Brythonic neighbours. Hence it is not unlikely that their speech was a hybrid between that of their Celtic overlords and that of the aboriginal population.

the Brythonic dialects assimilated many words recognisable as such in modern Welsh. Otherwise, England, Wales and the Scottish Lowlands remained a relatively homogeneous Celtic speech community till the Roman legions withdrew.

Before that date, there had already been raids by Teutonic tribes on the east coast of Britain, and what prompted the withdrawal was itself the challenge of a second great migration of considerable consequence to the linguistic map of Europe. During the century which followed (i.e. by about A.D. 510), Teutonic tribes had established one kingdom (*Vandal*) on the coast of North Africa, one (*Visigoth*) embracing what is now the greater part of Spain, all Portugal and a corner of South France, one (*Ostrogoth*) embracing all Italy, Switzerland and Austria, one sizeable *Burgundian* kingdom in south-east France, that of the *Franks* including nearly all of the rest of France other than Brittany, with West Germany and the Lowlands, and several small kingdoms in the eastern half of Britain south of Edinburgh in Scotland. After the Frankish occupation of Channel ports, invasion of Britain from the Lowlands seems to have intensified. By about A.D. 650 Teutonic invaders had occupied all England except Cornwall and Devon in the West and, in the North, Cumberland and Westmorland. The last-named region was part of the Celtic kingdom (*Cambria*) which also included Strathclyde, i.e. the Scottish counties west and south of Glasgow.

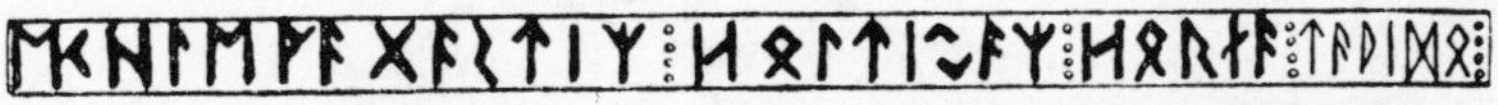

Fig. 2.   Earliest Teutonic Inscription, in Runic signs.

Though a Teutonic dialect of one sort or another wholly displaced the pre-existing speech of the territory invaded in Britain alone, the effect of the same linguistic migration during the dissolution of the Western Empire of Rome has left traces in the vocabularies of all descendants of Latin. We have already noted under *Reich* (p. 25) one example of a Teutonic word common to French, Italian and Spanish. Another, of the same ancestry as *blank*, means *shining* in Swedish, Danish, German and Dutch, used in the last synonymously with *wit* (O.E. HWIT). From this common Teutonic word comes *blanc* in French, *bianco* in Italian, *branco* in Portuguese, *blanco* in Spanish for Latin *albo* as in *albino*. In Modern English a *blank* page is (usually) a *white* one; but the word, though Teutonic, seems to have disappeared in O.E. and to have come back (like *war*, *ward* and *warden*) through French.

The influence of the Teutonic Goths and Vandals was transitory in Italy and in the Iberian peninsula; but that of the Franks was much more lasting in the territory on which they conferred their name. They and other Teutonic tribes bequeathed to the French language well over 400 words, including such common ones as the following. Besides *blanc(he)*, for colours we find *brun* (Du. *bruin*, Germ. *braun*,

Swed., Dan. and O.E. BRUN); *bleu* (Du. *blauw*, Germ. *blau*, Swed. and Dan. *blå* for Modern English *blue*); *gris* (Du. *grauw*, Germ. *grau*, Dan. and Swed. *grå*, O.E. GRÆG). Besides *riche*, among other adjectives, we meet *franc(he)* for *free* (because initially the Franks and their descendants were the *freemen* of the conquered territory). Like *blank*, *frank* (=*freely speaking*) came into English by the back door. Among other Teutonic intruders in French, we may note the nouns *jardin* (Old French

Fig. 3.   Map of Teutonic Invasions, from A.D. 400 to A.D. 600.

gardin, Germ. *Garten*), *guerre* for *war* (Old French *werre*), *canif* for *knife* (Swed. and Dan. *kniv*) and *bateau* for *boat* (Swed. *båt*, Dan. *båd*). Two familiar French verbs are of Teutonic ancestry: *choisir* (O.E. CEOSAN, Du. *kiezen*) for *choose*, and *danser* (Du. *dansen*, Germ. *tanzen*, Swed. *dansa*, Dan. *danse*) for *dance*.

In what is now England and in the Lowlands of Scotland, the linguistic effect of successive Teutonic invasions beginning at the time of the Roman withdrawal and extending thereafter over six centuries was far more profound and more lasting than in other parts of the Western Empire. Apart from local place names which an invading force with no maps necessarily adopts for planning a campaign, Celtic Britain does not seem to have contributed more than about a dozen native words to the vocabulary of O.E. This circumstance supports a tradition that the Brythons retreated with their families before the westerly invaders; but we have no contemporary written record of events before the invaders adopted the Christian religion. Christianity had been firmly established in Roman Britain, and if we have little evidence of the rôle of the native church in the conversion of the various tribes named in the Chronicle as Angles, Saxons, and Jutes, a sufficient explanation is that the native church was not in full accord with the papacy. What is beyond dispute is that Celtic missionaries from Scotland played the leading rôle in the conversion of Northern England, and it is highly significant that the Celtic form of the Roman alphabet supplanted the Teutonic *runes* (Fig. 2) which the invaders brought with them from the Continent for short inscriptions on wood or stone.

That the response to missionary effort was comparatively rapid was in some measure due to cultural links with the Frankish kingdom, whose first ruler (Clovis) had adopted Christianity. In the latter half of the sixth century a king of Kent married a Frankish princess who brought to her court a Roman bishop, whence the favourable reception of a papal mission in A.D. 584. By A.D. 650 the process of conversion was complete and therewith, on the horizon, a far higher level of literacy attained under Alfred, king of Wessex, two centuries later. Before Alfred's birth many of the petty English kingdoms had merged. There were now four: *Northumbria* (embracing North Lancashire, Yorkshire, Northumberland, Durham and the eastern fringe of the Scottish Lowlands); *East Anglia* (Norfolk and Suffolk); *Mercia* (all the Midland Counties including South Lancashire and Lincoln, between East Anglia and the Welsh border, north of Essex); *Wessex* (Devon, Somerset, Wiltshire, Dorset, Hampshire, Surrey, Essex and Kent).

During Alfred's boyhood the coasts of Britain had been unceasingly harassed by sea-borne Scandinavian warriors whose arrival brought linguistic eruption with a twofold effect on the English language in its earlier form. Between 839 and 878 an organised army of Scandinavian adventurers ravaged all East Anglia, Mercia, and the southern half of Northumbria. It penetrated Wessex, where it suffered defeat by Alfred's forces. Thereupon the leader of the expedition embraced the Catholic faith and became by treaty overlord of Mercia, East Anglia, Essex, and part of Northumbria. Throughout this region, the Norse settlers accepted as overlord Alfred's successor, Edward the Elder, in A.D. 924. The hegemony of Wessex was of short duration. From 900 to 939 migrants from Ireland (which the Norsemen had partially occupied) settled in Cambria, then predominantly Celtic, and briefly occupied York.

An English king, Athelstan, defeated a combined invasion by Scots in alliance with the Norse king of Dublin in A.D. 937; but there were ephemeral Norse occupations of York for nearly twenty years thereafter. From A.D. 940 to 942 a Norse invasion assimilated all Mercia; but again in A.D. 958 Northumbria and East Anglia acknowledged as overlord a West Saxon king. A second unification of England, like the first, was short lived. About A.D. 980 a succession of coastal raids by Norsemen was the prelude to a large-scale invasion (A.D. 1013) which drove an English king, then married to a sister of the Duke of Normandy, into exile at the Norman court. The leader of the invasion was the Danish King Swegn, whose son Cnut ruled all England except Wessex (A.D. 1016-1035). Cnut's two sons retained their father's throne till A.D. 1042, when the renegade Edward, so-called Confessor, returned from Normandy as heir to the Wessex throne with a following of Norman nobles and prelates.

The partial settlement of England by Norsemen in the ninth century was only one facet of a vast migration. Norsemen colonised Iceland about the same time and settled on the Baltic fringe of Russia. During the reign of Alfred the Great they penetrated France as far as Paris where the reigning monarch (Charles the Fat) bought them off. A little later (A.D. 911), they settled by consent in what was henceforth to be known as the Duchy of Normandy. There they adopted the local dialect of the French language; and thence they proceeded, with the encouragement of the Pope, to the conquest of Sicily (A.D. 1061-1100), at that time under Saracen rule. The invasion last mentioned set a pattern for three centuries of warfare in which rapacious Teutonic robber-barons, egged on by fanatical psychopaths with Papal blessing, contended with the armies of a more advanced civilisation.

From the foregoing record, it will be clear that Norse influence before the Norman Conquest was most effective in the northern part of England. To be sure, the part of Northumbria beyond its present boundary came under the Scottish crown in the first year of Cnut's reign; but the islands off the Scottish coast remained under Norse rule much longer. The Hebrides remained Norse till 1250. The Orkneys and Shetlands, in the outermost islands of which the Old Norse speech survived into the beginning of the nineteenth century, retained their allegiance to the Norwegian crown till about 1450. Except in Wales and in the part of England south of the Thames, the population of Britain at the time of the Conquest had indeed absorbed successive waves of settlers whose native speech was Norse; and the fact that the English speech community could so easily assimilate them is explicable only in terms of the family likeness of the overwhelming majority of words in the Low German and Scandinavian dialects. Hence, the effect on the vocabulary of English of the dilution of Low German stock during the 150 years after the beginning of Alfred's reign was not very considerable, and pertains largely to

Scandinavian words which are of different ancestry from Low German words of the same meaning.

We have seen (p. 30) that the two verbs *take* and *die* are both Norse intruders. So also are *call* (Swed. *kalla*, Dan. *kalde*), *cast* (Swed. *kasta*, Dan. *kaste*), *hit* (Swed. *hitta*, Dan. *hitte*) and *lift* (Dan. *løfte*). Besides *leg* for SCEANCA (*shank*, p. 26), our battery of specifically Norse nouns includes *inter alia*: *egg* (Swed. *ägg*, Dan. *æg*), *knife* (Swed. and Dan. *kniv*), *skin* (Swed. *skinn*, Dan. *skind*), *sky* (Old Norse for *cloud*) and *window* (Dan. *vindue* and Old Norse *vindr-auga=wind-eye*). Also Scandinavian are *same* (Swed. *samma*, Dan. *samme*) and *first* (Swed. *första*, Dan. *først*) for O.E. FORMA or ÆREST (Du. *eerste*, Germ. *erst*, cf. *erstwhile*). Aside from about one hundred of such specifically Norse intruders, the influence of the Vikings persists in hosts of British place names with such suffixes as -BY (*town*), -GATE (*road*), -FIRTH (*fjord*), -NESS (*headland*), -EY (*island*), e.g. *Grimsby, Ramsgate, Firth of Forth, Sheerness, Orkney*. In Scottish dialects, the Norse influence on pronunciation was appreciable in conserving the *k*-sound, e.g. *kirk* for *church*, *mickle* or *muckle* for *much* (O.E. MYCEL). In England as well as Scotland, it was responsible for the hard *g*- sound in *give, gift* (p. 22) and for the substitution of the *dh*- sound represented by TH in *father* and *mother* (in O.E. FÆDER and MODOR). Norse influence also accounts for the second member of such couplets as *ditch-dike* and *shirt-skirt*.

If the specifically Viking contribution to our vocabulary was comparatively small, the influence of Norse on English grammar was destined during the century after the Conquest, and later, to be very considerable. Thus the intrusion of *are* (*we are*, etc.) in the conjugation of *be* (p. 71) and the introduction of the pronouns *they—them—their* (p. 211) are undisputed examples of Norse usage. So also is the adoption of *shall* and *will* (Swed. *skall* and *vill*, Dan. *skal* and *vil*) as future auxiliaries. In view of what happened in North Britain where Norman influence was least, there is a strong presumption for the view that Norse influence contributed as much as, if not more than, that of the Norman conquerors to the abandonment of a characteristically Low German word order (see p. 222) and to a wholesale loss of terminals which O.E. shared neither with Norse nor with French.

Like that of Charlemagne, the court of the scholar warrior Alfred of Wessex (A.D. 871-901) had been a beacon in the surrounding darkness of Europe. He himself translated several devotional works and encouraged his subjects to read; and there is some reason to believe that he enlisted in this task monks with roots in the ancient native church from beyond the Welsh border. About fifty years after his death appeared several English translations of the Gospels—the Lindisfarne, Rushworth and Wessex versions. Before the Norman Conquest we may thus be sure that the English Church encouraged the preservation of a literary standard of English speech. We can scarcely doubt that its spirit of independence was uncongenial to the

MUSEUM EXHIBIT—THE TEUTONIC MIXED VERB "BE"

	MODERN GERMAN	OLD ENGLISH		ICELANDIC
	sein	beon *or* wesan		vera
	seiend	beonde *or* wesende		verandi
	gewesen	....		....
1. s.	ich bin	bio	*or* ic am	ég er
2. s.	du bist	bist	thu arth	thu ert
3. s.	er ist	bith	he is	hann er
Plur.	sind, seid, sind	bioth	sind	erum, eruth, eru
1. s.	ich war	ic wæs		ég var
2. s.	du warst	thu wære		thu varst
3. s.	er war	he wæs		hann var
Plur.	waren, wart, waren	wæron		vorum, voruth, voru
Pres. Subj.	sei-seien	sie-sien	beo-beon	sé, sért, *etc.*
Past Subj.	wäre-wären	wære-wæren		væri, værir, *etc.*

NOTES: *am, arth* (for *eom, eart*) are Anglian. In other dialects, *sint* and *sindon* occur as variants of *sind*.

Vatican at a time when the Normans had earned its benediction by starting (A.D. 1060) to drive the Saracens out of Sicily; and if we may properly speak of this exploit as the first Crusade, we may with equal propriety speak of the Norman invasion of England as the second. When William the Bastard, Duke of Normandy, landed (A.D. 1066) on the coast of Sussex, he unfurled a banner blessed by the Pope himself in anticipation of favours to come. Four years after the battle, the Conqueror secured the expulsion of the English Archbishop of Canterbury, and replaced him by Lanfranc, an Italian who had visited Rome to secure papal dispensation for William's marriage to his cousin Matilda.

While Norman barons largely replaced the English nobility and collaborated in building monasteries and cathedrals, a Norman hierarchy more subservient to Rome thus replaced the leaders of the English church and recruited its monasteries from those of the Continent. Inevitably, the cultivation of English as a medium of religious instruction languished. Less than two centuries after the Conquest, the English of the English versions of the Gospels was a dead language to people of

English stock. Greek scholarship such as the Celtic monasteries had cultivated disappeared under a régime which had no inclination to favour intercourse with the rival Byzantine Church. A century after William's conquest the nobility, abbots, bishops and lawyers were almost exclusively of Norman origin. Besides these, architects and artisans, builders of the fortresses, castles, cathedrals, abbeys and parish churches of the same century, were Norman immigrants, with whom came merchants from Norman cities to settle with Flemish weavers in London and other, then small, English towns.

Before the twelfth century, descendants of the craftsman and merchant settlers had ceased to be a people apart, and spoke an English diluted with a modicum of Norman French words. However, it is wrong to assume that the Norman dialect made the major contribution of French to the English of Wycliffe and Chaucer. For nearly three centuries embracing the so-called Hundred Years' War (A.D. 1337-1453), English-speaking English soldiers, including Geoffrey Chaucer (see below), were intermittently engaged in fighting on French soil. By inheritance and marriage, Henry II (1154-89) was Duke of Normandy, Count of Anjou and Duke of Aquitaine. Edward III, who had claimed the title of King of France in 1340, annexed by conquest Calais, part of Normandy and roughly half of France south of the Loire. By the decisive battle of Agincourt (1415) Henry V assured for his successor the overlordship of nearly all France north of the Loire. Fifty years later the only English foothold on French soil was the port of Calais.

In connexion with our main concern in this narrative, it is relevant to record that linguistic traffic was not wholly one-way. Side by side with words of Latin parentage —*septentrional, midi-meridional, orient(al), occident(al)*—French assimilated from the early Plantagenet period a Teutonic battery for the compass points, as below:

FRENCH	OLD ENGLISH	DUTCH	GERMAN	DANISH	SWEDISH
nord	north	noord(en)	Nord(en)	nord	nord
sud	suth	zuid(en)	Süd(en)	syd	söder
est	east	oost(en)	Ost(en)	øst	öst
ouest	west	west(en)	West(en)	vest	väst

Writers who deign to offer an explanation of the recrudescence of English as a literary medium commonly refer to the loss (1204) of Normandy with Anjou, Touraine and Poitou during the reign of John, the son of Henry II; but Aquitaine and Gascony remained English, and Brittany recognised Henry III, son of John, as overlord. To be sure, the reign of John may well have been a watershed, but if so for other reasons. The brother of John and successor of Henry II spent only two of the ten years of his reign in England. His crusading capers and his intrigues for influence as a continental potentate bled England to foot the bill for costly campaigns and an equally costly ransom, with consequences which outlasted the reign of John himself. Only onerous taxation of an emergent English-speaking bourgeoisie could pay the piper. Seemingly, the piper could call the tune. For we learn from one authority that 250 out of 760 boroughs which received royal charters of self-government during the two and a half centuries (1066-1307) between the Norman Conquest and the death of Edward I are assignable to the reigns of Richard I and John, a period (1189-1216) of twenty-seven years.

The reign of the much-maligned John ushers in the latter part of the thirteenth century, and the fourteenth century. Merchants, domiciled in towns whose charters guaranteed legal independence of rapacious feudal landlords, were becoming increasingly prosperous as a result of wool trade with the Continent. Noblemen who used their lands for rearing sheep were enriching themselves with business transactions which brought them into contact with merchants and money-changers whose native speech was English. In becoming a trading community, England had become a nation in correspondence with a larger world, and English was becoming, as never before, a medium for the written word. Substantial residences with bottle-glass windows made indoor reading possible for the more opulent burghers without recourse to artificial light. During the latter half of the fourteenth century secular grammar schools sponsored by the guilds gave English instruction in the new commercial arithmetic which came with the Hindu-Arabic numerals from Moorish universities; and the latter end of the century witnessed an outburst of literary activity, which followed very soon after a noteworthy event in the reign of Edward III. For the first time since the Norman Conquest, commoners could use English to plead in the courts.

Before A.D. 1362 it was customary to plead in Norman French, which had also been the language of Parliamentary debate. In one sense, Norman French remained the language of the Law till a revolution put Cromwell in power. At that time small-holders had a great grievance. Wealthy landowners with skilful lawyers were seizing from the peasantry what had once been common land for grazing; and the Levellers in Cromwell's following denounced bitterly a practice which antedates parliamentary institutions. The Norman kings had not promulgated an all-inclusive fixed system of written law, and statutes enacted after Magna Carta were recorded in Norman French or in Latin till A.D. 1483. None the less, use of Norman French for legal purposes lingered long after it ceased to be the language of the Statute Book. Much of the Law of England, especially as affecting ownership of land, is embodied in what judges have ruled to be accepted as such from earlier times. To interpret this *Common* Law, outside the contents of the Statute Book, judges themselves rely on reports of court proceedings in the past, and Norman French remained the language of such reports till Cromwell's time. Its use came back again at the Restoration; but an Act of Parliament finally abolished it in A.D. 1731.

In the fourteenth-century setting of increasing literacy, churchmen of native

Fig. 4. Map of Celtic Monasteries and Christianisation of Britain.

descent in the newly-founded universities boldly challenged an alien hierarchy, and exhorted people to read the scriptures in their own language. The earliest version of the period was completed shortly before the death (A.D. 1384) of John Wycliffe. How far he was actively engaged in the work of translation is not clear. What we know certainly is that a far better translation which appeared about ten years later was the work of disciples inspired by his teaching. The so-called Wycliffe Bible is a far more bulky work than any of its predecessors in the native tongue. For that reason the man to whose inspiration we owe its production must rank with Chaucer as one of the architects of Modern English; and as such his life is relevant to our story of the Mother Tongue.

Born in the Yorkshire village of Richmond (A.D. 1324), he entered the newly-founded Queen's College of Oxford at sixteen years of age, and became a Fellow of Merton College in 1356. He studied Aristotle in the Latin translations of the time, and won high regard for his powers of public argument at a time when University authorities were faced with a threat from new orders of mendicant preachers, more especially the Dominicans, eager to control education at all levels. He wrote many religious treatises, some exposing the "errors and heresies of friars". As champion of its rights, the University rewarded his services by appointing him Master of Balliol College. In 1367, he defended Edward III when the King refused to pay tribute exacted by the Pope from King John and his successors. Wycliffe's eloquence earned him the esteem and protection of the King, of Parliament and of the powerful Duke of Lancaster, John of Gaunt. In 1372, he became Professor of Divinity at Oxford; and in 1374 he retired to the vicarage of Lutterworth in the Midland county of Leicester. There he may well have devoted himself to the great task we associate with his name.

Also to the latter half of the century, which witnessed the appearance of the first complete English Bible, belongs the work of Geoffrey Chaucer, born about sixteen years after Wycliffe. Chaucer is noteworthy as the first man to write English for fun in a big way. We know him best for a collection of stories in rhyme called the *Canterbury Tales*. In this collection, one or other member of a company of men and women on a pilgrimage to the shrine erected on the spot where soldiers of Henry II dispatched the tempestuous Roman bishop Thomas à Becket recounts a tale while they travel towards Canterbury. The *Prologue* gives us a description of each of the pilgrims, and with each a glimpse of some social stratum in the England of Chaucer's time. From what the *Prologue* tells us, we learn much of what we know about the customs of a time when England was becoming a trading nation with a considerable literate stratum.

Chaucer was born at a time when a merchant class, prospering through the wool trade with Flanders, was beginning to mix and to marry with the land-owning nobility. His father, a London wine merchant, had married the heiress of a money-changer.

He was wealthy and well connected enough to place his son on the way to social advancement as a page in the household of the Countess of Ulster. After that, the youth studied at the great law school called the Inner Temple. He fought in the campaign of 1359-60 under Edward III, when the English king invaded and temporarily conquered France. There he was a prisoner for a short time till ransomed for £16. He then remained a little longer at Calais as a courier. His fortunes improved greatly after marriage in 1366 to a Lady of the Queen's Bedchamber, herself the daughter of a knight.

His wife's sister, long the mistress of John of Gaunt, Earl of Richmond, Duke of Lancaster, and then the most powerful of English noblemen, eventually became the Duke's third wife. In 1367 Chaucer received a pension from the king and a position in his household. Between 1370 and 1380 he engaged in diplomatic service on the Continent, and on one of his missions he made the acquaintance of the Italian poet Petrarch at Padua. During this period he became Controller of Customs and of the Subsidy of Wools, with a handsome residence in London. Both he and his wife received ample pensions from John of Gaunt. In 1385 Chaucer took up residence near London, in Kent, where he became a Justice of the Peace of the County, and a Knight of the Shire in the Parliament of 1387. After the death of Edward III, other royal appointments and pensions followed in the reigns of Richard II and of Henry IV. Chaucer died in 1400 at about sixty years of age. He seems to have done no literary work till his fortunes improved by marriage. Indeed, he finished only one of his books, the *Romance of the Rose*, before 1369. By then he had gained worldly prosperity. Nearly the whole of the *Canterbury Tales* belongs to the last five years of his life.

But for two circumstances, the stage was now set for a great step forward towards greater prosperity and greater literacy. For nearly a century after Wycliffe's death, futile disputes between contestants for the crown (one episode being the so-called Wars of the Roses) dissipated the nation's resources, and throughout this period the only reading matter available to those who were able to read was manuscript copied by a scribe or scrivener with his own hand. Only through a scrivener could a writer reach his public; but there was otherwise no lack of instructive readable material. Even in twelfth-century England, the more important surviving scientific treatises of antiquity, such as those of Euclid and Ptolemy, were available in Latin translations from Arabic versions made by Adelard of Bath, a monk who disguised himself as a Moslem to study in the Moorish universities of Spain.

In the time of Chaucer and of Wycliffe, there were in circulation hand-copied manuals of commercial arithmetic and manuals of navigation called *rutter*-books for the use of the master mariner. Despite this, reading of any sort, and especially for pleasure, was a luxury. Only the prosperous few could hope to possess copies of the products of a scrivener's laborious penmanship; and while this state of affairs persisted, there could be no rigid standard of spelling. The spoken word must needs remain the chief instrument of instruction or persuasion. There was no agency to promote the circulation of translations of foreign literature into the Mother Tongue, and little but the evangelical enthusiasm which sustained the labour of Wycliffe to encourage the undertaking.

Thus the story of the English language is not complete if we fail to take stock of two circumstances which happened before a Tudor dynasty ended a dreary and devastating dynastic struggle. Each is one of our many debts to Chinese civilisation. One was the availability of a writing surface considerably less costly than the parchment of the chroniclers. The other was a mechanical substitute for the scrivener's art. The capture of Samarcand by Moslems in A.D. 750 signalises the date when the use of paper began to spread westwards. In succeeding centuries, Moslem invaders brought it into Spain and into Sicily with a recipe for making the fibre basis from rags. By A.D. 1200 it was beginning to compete with costlier parchment made from animal membranes in the neighbouring Christian countries of the West, where the spread of water-mills provided power to break up the pulp. Before Chaucer or Wycliffe began to write, there were paper mills in Germany, and at the time of their deaths, in England also. Playing cards produced by the Chinese device of block printing were already in use.

Printing from movable type began in Germany about A.D. 1450 and spread very rapidly to Italy, to France, to the Low Countries and to England. William Caxton, who started printing English books in Holland, set up the first printing business on his native soil in A.D. 1476. Meanwhile, the end of the Hundred Years' War had effectually terminated English commitments on the Continent, and less than a decade later, the start of the Tudor dynasty ended half a century of civil strife. Fifty years after, the press which issued Martin Luther's tract *To the Christian Nobility* could dispose of 4,000 copies in five days; and 24,000 copies of one of the works of the scholar Erasmus sold in the first few decades of the same century. These are small figures beside a 50,000 edition of a modern best-seller; but they register an unprecedented advance in the accessibility of the written word to a human community, in an age when the production of a single complete copy of Holy Writ had lately been a creditable half-yearly product of penmanship.

Inevitably, the output of writing in the Mother Tongue leapt upwards in the half century which followed the introduction of printing into England. Since one master printer in the capital city now made decisions formerly at the discretion of local penmen, the spelling of English began to be more uniform. Apart from this, printing from movable type had little direct effect on the language. What changes of standard English grammar occurred between A.D. 1400 and 1800 were changes for which we can find local precedents before printing began. It would be too much to say that printing directly contributed much to this process; but its influence on our

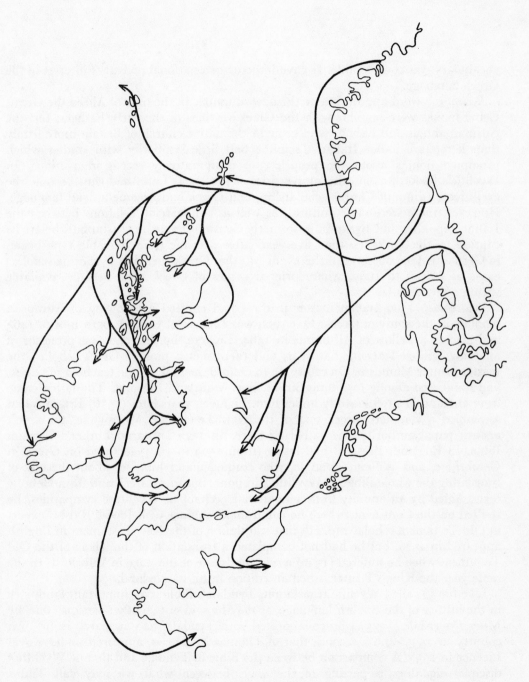

Fig. 5.   Map of the First Great Norse Invasion—time of Alfred the Great.

vocabulary was considerable. It gave impetus to a national revival of interest in the Greek language.

Revival is a word appropriate to the new situation. In the time of Alfred the Great, Celtic monks were familiar with the Greek writings of the early Fathers; but the Norman abbots and bishops who brought the native church of Britain more firmly than heretofore under Italian discipline had little sympathy with studies which prompted doubts about the propriety of comparatively recent innovations. In Wycliffe's Oxford, as in other universities of the West, Latin had thus become the exclusive medium of Church scholarship, and Greek had become a dead language. However, there were close cultural, as well as commercial, relations between the Italian republics and Byzantium (formerly Constantinople, now Istanbul) before its capture by the Turks less than five years after printing from movable type began in Germany. One outcome of this event was that Greek-speaking Byzantine scholars came as *émigrés* to Italy, where printed copies of Greek texts became available within a few decades.

Before A.D. 1500 Italian master printers had enlisted a following of European scholars in the study of Greek. One such was Linacre of Oxford, born in A.D. 1464 and elected a Fellow of All Saints in 1484. Linacre, by first choice a professor of anatomy, visited Italy in that year, and there met a pioneer Greek scholar, the master printer Manutius. On returning to Oxford, he took up the teaching of Greek, and numbered among his pupils Sir Thomas More and Erasmus. The latter came from Holland in 1498 to study under him. Eighteen years later (1516) Erasmus had assembled a complete Greek text of the New Testament. Meanwhile, the revolt against papal authority was gathering force. In 1522 appeared Luther's German Bible. In England, Erasmus had lately (from 1509 to 1514) lectured on Greek in Cambridge, and William Tyndale, who studied under him, set about the task of translating the whole Bible, as Wycliffe had done, but from Greek and from Hebrew texts. Aided by an annuity from a London merchant of Wycliffite sympathies, he resided on the Continent, where he could make contact with Jewish Rabbis expert in Old Testament scholarship. His first translation of the New Testament in English appeared in 1526, but he had not completed a translation of the whole of the Old Testament when he suffered (1536) a reformer's fate at the stake in Vilivoord. In the same year the King's Printer issued an edition in his native land.

Like the so-called Wycliffe translation, Tyndale's Bible is an important landmark in the history of the English language, as may be said of two other versions: one, by Miles Coverdale (1535) who collaborated with Tyndale, had appeared in his own country in 1535; and a second, that of Thomas Matthews, appeared under Royal Licence in 1537. A comparison between the Bible of Tyndale and that of Wycliffe's disciples signalises a parting of the ways between what we may call Tudor English and the Later Middle English of Wycliffe and Chaucer. The English

Church had now won freedom from foreign control, and its Archbishop Cranmer authorised that the copy of an English Bible should be available in a convenient place in every church where all parishioners might read it. With minor editorial changes by a panel of bishops, the so-called *Great Bible* of Cranmer was essentially Tyndale's own version.

Throughout the reigns of Henry VIII and Edward VI, it remained the version authorised by the English Church. It regained its former status under Elizabeth I, in whose reign Archbishop Parker completed another revision. When James I authorised preparation of the 1611 Bible, since known as the Authorised Version (A.V.), he enjoined those who undertook the task to adhere closely to its predecessor, in effect the translation of Tyndale. Five years before its completion and three years after the death of the last Tudor monarch, a London company sent out an expedition to settle the territory of Virginia, so-named by Raleigh in honour of the presumptively Virgin Queen. Thenceforth we may speak of what we may more properly call Anglo-American.

Thus the social background of what is now the Anglo-American language, and as such also the language of Australasia, is divisible into seven periods, each with linguistic features of its own. First, we may separate as *early* Old English (or Anglo-Saxon) the period A.D. 550-850, i.e. before the Norse settlements. Next, as *late* Old English a period which ends soon after the Norman Conquest. Then comes a somewhat obscure *transitional* period, with few evocative remains in writing, from about A.D. 1100 to 1250. Thereafter, we may speak of English before its reinstatement in the courts of law, i.e. during the succeeding century, as early Middle English, in contradistinction to late Middle English between 1362 and the beginnings of printing in England. What we shall here call Tudor English begins but a few years before the start and terminates but a few years after the end of the Tudor dynasty, i.e. only seventeen years before the *Mayflower* sailed. The division between the Tudor and the succeeding Anglo-American period is not wholly arbitrary. It was the prelude to a closer fusion of Northern and Southern dialects brought about in no small measure by the Scottish entourage of a Scottish king and by presbyterian divines who found a home in England. A century later, the union (1707) of England and Scotland under one parliament consolidated the same process.

The main impact of the Scandinavian contribution already mentioned is assignable to the second and third of these periods. The influence of French was negligible before the predecessor of William the Conqueror packed his court with Norman favourites, and it continued to gather momentum throughout the Middle period. Its outcome for the vocabulary of English and for the pronunciation of native words was immense. Apart from reinforcing the influence of Norse settlers on its word order and the decay of its flexional (p. 173) system, its impact on the grammar of English is noteworthy in only one respect, namely the plural form of the noun.

One and the same O.E. noun had more than one plural (as well as singular) form, e.g. for *stones* we meet *stanas, stana, stanum*; for *houses* there were *hus, husa, husum*; for *answers* there were *andswara, andswarena, andswarum*; for *names* there were *naman, namena, namum*. Such were the main types, and one of three forms with final -S was in a minority. Contrariwise, the -S terminal was predominantly the hallmark of the French plural, e.g. *homme—hommes* and *femme—femmes* for *man—men* and *woman—women*. Since Scandinavian has no plural of this sort, there can be little doubt that French usage was responsible for the predominantly -ES type plural of Chaucer's time, albeit there still persisted so-called weak forms such as *oxen* (cf. *naman*), since accommodated to the common pattern. For instance *eyen* for *eyes* and *shoon* for *shoes* persisted long after Chaucer's time.

A remarkable feature of the impact of French on the vocabulary of English, but not widely recognised as such, was the equipment of the latter with a considerable battery of new terminals. Some of these are of trivial interest e.g. *-ess, -age, -ee,* as in *shepherdess, garage* and *employee*. The suffix *-able* is more noteworthy, because it now attaches itself to almost every verb to make adjectives such as *readable, lovable*. Most interesting of all are *-ite* (in *erudite*), *-ate* (in *sedate*), *-ous* (in *anxious*), *-ic* (in *historic*) and *-aceous* (in *herbaceous*). All these have proved highly fertile for formation of scientific terms. The first four (cf. *nitrite, nitrate, nitrous, nitric*) are (p. 250) the king-pin of the great reform of chemical nomenclature at the beginning of the French Revolution, when an Anglo-French united front laid the foundations of what was to become the world-wide vocabulary of Western science. This aspect of the impact of the Anglo-French set-up in the four centuries following the Norman Conquest is the topic of Chapter 7.

French words displaced many native ones during that period, relegated others to a minor rôle (cf. WYRT, p. 29), but supplemented many with synonyms, whence an enormous number of such Anglo-French couplets as: *begin—commence, buy—purchase, forgive—pardon, hang—suspend, work—labour*. An example, which emphasises that the intruder did not always win the struggle for existence, demonstrates this. The reader should recall that English writers of the Tudor period use *quoth*, a past tense form (CWÆTH) of the O.E. verb CWETHAN, now a poetic fossil. Of two French verbs which respectively mean *follow* and *follow after, pursue* and *pursuit* from *poursuivre* are in common currency. *Sue* from *suivre* survives only in law, but briefly enjoyed its original and more general meaning, as comparison of three versions of Matt. ix. 9 shows:

> *Old English*   A.D. 995   And he cwæth to him, Fylig me.
> *Wycliffe*   A.D. 1389   And he saide to hym, Sue thou me.
> *Tyndale*   A.D. 1526   And he said to him, Folowe me.

In the period 1350-1450 when there was still a prosperous trade in wool with the Low Countries, some Flemish words also came into English. *Rabbit*, for the Teutonic word *coney* still current in the fur trade, is an example of such. Earlier still, in the Middle Period, English had absorbed a not inconsiderable battery of words from Moslem science and commerce with the Moslem world. The Tudor period is note-worthy for the assimilation of not a few Italian words: but what is most characteristic of the Tudor period is a foretaste of a linguistic invasion which did not gain momen-tum till the end of the eighteenth century. Till about A.D. 1750 men of science turned chiefly to Latin for the bricks from which to build new words; but often such bricks were words borrowed by the Romans from their Greek schoolmasters. From A.D. 1750 till today, science has turned to Greek rather than to Latin for the raw materials of its dictionary.

An enormous proportion of the words in a dictionary of the Anglo-American language is either traceable to the spoken Latin of Gaul through Norman French or directly taken after a much longer lapse of time from Latin authors who wrote when Rome was still mistress of the Western world. Many others come directly from Greek authors who wrote in the long period (roughly 450 B.C. to A.D. 450) when Greek was the language of instruction in all outstanding branches of natural science, mathematics and philosophical disputation of the Western world. Latin translations from Arabic of the great scientific works of the Greeks when the Moorish universities of Spain were pre-eminent in the Western world have also conspired to contribute not a few words of Arabic and Persian origin to our vocabulary. Besides this, the dominant rôle of the English speech community in trade and in colonisation during the past four centuries has led to the assimilation of familiar words from Russian, Hindustani, and even the Amerindian languages.

Because of the vast store of word materials directly or indirectly derived from Latin and more recently from Greek besides other sources, it is now true to say that the majority of words in a modern English dictionary are *not* native words. In spite of this, English remains a Low German language if only because the overwhelming majority of words we still most commonly use are of O.E. stock. Thus 92·5 per cent. of the words in the Authorised (A.D. 1611) Version of the New Testament are native English, and it would be difficult to pick up even a current scientific textbook with less than 65 per cent. The explanation of the paradox, that a small minority of the total number of words in most of our books is of alien origin though most words in our dictionary are indeed aliens, lies in the fact that nearly all words we most rely on when we write spontaneously are native. To be sure, we can indeed make isolated meaningful sentences without using a single native word. The following examples show how we might convey the same news item first in words which are all native, then in words which are all foreign:

Speed fiends spread fear among good townsmen.
Ace motorists terrorise honest citizens.

Such examples might suggest that it is just as easy to write Modern English without using words of native English stock as to write Modern English without using borrowed words. In fact, it is not. So long as we are writing or talking about familiar things which call for the use of no highly technical words, we can express ourselves simply and clearly without using a single borrowed word, but it would be difficult to string together even 100 non-native words about any topic in an understandable sequence. One reason for this is clear if we ask ourselves what forces or tempts us most to borrow. The answer is simple. We are most prone to do so when we have to find names for new things; but words we use most often are not names for any particular thing.

That this is so gives us a clue to one prerequisite for exploiting the advantages of our hybrid heritage to the fullest possible extent. We can do so only if we can recognise which words are of native (or Scandinavian) origin and which are not. We can often do so by the way in which we spell them, and this will be our next theme. Otherwise, we can rely on the fact that the grammatical cement of the vocabulary of Anglo-American remains essentially Teutonic. We may thus list certain classes of words which are wholly, or almost wholly, native, or of Scandinavian origin:

1. The articles (*a*, *the*), demonstratives (*this*, *that*), personal pronouns (*I*, *him*, etc.), interrogative pronouns and adverbs (*who*, *what*, *how*, *when*, *where*, *why*, etc.).

2. The numerals, except *second* (Lat. *secundus*) and *million*, both French.

3. All monosyllabic* prepositions (*to*, *for*, etc.), conjunctions (*and*, *but*, etc.), and adverbs of time (e.g. *soon*, *then*) or place (e.g. *here*, *there*), exceptions (both French) being *round* (=*about*) and *save* (=*but*).

4. All adjectives and adverbs which have comparative and superlative forms derived from different roots (e.g. *good* or *well*, *better*, *best*).

5. All nouns which have plural forms which do not end in -S (e.g. *man*, *mouse*, *child*, *ox*, *sheep*).

6. With the exception of *strive* (from Old French *estriver*), all strong verbs, i.e. those which exhibit internal vowel change as illustrated by *find—found* or *give—gave*.

7. Mixed verbs and all helper verbs (*have*, *ought*, *shall*, *will*, *must*, *may*, *let*) except *use* (French) as in *we used to go*.

Two of the above list call for comment. Item 6 may be an example of the exception which proves the rule. Like *blank* (p. 53) we do not meet *strive* in any English texts before the Middle period, i.e. when *estriver* was already current in French. It does not follow that it was not part of the native stock-in-trade; but if not, scholars, who prefer to rely on documentary evidence, have to explain why a word which came into English by the back door recovered a Teutonic flexional form which had disappeared in a French verb, itself manifestly of Teutonic origin (p. 150). Thus

---

* *Because* is a hybrid written as such (=*by cause*) in Middle English.

estriver is equivalent to Icelandic *stritha*, Swed. *sträva*, Dan. *stride*, Du. *streven*, Germ. *streben*, all of them strong verbs. Surely, it is more likely that an adopted Norse strong verb, which had not gained literary currency, acquired popularity from its equivalent Old French intruder with the same parentage.

As regards item 7, the only mixed verbs to notice are *be*, etc., and *go—went*. The former derives its components from four sources present respectively in *be*, *is*, *were* and *are*. The first three turn up also in German and Dutch, the last two in Scandinavian. Only the third is common to all Teutonic languages. The equivalent is also a mixed verb in French compounded of Latin *stare* (*stand*) and mixed Latin *esse—fui*, corresponding to *is* and *be*. The French equivalent of *go*, etc., is likewise a mixed verb—*je vais* (I go) but *j'allais* (I went). *Go* (O.E. GAN, Du. *gaan*, Germ. *gehen*, Swed. and Dan. *gå*) is a mixed verb in all Teutonic languages. In O.E. the past tense was EODE which persisted in Chaucer's time as *yede*. In German and Dutch the past comes from an obsolete verb corresponding to O.E. GANGAN. This persists in Scots dialect, as in the expression *gang one's own gate* (*gate* being the Scandinavian word for *road* as in *Ramsgate*). O.E. had another verb FARAN whose equivalent (Germ. *fahren*, Swed. *fara*) in other Teutonic languages means *go in a conveyance*. It persists in the noun *fare* (conveyance cost), in *farewell* (have a good journey) and as a verb in the expression *go further and fare worse*. We have still to account for *went*. The O.E. verb WENDAN (Du. and Germ. *wenden*, Swed. *vända*, Dan. *vende*) means *turn* in its most general sense but like its equivalent in German or Swedish has the more specialised meaning *turn one's steps*, as when one says poetically *wend one's way*. *Went* is a shortened form of the past *wended*, and ousted *yede* of late Middle English.

It would be convenient if we could truthfully add that words with native affixes are all native. Actually, several French and Latin affixes attach themselves to native words (e.g. *pro-war*) and native ones to newcomers. This is so of *-ness* as in *tenderness*; *-dom* as in *officialdom*; *mis-* as in *miscalculate*; *fore-* as in *fore-ordained*; *-ly* as in *verily*; *under-* and *over-* as in *underrate* and *overestimate*. The following, though of limited range, are reliable: *-ship*, *-hood*, *be-*, *for-* and *ful-*, as in *lordship*, *manhood*, *behead*, *forgive* and *fulfil*.

We have already met one example (NIMAN, p. 30) of an O.E. verb which disappeared early in competition with Scandinavian *take*, and, like FARAN, two examples (p. 30) of O.E. verbs used only in set expressions, as in the King James Bible (WEORTHAN, Ezek. xxx.2, and WUNIAN, Num. xxii.30). From the source last named one may cite *abide* and *dwell*. The former, from ABIDAN, is a derivative of the same root as BIDAN, which survives in *bide one's time* with the same meaning (*delay*, *tarry*) as DWELLAN. The original meaning of the last named survives in the expression *dwell on*, etc., but the more usual meaning of *dwell* is now akin to its Scandinavian kinsman (Iceland *dvelja*, Swed. *dväljas*, Dan. *dvæle*). The word *abode* from ABIDAN recalls the Swed.-Dan. verb *bo* (Iceland *bua*) with the same meaning as *dwell*.

Unrelated to BIDAN is the O.E. verb BIDDAN, which is *bid* in the 1611 Bible, now replaced by *command, beg* or *implore.* Another verb on the lips of the Pilgrim Fathers was *trow* from native TRUWIAN with the same meaning as the Swed.-Dan. verb *tro* (Iceland. *trua*). The more familiar *believe* is a Middle English corruption of GELIEFAN, which is recognisably equivalent to Dutch *geloven* and German *glauben.*

Of O.E. verbs whose descendants survived into the Tudor period, one is of interest because it covers in Anglo-American the meaning *to be called* = *have the name,* and as such survives in all the sister Teutonic languages. HATAN tallies with Du. *heten,* Germ. *heissen,* Swed. *heta,* and outlasted the introduction of printing with the poetic mis-spelling *hight.* The corresponding active O.E. verb (*name*) was NAMIAN, equivalent to Du. *noemen,* Germ. *nennen,* Dan. *nævne,* Swed. *nämna.* Reminiscent of *hight* is *dight* (= *adorned*), resurrected by Sir Walter Scott from DIHTAN; and reminiscent of WUNIAN is WENIAN which has left as a poetic survival *I ween* etc. The past tense form (*quoth* = CWÆTH) of the O.E. verb CWETHAN was very much alive in Shakespeare's time, as were also the forms *wot* and *wist* from WITAN (*know*), corresponding to Du. *weten,* Germ. *wissen,* Swed. *veta,* Dan. *vide.* A reader who dips into the work of Chaucer or of his contemporaries will probably meet the Middle English form of two verbs easy to confuse. CLYPPAN now survives only in *paper-clip,* and is a word since replaced by the French *embrace.* It lingered in poetry till the time of the American Revolution, as in Cowper's poem, where we read: *Yon fair sea that cleps thy shores.* CLIPIAN meant *call,* and hangs on in Milton's pompous *by Heaven y-clept Euphrosyne,* where we also get the last English relic of Y- for the unwanted GE-. Neither of the verbs last mentioned appears to have any connexion with *clap* from Norse KLAPPA or *clip* from Norse KLIPPA as in *clippers.* We do not know the origin of *clasp;* possibly it was a mix-up of *grasp* and CLYPPAN. At least, people grasp one another when they *clip* in Chaucer's sense.

Two other native verbs call for comment. One is SELLAN, also spelt SYLLAN (= *give*), as in the O.E. Lord's Prayer (p. 35). It comes from the same source as SELLAN (= *sell*), the latter being equivalent to Dan. *sælge,* Swed. *sälja.* As used in the O.E. Gospels, SYLLAN has disappeared in competition with GIEFAN, with the same ancestry and meaning as Du. *geven,* Germ. *geben,* Dan. *give,* Swed. *giva.* Also noteworthy is TÆCAN (= *teach*), which has supplanted LÆRAN with the same ancestry and meaning as Du. *leren,* Germ. *lehren,* Dan. *lære,* Swed. *lära.* It comes remotely from the same source as TACEN, which survives as *token,* being equivalent to Du. *teken,* Germ. *Zeichen,* Dan. *tegn.*

QUIZ CORNER 2

Quiz 1

Comparison

The class of words called adjectives is the class of words to which we add the terminals -ER and -EST when we *compare* one thing or person with another. Sometimes one -ER and one -EST form serve for two or more dictionary words. The -ER and -EST forms of some dictionary words have disappeared. The -ER and -EST forms of a dictionary word which has itself disappeared take their place. Fill in:

MODERN ENGLISH	OLD ENGLISH	DUTCH	GERMAN	SWEDISH	DANISH
1.	SWETE	ZOET	SÜSS	SÖT	SØD
2.	SWETRA	ZOETER	SÜSSER	SÖTARE	SØDERE
3.	SWETEST	ZOETST	SÜSST	SÖTAST	SØDEST
4.	DEOP	DIEP	TIEF	DJUP	DYB
5.	DEOPRA	DIEPER	TIEFER	DJUPARE	DYBERE
6.	DEOPEST	DIEPST	TIEFST	DJUPAST	DYBEST
7.	EALD	OUD	ALT	GAMMAL	GAMMEL
8.	IELDRA	OUDER	ALTER	ÄLDRE	ÆLDRE
9.	IELDEST	OUDEST	ALTEST	ÄLDST	ÆLDST
10.	GOD	GOED	GUT	GOD	GOD
11.	BETERA	BETER	BESSER	BÄTTRE	BEDRE
12.	BETEST	BEST	BEST	BÄST	BEDST
13. ..... *or*	LYTEL *or* SMÆL	KLEIN	KLEIN	LITEN, LILLA *or* SMÅ	LILLE *or* SMÅ (pl.)
14.	LÆSSA	KLEINER	KLEINER	MINDRE	MINDRE
15.	LÆST	KLEINST	KLEINST	MINST	MINDST
16.	FEAWA	WEINIG	WENIG	FÅ	FÅ
17.	FEAWRA	MINDER	MINDER	FÄRRE	FÆRRE
18.	FEAWEST	MINST	MINST	MINST	FÆRREST
19.	MYCEL *or* FELA	VEEL	VIEL	MYCKEN	MEGET
20.	MARA	MEER	MEHR	MERA	MERE
21.	MÆST	MEEST	MEIST	MEST	MEST
22.	MANIG	MENIG *or* VEEL	VIELE	MÅNGA	MANGE

MODERN OLD ENGLISH	ENGLISH	DUTCH	GERMAN	SWEDISH	DANISH
23.	MARA	MEER	MEHR	FLERA	FLERE
24.	MÆST	MEEST	MEIST	FLESTA	FLEST
25.	YFEL or WOH	KWAAD or SLECHT	SCHLECHT	DÅLIG	DÅRLIG
26.	WIERSA	ERGER or SLECHTER	SCHLECHT-ER	VÄRRE or SÄMRE	VÆRRE
27.	WIERREST	ERGST or SLECHTST	SCHLECHT-EST	VÄRST or SÄMST	VÆRST
28.	GEONG	JONG	JUNG	UNG	UNG
29.	GINGRA	JONGER	JUNGER	YNGRE	YNGRE
30.	GINGEST	JONGST	JUNGST	YNGST	YNGST

Quiz 2

English before the Norman Conquest

Clues:

(1) Treat the terminals in bold type with the same proper contempt as the coarse and brutal Norman soldiery showed.

(2) Read **the** for SE and **that** for THE (p. 212).

(3) Look up SC in the spelling quiz of p. 115.

(4) For MID and AC, see pp. 39 and 187.

1. AN MANN HÆFDE DOCGA**N**.

   ....

2. SE MANN WÆS HWIT. HIS HUND WÆS BLÆC AND ÆC WÆS, EALD.

   ....

3. SE DOCG**A** ÆT BAN. SE MANN ÆT FLÆSC.

   ....

4. THA BAN WÆR**ON** HEARD AND TH**ÆT** FLÆSC WÆS GOD.

   ....

5. SE HUND DRANC WÆTER AC SE MANN DRANC WIN.

   ....

6. SE MANN WEOX THYNNE AND SE DOCGA WEOX GREAT.

   ....

7. SONA WÆS SE HUND DEAD AC SE MANN IS NU MID US.

. . . .

8. HWÆT LEORNIATH WE FRAM THISSUM?

. . . .

9. MANN LIFETH LENGEST THE NE DRINCTH WÆTER.

. . . .

10. WIS MANN NE GIEFTH GOD FLÆSC TO HUNDUM.

. . . .

Quiz 3

Helper Verbs

The Helper Verbs shown here can all precede the dictionary form of another verb without needing anything to replace our empty word *to* (TE, ZU, ATT, AT) between them, as in (*fill blank*):

(D, G, d or S)*		ENGLISH
(...)	VI SKAL GÅ NU	. . . .
(...)	KAN DU KOMMA IGEN?	. . . .
(...)	MAG IK KOMEN?	. . . .
(...)	ICH HATTE IHN GESEHEN	. . . .
(...)	VIL DU LADE HAM KOMME HER?	. . . .

Note:

The German SOLL-SOLLEN retains its original meaning, i.e. . . . . . . in the Tenth Commandment, not as a time marker in VI SKAL GÅ NU. The Swedish MÅ and its German equivalents do not take the place of MAG-MOGEN, MOCHTE-MOCHTEN in Dutch, which tallies with English. The corresponding German equivalents signify *like-liked*. With this proviso, fill in the English equivalents for:

---

* *D* = Dutch, *G* = German, *d* = Danish, *S* = Swedish.

1a. ......   1b. ......
2a. ......   2b. ......
3a. ......   3b. ......
4a. ......   4b. ......
5a. ......   5b. ......
6a. ......   6b. ......
7a. ......   7b. ......
8a. ......   8b. ......

	DUTCH	GERMAN	SWEDISH	DANISH
1a.	HIJ IS	ER IST	HAN ÄR	HAN ER
	WIJ ZIJN	WIR SIND	VI ÄRO	VI ER
b.	HIJ WAS	ER WAR	HAN VAR	HAN VAR
	WIJ WAREN	WIR WAREN	VI VORO	VI VAR
2a.	HIJ HEEFT	ER HAT	HAN HAR	HAN HAR
	WIJ HEBBEN	WIR HABEN	VI HA(VA)	VI HAR
b.	HIJ HAD	ER HATTE	HAN HADE	HAN HAVDE
	WIJ HADDEN	WIR HATTEN	VI HADE	VI HAVDE
3a.	HIJ KAN	ER KANN	HAN KAN	HAN KAN
	WIJ KUNNEN	WIR KONNEN	VI KUNNA	VI KAN
b.	HIJ KON	ER KONNTE	HAN KUNDE	HAN KUNNE
	WIJ KONDEN	WIR KONNTEN	VI KUNDE	VI KUNNE
4a.	HIJ MOET	ER MUSS	HAN MÅSTE	HAN MÅ
	WIJ MOETEN	WIR MUSSEN	VI MÅSTE	VI MÅ
b.	HIJ MOEST	ER MUSSTE	HAN MÅSTE	HAN MÅTTE
	WIJ MOESTEN	WIR MUSSTEN	VI MÅSTE	VI MÅTTE
5a.	HIJ MAG	(ER MAG)	(HAN MÅ)	HAN MÅ
	WIJ MOGEN	(WIR MÖGEN)	(VI MÅ)	VI MÅ
b.	HIJ MOCHT	(ER MOCHTE)	(HAN MÅTTE)	HAN MÅTTE
	WIJ MOCHTEN	(WIR MOCHTEN)	(VI MÅTTE)	VI MÅTTE

DUTCH	GERMAN	SWEDISH	DANISH
6a. HIJ WIL WIJ WILLEN	ER WILL WIR WOLLEN	HAN VILL VI VILJA	HAN VIL VI VIL
b. HIJ WILDE WIJ WILDEN	ER WOLLTE WIR WOLLTEN	HAN VILLE VI VILLE	HAN VILLE VI VILLE
7a. HIJ ZAL WIJ ZULLEN	(ER SOLL) (WIR SOLLEN)	HAN SKALL VI SKOLA	HAN SKAL VI SKAL
b. HIJ ZOU WIJ ZOUDEN	(ER SOLLTE) (WIR SOLLTEN)	HAN SKULLE VI SKULLE	HAN SKULLE VI SKULLE
8a. HIJ LAAT WIJ LATEN	ER LASST WIR LASSEN	HAN LÅTER VI LÅTA	HAN LADER VI LADER
b. HIJ LIET WIJ LIETEN	ER LIESS WIR LIESSEN	HAN LÄT VI LÄTO	HAN LOD VI LOD

Quiz 4

Teutonic Affixes

The following native prefixes attach themselves to nouns and to verbs:

BE-, BY-, FOR-, FORE-, FUL-, MIS-, OUT-, OVER-, UNDER.

Some of these attach themselves more or less readily to roots of Latin origin, as in:

foreordain miscalculate, outmode, overstatement, underestimate.

Give the modern form of the O.E. words:

1. UTLAGU	......	7. UNDERLING	......
2. OFERMICEL	......	8. FORGIEFAN	......
3. MISLÆDAN	......	9. BECWETHAN	......
4. BIWORD	......	10. FULLFYLLAN	......
5. BECUMAN	......	11. BEHEAFDIAN	......
6. FORBEODAN	......	12. FORHEAFOD	......

The following native suffixes attach to nouns:

-DOM, -EN, -ER, -HOOD, -NESS, -SHIP.

Of these, -DOM, -ER, -HOOD, -NESS, and -SHIP may attach themselves to roots of Latin origin, as in: * *martyrdom, armourer, parenthood, tenderness, scholarship.*

Give the modern form of the O.E. words:

1. MÆGDEN	......	7. BLINDNES	......
2. BÆCERE	......	8. FIXEN	......
3. CNIHTHAD	......	9. CILDHAD	......
4. BITTERNES	......	10. FREONDSCIPE	......
5. CYNINGDOM	......	11. IDELNES	......
6. FOLGERE	......	12. HLAFORDSCIPE	......

The following are native suffixes attached to adjectives:

-EN, -FAST, -FOLD, -FUL, -Y, -ISH, -LY, -SOME, -WARD.

Some of these attach themselves to roots of Latin origin, as in: *beautiful, rosy, stylish, miserly, venturesome.*

Give the modern form of the O.E. words:

1. ÆSCEN	......	9. MANIGFEALD	......
2. LUFSUM	......	10. HUNGRIG	......
3. STEDEFÆST	......	11. HWÆTEN	......
4. WUNDORFULL	......	12. FORTHWEARD	......
5. NORTHEWEARD	......	13. ANLIC	......
6. DÆGLIC	......	14. ENGLISC	......
7. CILDISC	......	15. WYNSUM	......
8. THYRSTIG	......	16. LEADEN	......

---

* The French -EUR in *masseur* usually becomes -OR in English. In such words -OR has the same significance as the native -MAN and -ER (*workman, worker*). It is not surprising that we find -ER attached to words of Latin origin and -OR in words (e.g. *sailor*) of native origin.

Quiz 5

Some Strong Verbs

DUTCH	HIJ KAN, TE *or* WIJ VINDEN	IK VIND	IK VOND *and* WIJ VONDEN	IK HEB GEVONDEN
GERMAN	ER KANN, ZU *or* WIR FINDEN	ICH FINDE	ICH FAND *and* WIR FANDEN	ICH HABE GEFUNDEN
SWEDISH	HAN KAN, ATT *or* VI FINNA	JAG FINNER	JAG FANN *and* VI FUNNO	JAG HAR FUNNIT
DANISH	HAN KAN *or* AT FINDE	JEG *and* VI FINDE	JEG *or* VI FANDT	JEG HAR FUNDET
ENGLISH (A.D. 900)	WE CANN FINDAN	IC FINDE *and* WE FINDETH	IC FAND *and* WE FUNDON	IC HÆBBE GEFUNDEN
ENGLISH (A.D. 1300)	WE CAN, TO *or* WE FINDEN	I FINDE *and* WE FINDEN	I FOND *and* WE FONDEN	I HAVE YFONDEN

DUTCH

1.	zingen	zing	zong	gezongen
2.	zinken	zink	zonk	gezonken
3.	geven	geef	gaf	gegeven
4.	zien	zie	zag	gezien
5.	vliegen	vlieg	vloog	gevlogen
6.	vriezen	vries	vroor	gevroren
7.	vallen	val	viel	gevallen
8.	houden	houd	hield	gehouden
9.	staan	sta	stond	gestaan
10.	komen	kom	kwam	gekomen
11.	gaan	ga	ging	gegaan
12.	liggen	lig	lag	gelegen

GERMAN

singen	singe	sang	gesungen
sinken	sinke	sank	gesunken
geben	gebe	gab	gegeben
sehen	sehe	sah	gesehen
fliegen	fliege	flog	geflogen
frieren	friere	fror	gefroren
fallen	falle	fiel	gefallen
halten	halte	hielt	gehalten
stehen	stehe	stand	gestanden
kommen	komme	kam	gekommen
gehen	gehe	ging	gegangen
liegen	liege	lag	gelegen

SWEDISH

sjunga	sjunger	sjöng	sjungit
sjunka	sjunker	sjönk	sjunkit
giva	giver	gav	givit
se	ser	såg	sett
flyga	flyger	flög	flugit
frysa	fryser	frös	frusit
falla	faller	föll	fallit
hålla	håller	höll	hållit
stå	står	stod	stått
komma	kommer	kom	kommit
gå	går	gick	gått
ligga	ligger	låg	legat

DANISH

synge	synger	sang	sunget
synke	synker	sank	sunket
give	giver	gav	givet
sige	siger	sagde	sagt
flyve	flyver	fløj	fløjet
fryse	fryser	frøs	frosset
falde	falder	faldt	faldet
holde	holder	holdt	holdt
stå	står	stod	stået
komme	kommer	kom	kommet
gå	går	gik	gået
ligge	ligger	lå	ligget

Strong Verbs and Irregular Weak Verbs

Study the forms of the strong verb class in the Teutonic languages and complete the following quiz which includes both strong verbs and weak verbs which undergo vowel change in some or other form:

I. Others like *begin—began—begun* and *sink—sank—sunk* are:

1. ...... 2. ...... 3. ...... 4. ......
5. ...... 6. ......

II. Others like *cling—clung* and *fling—flung* are:

7. ...... 8. ...... 9. ...... 10. ......
11. ...... 12. ......

III. Others like *find—found* are:

13. ...... 14. ...... 15. ...... 16. ......

IV. Others like *steal—stole—stolen* and *bear—bore—born* are:

17. ...... 18. ...... 19. ...... 20. ......
21. ...... 22. ......

V. Others like *bid—bade—bidden* and *eat—ate—eaten* are:

23. ...... 24. ...... 25. ......

VI. Others like *forsake—forsook—forsaken* are:

26. ...... 27. ...... 28. ......

VII. Others like *arise—arose—arisen* are:

29. ...... 30. ...... 31. ...... 32. ......
33. ...... 34. ......

VIII. Others like *choose—chose—chosen* are:

35. ...... 36. ......

IX. Others like *grow—grew—grown* are:

37. ......   38. ......

X. Others like *cut—cuts—cutting* are:

39. ......   40. ......   41. ......   42. ......
43. ......   44. ......   45. ......   46. ......
47. ......   48. ......   49. ......   50. ......
51. ......   52. ......   53. ......

XI. Others like *buy—bought* or *creep—crept* are:

54. ......   55. ......   56. ......   57. ......
58. ......   59. ......   60. ......   61. ......
62. ......   63. ......   64. ......   65. ......
66. ......   67. ......   68. ......   69. ......
70. ......   71. ......   72. ......   73. ......
74. ......   75. ......   76. ......   77. ......
78. ......

XII. As for *shave—shaves—shaving—shaved—shaven*, give all the forms of:

79. *stick*   ....
80. *sit*   ....
81. *get*   ....
82. *tread*   ....
83. *stand*   ....
84. *wake*   ....
85. *bite*   ....
86. *shine*   ....
87. *fly*   ....
88. *draw*   ....
89. *lie*   ....
90. *go*   ....
91. *bring*   ....
92. *teach*   ....
93. *fall*   ....

94. *hew*	......	......	......	......
95. *beat*	......	......	......	......
96. *hang*	......	......	......	......
97. *hold*	......	......	......	......
98. *shoot*	......	......	......	......
99. *strike*	......	......	......	......
100. *chide*	......	......	......	......

Quiz 6

English with the Old Look (A.D. 1000)
  Clue: neglect letters in bold type.

SE EALDA MAN BENEOTHAN THAM **TRE**OWE NEAH TH**Æ**RE BRYCGE
WUNETH ON THAM HUSE UP**PAN** THAM HYLLE BEGEONDA**N** THAM
STREAME MID HIS HUND**E** AND TWAM CAT**TUM**. HIS WIF IS NU
DEAD. HE NE HÆFTH BEARN AND FRIEND NE CUMATH OFT TO HIS
DORE. ON THAM GEARD**E** BEHINDA**N** HIS HUSE BEOTH TWA GÆT,
FEAW**A** HEN**NE** AND BE**ON**. HE MACETH CIES**E** TO ET**ENNE** OF THAM
MEOLC**E** FRAM HIS GAT**UM** AND BÆCTH HIS AGENA**N** BREAD.
THURH THONE SUMOR HÆFTH HE MANIG ÆGRU FRAM HIS
HEN**NUM** AND FISCAS OF THAM LYTELA**N** BROCE WITHIN**NAN** HIS
GEARD**E**. THONNE CYMTH HÆRFEST THA BYGTH HE MEOLU HIS
BREAD TO MAC**IENNE**. HE GADERATH ÆPPLAS OF THAM TRE**OWUM**
AND HONIG FRAM THÆRE HYFE**ON** HIS GEARD**E**. THONNE CYMTH
WINTER THA IS SNAW OFER THAM GRUND**E**. THURH THONE DÆG
MÆG HE GADERIA**N** WUD**U** FRAM THAM FELD**UM** NEAH HIS HUS TO
MAC**IENNE** FYR. WULFAS BEORCATH TOFORAN HIS HUSES DORE
THURH THA LANGA**N** NIHT. HIS HEORTE IS GLÆD**U** THONNE
CYMTH LENTE**N**. THA DÆGAS WEAXATH LENGRA**N**. SEO SUNNE
SCINTH. TREO BEOTH GRENE AND HEOFONES FUGLAS SINGATH
ONGEAN. SONA CYMTH HIS ENDE AC HE NE IS SARIG. DÆGLICE
THANCETH HE HIS GODE FOR LANG**UM** LIFE AND NE WYSCTH
LENG TO LIB**BAN**NE WITHUT**AN** HIS GODA**N** WIFE.

3

The Limitations of the Latin Letters

The first chapter of this book has sufficiently illustrated one way in which an intelligent adult or adolescent reared within the Anglo-American speech community can advantageously exploit its hybrid ancestry. He (or she) can mitigate the tedium of the initial stages of becoming familiar with a sufficiently large vocabulary of a Teutonic or Romance language—even of Greek also—by seeking to form lively associations to previously unfamiliar words. In the context of our first chapter, lively association signifies recognition of the common parentage of an alien and of a native word with the same or an intelligibly related meaning. Such recognition presupposes some knowledge of what different sound values identical alphabetic signs used by different speech communities may have. It also calls for some knowledge about how sound values of words diverge in the gradual process whereby locally intercommunicable dialects have become less and less recognisably alike. On the printed page, we can discuss this process meaningfully only if we are first conversant with correct interpretation of alphabetic signs, our theme in this chapter.

Equipped with a little premedication of both sorts last mentioned, a beginner can make the learning process less wearisome in another way, i.e. by intelligent anticipation of the likely appearance a Teutonic, Romance or Greek word equivalent to an Anglo-American one will have on the printed page. This is possible only if one can identify at sight whether a word (as written) is of such and such ancestry, whence with a likely equivalent cousin in one or other of the parental clans. In our last chapter we have seen how it is possible to recognise the Teutonic ancestry of a very high proportion of Anglo-American words which greet the eye most often in print or typescript; but such words make up a small fraction of entries in *Webster's* or the *Oxford Dictionary*. Too few of us realise that one should be able to identify the parentage of a very high proportion of the more considerable residue of entries by the way in which we spell them.

In addition to the circumstance that we can intelligibly discuss laws of sound change set forth in our next chapter only if we first acquaint ourselves with the manifold conventions of spelling, there is therefore another reason why we should make an effort to understand the vagaries of spelling on a broad front. Nowadays, neither school nor college courses within the English-speaking part of the world do much to divulge the many clues to word origin which we can get from spelling; and we can do justice to them only if we now digress to fill a deplorable gap of early education. In short, our survey may best start by disposing of several misconceptions about the origins of writing, alphabetic or otherwise.

In particular, one should dismiss the supposition that writing began as a deliberate invention to make it possible for human beings to communicate at a distance. Least of all should we interpret as truly primitive the romanticised exhibits of pictorial messages from nomadic American Indians whose settled ancestors could boast of a sophisticated calendrical script before the arrival of the white man. We should also at all times recall that, a millennium after its modest beginnings, the first people to use alphabetic writing for recording inventories of cargoes, personal ownership, the burial place of a relative and so forth had no prevision of its eventual use either to supersede pictorial writing as a repository of the celestial lore of the temple observatories of a calendar priesthood or as a medium in which to preserve the heroic

Fig. 6.   Japanese Katakana Syllabary.

exploits of a tribal tradition, the corpus of tribal law (as in Hebrew and Greek) or (as uniquely in Greek) the set words of participants in the public ritual of the tribal dance.

The scripts of the world are of three sorts. Being no more than an *aide-mémoire* for keeping track of the seasons, the earliest writing presumptively had only two ingredients—repetitive strokes to represent numbers, and pictorial symbols for calendar units. What remains of the earliest (*Maya*) civilisation of the American continent did not get much beyond this stage. By incorporating other pictorial elements, writing of this sort eventually found a place for pictorial signs to catalogue names for possessions and to record human happenings. Such is the stage to which our earliest records of Egyptian and Mesopotamian civilisation testify; but already the pictorial origin of many word signs had then ceased to be easily recognisable. Eventually, the word-sign loses any visible resemblance to the parental picture; and each is as arbitrary as & (&) for *and*, + for *plus* and √ for *square root*. Writing of this sort has persisted in China till today.

If every word one needs to use has to have its own sign, it goes without saying that such *sign-writing*, as we may call it, entails an enormous burden on the memory of a learner. It is therefore tolerable only to a priestly or scholar caste intent on preserving a privileged status; and a new break through the sound barrier is essential to the realisation of a larger literacy, as commerce by land and sea expands. That is why the new régime of continental China is promoting the introduction of a script less burdensome from a tuitional viewpoint and more *en rapport* with other forms of writing in the world of today. One of the difficulties which beset its task gives us a clue to how an educationally more economical writing technique came into being. Basically, the languages of China consist of monosyllables of a very simple type, almost exclusively like DO—RA—MI—FA, etc. Even with due allowance for what one can convey by tone and stress, this pattern admits of relatively few combinations. So the same spoken word may have many meanings, clarified in common speech by coupling of the sort which comes through into pidgin English as *look-see*, etc. A single element of such a couplet might thus be hopelessly misleading, if represented in writing by signs which reproduce its pronunciation faultlessly.

Be it said that New China faces another obstacle to writing reform, and can surmount it only by promoting one standard language for the vast territory it embraces. The speech of the South is no longer intelligible in the North and *vice versa*. Nevertheless, literates from all parts of China interpret with the eye signs for words which are totally different to the ear. This should not be difficult to understand. A Swede, a Frenchman and a Welshman interpret '5' on the written page in the same sense despite the fact that they identify it with what they represent in *sound-writing* respectively as *fem*, *cinq* and *pump*. Albeit in the past largely the preserve of a prosperous merchant and scholar caste, sign-writing of the sort which China has hitherto used has thus been the only truly national language. Hence any attempt to convey in print the *sounds* people utter in different parts of China will create a new problem unless it is possible to introduce a standard of the spoken word common to the whole country.

The transition from sign-writing to the more economical device of *sound-writing* has come about in two ways. One way is comparatively easy to conceive in terms of culture contact between an already and a not as yet literate community when each of two conditions holds good: (a) the parent culture uses a language rich in simple monosyllables of the sort so characteristic of Chinese dialects; (b) the pupil culture consists of words made up of a small range of syllables of the same type, as in the familiar Japanese and Polynesian place names TO-KI-O, YO-KO-HA-MA, O-SA-KA, FI-JI, WAI-KI-KI, HO-NO-LU-LU. If unable to understand the language of his teacher, the not as yet literate learner can then associate only the sounds the teacher utters with the signs he points to. Such *syllabic* writing, which the Japanese still use (more or less mixed up with Chinese signs for whole words), has emerged many times in the past—in Asia Minor, in Senegal, in Cyprus and in Crete. This is possible because the number of different syllables in use among many speech communities is very small—little more than fifty. Contrariwise, it is far past the thousand mark for Greek, Latin, or Anglo-American.

In contradistinction to syllabic, alphabetic writing, which can adequately serve the needs of speech communities with a vast range of syllables (as is true of the Indo-European group), has arisen only once in the history of the world. That its parent was a Semitic script is intelligible if we know that: (a) most root words in the older Semitic languages conform to the pattern of *David, Moses, Balaam*, etc.; (b) while the vowels within this three-consonant framework may vary, each such framework has a unique core of meaning, as have *men* and *man* or *goose* and *geese*. Though it may be inconvenient to have no signs for vowels, it is therefore possible to decode a message by recourse to signs standing only for the initial *consonant* sounds of the two syllables; and the earliest type of alphabet, probably one (Fig. 7) used by Hebrew slaves in the Egyptian mines somewhat before 1500 B.C., had no vowel signs. Indeed, to this day Hebrew and Arabic scripts are essentially based on a consonantal alphabet, useless as such to those whose language can accommodate many words with no common core of meaning within one and the same consonant framework. For instance, M.N (with a dummy dot for the lack of a specific vowel sign) might stand in Anglo-American for *man, men, main, mane, mean, mien, mine, mown, moan, moon* and (in most dialects) *morn* and *mourn*.

When Greek-speaking people, who had hitherto limped along as best they could with the Cypriotic or Cretan syllabaries, took over (*circa* 750 B.C.) such a battery of consonant signs from their Semitic Phoenician trade rivals, they were already acclimatised to the use of syllables of the simplest possible sort, i.e. composed of one vowel, as is O in TO-KI-O. Accordingly, to represent vowels they adapted alien signs for sounds alien to Semitic script. The earliest Greek alphabetic writing is the parent of Etruscan (whence Latin) and of other Italic scripts. Their divergence came about through a variety of circumstances which have obliterated any trace of the ancestry of many of the world's alphabets, though all are traceable to the same Semitic source.

Even today, the correspondence of many signs of the Greek and of the so-called Roman alphabets is easily recognisable. Some discrepancies illustrate reasons for divergence mentioned later. Thus X has different sound values *kh* (Greek) and *ks* (Latin) conceivably associated with the sound shift *s-h* mentioned later (p. 136). Latin retains H with its primitive value. Possibly among those who used eastern Greek dialects which dispensed with the *h*-sound (as do all modern descendants of Latin), the Greeks adopted H to represent a long *e* (*eta*) as in *élite* in contradistinction to the short *e* in *wet* represented by E (*epsilon*). Others, however, used marks possibly by splitting H to represent a rough breathing (Ⱶ) or lack of the same (ᚺ) whence eventually ῥ signified what Anglo-Saxon and Viking scribes represented by HR and Welsh by RH as in *diarrhoea* and *rheostat*, and ῤ the unaspirated (*r*) equivalent.

Two Phoenician signs which gave rise to F (*digamma*) and Q (*koppa*) dropped out of Greek scripts very early. Through Etruscan, Latin retained these and adapted them to sounds (*f* and *kw*-) alien to Greek speech. Etruscan retained the Greek θ (*theta*) for the *th*-sound written as θ in manuscripts of the classical period, and φ (*phi*) for the Greek *ph*-sound (eventually displaced by *f*-). Since both sounds were alien to Roman speech, these signs left no trace in the Latin script. The same is true of

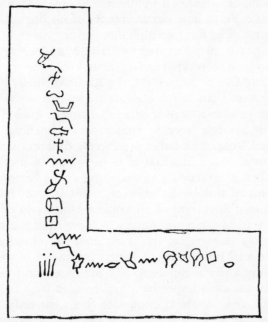

Fig. 7.   A workman's inscription on a mine shaft, Sinai Peninsula.

another Greek letter, ψ (*psi*) for *ps*-, whose origin we cannot trace to the Semitic battery—or with assurance to any other source.

If we wish to exploit intelligently the use of the English hybrid heritage as a passport to language learning, each of the several circumstances contributory to this conspiracy of concealment has, in some measure, relevance. To start with, we must take cognisance of the modest beginnings of alphabetic writing. Those who first used it did so for brief annotations to date an event, to label an article as its owner's property, to record a debt or to commemorate a death.* In the beginning, they

---

* For instance, a very early (sixth-century B.C.) example of written Latin inscribed (Fig. 11) on a brooch-pin states, *Manius made me for Numasius*; and the earliest example (Fig. 2) of Teutonic writing is (in Runic signs) an inscription on a drinking vessel, *I Liugast the Holting made this horn.*

recorded such short messages with no fixed convention for writing up or down if vertically, or right or left if sideways (Fig. 10). When the need for a convention for a longer communication became imperative, one community (e.g. Oscan) might write from right to left, another (e.g. Greek and Latin) left to right, another (like Hebrew in the Israeli of today) vertically from top to bottom. The subsequent appearance of what was once the same letter, e.g. Latin and Greek for our L and D (in Fig. 8) may thus partly depend on whether it finally settled down sideways or upright.

This is but one example of how circumstances of no linguistic significance contributed to the outcome. The form an alphabet (or any other such) sign eventually assumes also depends partly on the writing tool (brush, knife, style) and partly on the surface (papyrus, wood, stone, wax). The Greeks took over papyrus from the Egyptians at an early date. Before Caesar's conquest, the Romans chiefly used wax, on which it is easier to trace curves than to cut a clean angle. Anyone who has used a penknife knows that the reverse is true if one is cutting a *Runic* (p. 53) letter on a wooden surface. This has relevance to contemporary spelling habits, because U and V of the so-called Roman alphabet are merely different ways of writing what was the sign for a vowel sound like that of U in *full* or for a consonant sound like that of W in *wood* when it preceded a vowel sound at the beginning of a word.

From the viewpoint of this book, however, what is most important about the process that has led to obliteration of all ancient landmarks of the once common alphabet arises partly from a circumstance which we shall shortly recognise as the pace-maker of language change, i.e. that pronunciation changes locally in a comparatively short span of historic time, whence the range of sounds employed by different speech communities is different. For instance, most readers of this book will know that the two sounds respectively represented by TH in *thin* and *then* are foreign to the French, few of whom enunciate them correctly, unless expensively educated with that end in view. It follows that any illiterate community which gets its alphabet from another already literate—usually from missionaries, Christian, Moslem, or Buddhist—may find itself equipped with some signs which have no pay-off for sounds in use and no signs for some essential sounds. In such circumstances, a missionary or native innovator deals with the situation with the limited means at his (or her) disposal in one of four different ways:

(i) by inventing entirely new signs, e.g. addition of J and W to the original Latin battery;

(ii) by making arbitrary combinations for which the parent battery provides no signs, e.g. TH (as in *thin*) and NG (as in *singer*);

(iii) by borrowing from another alphabet, e.g. Greek *K, Y, Z* added to the late Roman alphabet, or (as is true of several scripts equipped by missionaries for central Africa and Oceania) from the International Phonetic Alphabet devised by phonetic experts of our own century;

(iv) by giving a pre-existing, now redundant, sign a new value, cf. the several values (p. 21) of mediaeval J as an alternative (p. 93) to the Roman I.

A few words about the International Phonetic Alphabet (I.P.A.) for any reader not familiar with it will make it more easy to plot our itinerary through the exploitable vagaries of English spelling, if we keep a firm foothold on the solid ground of our consonants, eschewing the quicksands of our vowel values. The International script adheres to the more customary Anglo-American values of B, D, F, H, K, L, M, N, P, R, T, V, W, Z. As regards G and S it prescribes the values in *goat* and *sit*. Concerning our other consonant signs, two are genuinely Roman but redundant, viz. Q (U) =$k(w)$ and X =ks, Y is the Greek capital for a vowel sound somewhat like *u* in Scots *gude lassie*, and the artificial J stands for a compound. In conformity with widespread usage (all modern Teutonic languages and Italian), the International system assigns the last named to replace Y as in *yes*. None the less, the Roman alphabet, augmented with Greek or hand-made signs, makes no provision for several Teutonic consonant sounds, nor for at least one of the modern descendants of Latin. With respect to Anglo-American we may exhibit the shortcomings of the Roman battery of signs by recourse to conventional arbitrary combinations as below, with International symbols in parentheses:

th (θ) as in *thin*
dh (ð) as in *then*
sh (ʃ) as in *shin*
zh (ʒ) like SI in *collusion*
nh (ŋ) like NG in *singer*—not NG as in *finger*
kh (χ) as in Scots *loch*

Two Anglo-American consonant sounds are compound: *tsh* (tʃ) as in *catch*, and *dzh* (dʒ) like J in *jam*.

Phonetics, which is the scientific study of pronunciation from a physico-anatomical viewpoint, is outside the intention of this book; but a word of explanation of the above conventions is relevant as bearing both on the most common of all types of sound shift in the evolutionary history of a language and on certain anomalies of spelling. We may arrange many of our consonants in two series, commonly named *voiced* and *voiceless*, thus:

voiced	b	d	v	g	z	dh	zh
voiceless	p	t	f	k	s	th	sh

An important feature of this twofold split is that we cannot quickly pronounce one of the upper series before or after one of the lower without substituting the corresponding member of the same line. For instance, we can say and write *caps*, but we say *cabz* where we write *cabs*. We write *cats* as we say it, but for what we write as *cads* we actually say *cadz*. Similarly, we pronounce the D as *t* in *laughed*, because the GH here stands for the voiceless *f*-sound. For an understanding of what follows, the reader needs to know that the sound range of a speech community need not, as is true of Anglo-American, have any one pair or both members of the same pair. Roman speech had the voiceless *f*-sound but not its voiced partner (*v-*). Like Spanish and Welsh, it had the voiceless *s*-sound but not its voiced (*z-*) partner. It had neither the *th—dh* nor the *sh—zh* pairs. When Celtic monks transmitted to their Teutonic converts the alphabet of Roman Britain not as yet augmented with Greek *K* and *Z*, and without the now redundant Q, it was defective for the end in

Fig. 8. | Tyrian | Early Greek | Later Greek | Roman | Russian

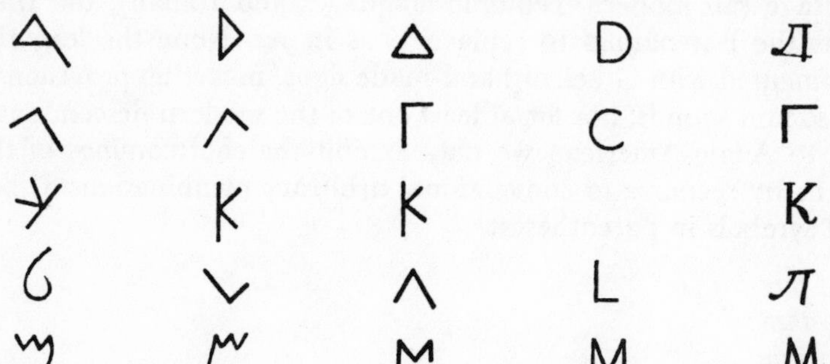

view, having no provision for the native voiced sounds *v*, *z* and *dh* or for the voiceless *th* and *sh*, the last being an intruder into the primitive Germanic sound battery.

Let us first consider representation of the *v-* sound in successive stages of Old, Middle and Tudor English. In O.E. it did not occur at the beginning of a word. Contrariwise, the voiceless *f*-sound did not occur between two vowels. Little or no ambiguity could therefore arise from use of the Latin F for both the voiceless *f-* and the voiced *v*-sound. It is instructive to notice that Welsh, with no voiceless *f*, uses Roman F for the native *v*-sound as in Anglo-American *of*. In loan words the alien voiceless *f*-sound has the sign FF as in *off*. This is on all fours with the German and French use of SS for the voiceless *s*-sound (as in *hiss*) and S for its voiced (*z*-) partner (as in *his*), the last-named sound being absent in Welsh and in Spanish, as in the Latin of the Republic.

The adaptation of the symbol V to its present use in Spanish, Italian, French and (through French) in Anglo-American is intelligible only if we recall (p. 88) that U and V in Latin script are different ways of writing the same two sound values, as dictated by writing surface or tool. Thus in stone inscriptions (always written in capital letters) we meet V. As already mentioned, it usually stood for a vowel sound; but before about A.D. 50 it had the consonantal *w*-value of *wood* before a vowel, or after Q at the beginning of a word, cf. Latin *vir* and O.E. WER in WERWOLF (p. 28). Thereafter *w* gave place to *v*. Possibly to emphasise its use as a consonant, Celtic and Teutonic scribes of O.E. doubled it, writing UU or VV, whence its name. Later scribes introduced a Runic sign very much like the rune (þ) for *th*, but happily the Norman scriveners reinstated the double U (or double V) linked together as a single sign. In Middle English texts we find U and V used interchangeably (p. 28); but early continental printers adopted a convention which had already gained some favour in England in the Tudor period, i.e. to restrict V for use to represent the consonantal *v*-sound and U to represent a vowel. The current phonetic differentiation of the two signs was not universal in Britain till a century after the end of the Tudor period.

Those who introduced the Celtic-Latin alphabet into English use at first adopted the arbitrary convention TH for both the *th*- and *dh*-sounds absent in Roman speech. Scribes of later O.E. reintroduced the runic sign þ indifferently for both. Others used ð ambiguously, where modern Icelandic script retains þ (called *thorn*) for *th* and prescribes ð (called *edda*, pronounced as in *heather*) for *dh*-, as defined above. The only other anomalies of O.E. spelling relevant to the theme of this chapter arise from changes of pronunciation which may have been incipient when the first Teutonic hordes overran Britain, and had reached a standstill, except in the North, before the end of the transitional period between the late Old and the early Middle period. These, which concern the hard C (=*k*) and G (=*g*) of *coat* and *goat* will enlist more detailed attention in the next chapter.

Since C has two sound values in Anglo-American and French, one being redundant, the other equivalent to Greek K, we may usefully digress here to consider the divergence of the Roman alphabet from an ancestor common to that of Greek and Etruscan. We have seen that one reason for obliteration of family likeness between descendants of the same alphabetic sign is that local changes of pronunciation after its adoption lead to local changes of its sound value. For instance, the Roman representation of the Greek letter φ by PH in Caesar's day was in all probability a tolerably faithful representation of its pronunciation. Before the end of the Western Empire, F replaces it in Greek words borrowed by Latin writers. That it had then come to stand for the *f*-sound (as in Anglo-American words of Greek origin) is clear. Similarly the *v*-sound later replaced the *b*-sound in Greek. That is why the sign for the former in the Russian (a modified Greek) alphabet is like our B (Greek β).

Correspondence between the order in which Greek and Roman pupils learned the letters of the alphabet is too close to be an accident, and it is sufficiently clear that Latin C in the third place corresponds to Greek *gamma* (Γ). One may surmise either that early Latin had no voiced equivalent (*g*-) of the *k*-sound or that their Etruscan teachers had none. What is certain is that the ancestral *gamma* stood in for the voiceless sound, and that the voiced equivalent for which a modified C (=G) intruded later occurs in far fewer Latin words. By the time the legions withdrew from Britain, changes where either the *k*- or the *g*-sound preceded one of the several *front* vowels (E and I, in *inkwell* and *élite*) had probably begun independently in different parts of the Empire. In Modern French words, we find *s*- (as in *ceiling*) where there was once *k*-, and *zh*- where there was once the hard *g*- of *goat*. Before the Norman Conquest the early O.E. *k*- (=C) and *g*- before a front vowel had likewise changed their values: the former to *tsh* as in *child* (O.E. CILD), the latter to the sound we now represent by Y in *yes* (J in the International script). Though otherwise purely Roman, the alphabet of Celtic monks in Britain had assimilated Greek *Y* for a vowel sound in all probability like that of U in French *lune* and in Scots *gude*. Pronounced quickly before a vowel, this simulates the *y*-sound of *yes*, whence its use in many native words which originally had G in its place. After the Norman Conquest the new convention CH looked after the *tsh*-sound in native words, but C remained ambiguous because it could stand for the *s*-sound in French loan words, whence perhaps the half-hearted reintroduction of Greek *K* and of the Roman QU, the latter both for French loan words and for O.E. words with CW (e.g. CWEN = *queen*).

In borrowed French words G was also ambiguous for the reason given, having in modern French its *zh*- value in *garage, barrage, camouflage, blancmange* and *entourage*.* For this novel sound, represented in some French words by J, users of the Roman alphabet in Caesar's time had no need to provide. Usually, we represent it in Anglo-American spelling by S- or SI-, as in *pleasure* and *effusion*, because it replaces the

---

* The initial hard *g* of Latin which in modern French becomes *zh* (=French J) before a front vowel, also does so in a few words before a back one. Thus Latin *gaudia*, cf. Harrow school song *gaudeamus igitur* (=let us therefore be joyful), is the parental form of *joie*, English *joy*. Since J occurs in words of different linguistic origin and may replace Latin I (=*i*) or DI (=*di*) before a vowel, phonetic spelling here combines with elimination of the second consonant to make the Roman ancestry of the word unrecognisable. Thus the Latin adjective *iuvene* for *young*, (cf. *juvenile*) in the second line of the song mentioned (*iuvenes dum sumus* =while we are young) becomes *jeune* in modern French. The Latin words *diurno* and *diurnale* (Eng. *diurnal*) become *jour* (*day*) and *journal*. The Teutonic intruder for *garden* (Germ. *Garten*) becomes *jardin*. The flowering shrub *jasmin* is from Persian *via* Arabic.

s-sound in some French and Latin loan words. Where it now occurs in French as a substitute for the hard Roman G, corresponding loan words in English show G or J pronounced as *dzh*, as in *goal* or *jail*. We have already (p. 21) seen that J has many different sound values in European speech communities, and the reader may ask how we acquired this late innovation. The answer is that late mediaeval writers would often tack a tail on to the second I in Latin words or symbols such as *filij* (=FILII) and *vij* (=VII). Before a vowel at the beginning of a word, the sound value of I approaches that of Y in *yes,* and it became customary to write I as J in such a situation. In French this Latin *i*-sound before a vowel approached the same

[βασιλεος ελθοντος ες Ελεφαντιναν Ψαματιχο
ταυτα εγραψαν τοι συν Ψαμματιχοι τοι Θεοκλ(ε)ος
επλεον ηλθον δε Κερκιος κατυπερθε υις ο ποταμος
ανιη αλογλοσος δ ηχε Ποτασιμτο Αιγυπτιος δε Αμασις
εγραψε δ αμε Αρχον Αμοιβιχο και Πελεφος ο Υδαμο]

Fig. 9.   Early Greek Lettering.

value as G before E and I (as above). Thus Latin *iuvene* is the parent of *jeune* (J=*zh*) in Modern French and *juvenile* (J=*dzh*) in Anglo-American.

It will now be abundantly clear that scribes of alien origin in the twilight of native literacy following the Norman Conquest had to tailor the alphabet to new requirements. Thereafter, changes of spelling during the transitional period underline both changes of pronunciation which had already, and changes of pronunciation which had not as yet, occurred. Thus substitution of KN for CN emphasises what we have other reasons for believing, namely that speakers in the Middle period fully pronounced the *k*- component. Contrariwise, we recognise as a *fait accompli* before the Middle period the change from the *sk*- to the *sh*-sound before a front vowel by the substitution first of SCH (as in Modern German), then of SH, for O.E. SC. By then, initial HL and HR for sounds roughly like those for which the Welsh respectively use LL*

---

* The Welsh sound spelt LL in LLANGOLLEN, where the International Eisteddfod holds its annual gathering, is difficult to convey to the vast majority (however few) who may read this book. Try to say TL as in *antler*, THL as in *monthly* and very quickly (as a Scots comedian might say it) CH-L in *Loch Leven*. Then mix thoroughly with mustard and pepper till the tongue adheres to one side of the cheek, while you are desperately getting back to L=*l*.

and RH had made way for L and R; and we may assume that pronunciation of these now tallied with our own, except that speakers probably trilled the second member of the pair as in Scots dialect. In Scots dialect O.E. HW- still survives, and the trivial substitution of WH- in the transitional period betokens that this compound was still very much alive throughout it. In O.E. manuscripts, H alone stands for the *h*-sound at the beginning of a word, but before T or at the end of a word it had a sound comparable to the *kh*- in Scots *loch*, represented in Scots dialect verse, as in German, by CH. Scribes of the transitional period substituted the Celtic ʒ (=G). Whence it is clear that the later GH of *knight*, like the initial K, was not as yet an acoustic cipher.

That the foregoing remarks are largely applicable to English pronunciation throughout, or at least till late in, the Middle period, we infer from the study of poetic metre, alliteration and rhyme. As regards the last, we may note that Chaucer, who correctly spells it as *delite* in accordance with its French origin, would never rhyme what we now spell *delight** with *right* or *night*. Likewise, no poet of his time would rhyme French *haughty* and *sprightly** with native *naughty* and *nightly*. As regards alliteration, no poet of Chaucer's time would pair off *knight* with *naught* or *where* with *woe*. Metre is instructive in so far as it labels the date at which certain syllables, e.g. -ED of weak verbs, ceased to be enunciated as we still do in *learned, hated, folded* and *beloved*. The final contraction to a double consonant as in *praised, used, loved, answered*, etc., gained ground in the seventeenth century. The final -ES of the plural noun, e.g. *thynges* for *things* in Tyndale's (1526) translation of the New Testament, lingered well into the Tudor period.

The foregoing remarks throw light on what we know of changes affecting consonants, but they do not satisfactorily answer the question: how can we possibly know anything about the pronunciation of vowels in O.E.? Comparison between dialect survivals and the sister languages (cf. Scots and Scandinavian *hus* for *house*) supplies one class of clues; but another class depends on the assumption that the scrivener of old time did in fact use his writing signs consistently, that he did so against the background of a standard dictated by Church Latin, and that vowel values of the latter tallied closely with those of contemporary Italian. This would not get us far, if we had no reason to believe that Italian vowel sounds of today are very much like those of Rome at the time when the legions withdrew from Britain. We have more than one good reason for believing this, in particular because change of pronunciation on a nation-wide scale occurs piecemeal and gradually. When a speech community consistently uses the same signs for the same sounds—as is conspicuously true of Italian, Welsh and Icelandic—we may infer that its pronunciation has not appreciably changed since it acquired its current script.

Writers on English pronunciation early in the Tudor period refer to Italian models; and Welsh (with much the same range of simple vowel sounds but somewhat

---

*   See E(v) on p. 101.

different spelling conventions) is of special interest as a standard. There is still extant an English hymn to the Virgin rendered about A.D. 1500 in Welsh orthography to convey to a Welsh-speaking pupil the correct pronunciation of the words. William Salesbury, a Welsh scholar who translated the New Testament into Welsh (1546-67), wrote a tract on English pronunciation in 1547 and another on Welsh pronunciation in 1567. As regards changes of English pronunciation thereafter, it is mentionable that shorthand, which came into prominence for reporting trials during the Civil War between Charles I and Parliament, takes its origin (1588) from the *Characterie* of Timothy Bright, an Elizabethan physician contemporary with Shakespeare.

If we rightly assume that the scrivener, before the days of printing, used his vowel signs in conformity with a standard set by Church Latin and close to the Italian of today, we can confidently infer that spelling reflects certain changes of vowel values in the period of transition from Old to Middle English. One example must here suffice to show how the spelling of native words changed after the Norman Conquest. In a large group of English words before A.D. 1150 (or thereabouts) we find A as in *ban, gat, ham* and *stan* (for *bone, goat, home* and *stone*). Thereafter, and throughout the Middle period, these give place to *boon, goot, hoom* and *stoon*.

It would be wrong to imply that spelling in the Middle period before printing began was consistent. At least one version of the English Bible of 1389 uses the Celtic ȝ, both where Chaucer and Tyndale use GH and where the consonantal Y as in *yes* had replaced early O.E. G, as in *nedlis yȝe* for *eye of a needle* (Mark x. 25) and *what wolen ȝe that I do to ȝou* (Mark x. 36). The source last quoted uses U both as a vowel sign and for the consonantal *v-* as in *twelue* and *belieue*. However, an early printed English Bible uses U only for a vowel and employs V only for the consonant represented ambiguously by F in O.E. texts. Since the *v*-sound occurs at the beginning of few, if any, O.E. words, use of the sign V in that situation (p. 100) is a useful signpost of word origin.

To some extent dialect differences account for inconsistencies of the scrivener's spelling before printing began; and their survival, as frequently mentioned before this, is one clue we have to changes of English pronunciation before phonograph records existed to satisfy our curiosity. Partly for this reason, but more so because one printer in the English capital (London) and later in the Scottish (Edinburgh) could do more work in a week than a hundred scriveners could do in a year, printing inevitably promoted more standardised spelling and encompassed a changing situation in a strait-jacket. Thenceforth spelling could never faithfully reflect contemporary pronunciation. To a large extent, in this historic context, the master printers adopted spelling conventions which severally perpetuate scripts tailored to the requirements of native words, French intruders and loan words from classical Latin or Greek. They did so partly by intention, as Caxton divulges, and partly also in conformity to pre-existing custom.

In days when there were no dictionaries, master printers, though more scrupulous about etymology than many scholars, inevitably made mistakes. However, such anomalies were comparatively few compared with those which have resulted from an already established tradition that familiarity with French is a hallmark of gentility, and from a deplorable inclination of some poets to write words which may (or may not) rhyme in the same way, if it is possible thereby to deceive the ear or to

Fig. 10.   Early Greek Lettering, written in all directions.

enlist the eye. *En passant*, we have noticed some such anomalies with reference to the intrusion of the authentic GH convention into unwanted situations (*haughty, sprightly, delight*). An even more deplorable example is the later substitution for early Tudor S of C, otherwise a signal of French ancestry, in the native set *since, hence, whence, thence, pence, mice, lice, once, twice, thrice*. In the poems of Sir Thomas Wyatt, contemporary with the appearance of the first printed English Bible, we find S for C in such words. Thus Tyndale renders Luke xxii. 34 as follows:

. . . I tell the, Peter, the cocke shall nott crowe this daye, till thou have thryse *denyed that thou knewest me.*

Aside from the foregoing, bogus scholarship and the misdemeanours of poets, among whom the Elizabethan Edmund Spenser is notorious, introduced many other anomalies. The D in *judge* from French *juge* (cf. Latin *judice*), the B in *debt* and *doubt* (from French *dette* and *doute*), the L in *false* and *fault*, and the S in *isle* (French *île*, Latin *insula*) are all referable to the delusion that words of French origin came into English directly from Latin (cf. the intrusive P in French *sept*, p. 150). The U in our native *tongue* seemingly results from a false analogy with its French equivalent *langue*. The B in *thumb* (native THUMA) and *crumb* (native CRUMA) is probably

Fig. 11. Early Latin Script, written from right to left.

there through false analogy with native DUMB and Latin *plumb*. The L in *could* (native CUTHE) is almost certainly referable to false analogy with *should* and *would*. Spenser's enormities, which include *quight* for *quite* as well as *delight* for *delite* to rhyme with *night* or *fight*, pinpoint the disappearance before the Elizabethan age of the guttural GH or ʒ for the H of O.E. of Chaucer's time.

The writer's aim in this context is not to reform English spelling for the benefit of those who approach its study as beginners; but the foregoing remarks put the spotlight on a fundamental difference between two ways in which we may advocate such reform. Like the late G. B. Shaw, we may assert that one sound should have only one sign. Alternatively, we may demand that one sign should have only one sound. The two claims are different, as one example suffices to show. In contemporary Anglo-American spelling, PH conveys only the sound represented by F in common words (other than *of*). As such, it is a signpost of Greek origin as in *Philadelphia* (= *brotherly love*). Thus two ways of writing the same sound, each unique, with the one notable exception mentioned, subject us to no uncertainty about pronunciation and tell us something important about origin. Incidentally, this means that they tell us something about meaning. Thus FILIAL affection does not mean the same as brotherly love.

Aside from unintentional and forgivable mistakes of master printers and deliberate falsifications by major poets such as Edmund Spenser, it is true to say that the consonant pattern of English spelling from the late Middle period onwards transmits to Anglo-American the trademarks of the ancestry of its vocabulary. Only one other qualification to this generalisation merits mention. Any loan word which is foreign to the range of sound values of the borrower necessarily conforms to a new pattern. Thus *typewriter* in Japanese becomes *tupuraita* in accordance with a native pattern which makes no provision for the compound consonant sound *pr* (represented as PEWR). It may also happen that a loan word, which is intrinsically assimilable, may by long assimilation conform to a native pattern. An outstanding example of this is the monastic Latin intruder which replaces the authentic O.E. WRITAN (*write*) in all its Teutonic sisters (Swed. *skriva*, Germ. *schreiben*, etc., for Latin *scribere*, whence *scribe* and French *écrire*). The only noteworthy Anglo-American example of this accommodation is *faith* (with the native *th*-sound). It comes through French from the same Latin root as in *fidelity* and in Fidel Castro.

Against the background of the foregoing reservations and of the foregoing post-mortem, we can now formulate a sizeable number of rules. A smart Alec could proffer exceptions to most of them; but all of them satisfy what contemporary statisticians designate as *significant at the 95 per cent level*, meaning that one will not be wrong more than five times per hundred, if one follows them. We shall therefore supplement the meagre indications of the ancestry of our Anglo-American vocabulary as stated at the end of Chapter 2 by listing: (a) which sounds are native or foreign to our Teutonic ancestry, and if foreign whence they come; (b) what signs have what sound values in one or other of the languages which have contributed to our contemporary stock-in-trade of words.

Starting with the sounds before we try to sort out their signs, we may proceed thus with recourse to the symbols used on p. 89:

A. TEUTONIC

(i) the *dh*-sound of TH in *then* occurs only in native words;

(ii) the *nh*-sound in *singer*, as opposed to the *ng* (or *nh-g*) sound in *finger*;

(iii) the *w*-sound in *weir* or *woman*;

(iv) the *y*-sound of Y in *yes* or *yard*, unless self-evidently a loan word, such as *yak* or *Yoga*.

B. TEUTONIC or GREEK

(i) the Teutonic *th*-sound of TH in *thin* occurs only* in non-native words of Greek origin.

---

* We have noticed above the only noteworthy exception (*faith*).

The latter are all scholarly (e.g. *theatre*, *theme* and *therapy*); and *thyme* (usually pronounced with initial *t*-), though now a folk word, is no exception, since it came into English from French, through Latin from Greek herbal medicine.

(ii) the *kn*-sound as in Greek was not uncommon in the Teutonic group, as in *knight* or *knife*; but it has come into English only at a highbrow level in biological terms with the Latinised (CN) spelling as in *cnidocil*.

C. FRENCH ONLY (or MAINLY)

(i) the *zh*-sound (=French J) in *pleasure—measure—treasure* and *effusion—evasion—collusion*;

(ii) the *dzh*-sound (=English J) with the same ancestry in *jam*, *judge*, *jelly* and *jail*. For reasons already explained, J replaces G with this sound in many Anglo-American words such as *genius*, *genuflexion*, *gesture*, *gentle*. It also occurs in (a) a few words of

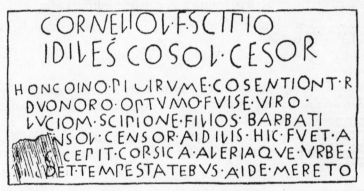

Fig. 12. Early Latin Script.

remote origin, e.g. *jackal*, *Jehovah* and *jasmin* (of which neither animal nor plant is European); (b) a very small group of words (*edge*, *sedge*, *bridge*) spelt in O.E. with the unpronounceable arbitrary combination CG (e.g. BRYCG). In all these few we now have DG for CG; but DG for the *dzh*-sound is not necessarily a trademark of native origin (cf. *judge* above).

(iii) the *v*-sound represented by V occurs at the beginning of very few (see p. 100) native words.

The reader who is not *au fait* with statistical jargon may need to know why this rule is significant at the 95% level. An examination of roughly 650 words which begin with V in Modern English gave the following result (in round numbers): (a) 93% Romance; (b) 2% Teutonic, including *Valhalla*, *Valkyrie*, *Viking* and *vole* from Scandinavian, *veld* and *vlei* from S. African Dutch, *voe* from Shetland Islands

Free Public Library
Cranford, N. J.

dialect, also *Vehmericht, Veneer, Verein* and *Volklied* from German; (c) 5% from Indic (*veda*), Slavonic (*vodka*), African (*voodoo*), Turkish (*vizier*), S. American Indian (*vacacha*), of mixed ancestry (*vermouth, Volapuk*) or eponymous, i.e. based on proper names (*volt, voltage, voltaic, voltameter*). Indeed the only familiar native words with initial V are: (i) VANE of a weather-cock, from O.E. FANA (Swed. *fana*, Dan. *fane*, Du. *vaan*, Germ. *Fahne*) signifying *flag*, also a pan-Teutonic word (Swed. *flagg*, Dan. *flag*, Du. *vlag*, seventeenth-century Germ. *Flagge*), though not found in O.E. texts; (ii) VIXEN from O.E. FIXEN with fem. ending -EN from *fox* like Germ. *Fuchs—Füchsin*; (iii) VAT from O.E. FÆT (Old Norse *fat*, Du. *vat*, Germ. *Fass*)—the corresponding Dutch and German verbs *vatten* and *fassen* signify *contain* (possibly from the same root as Swed. *fatta*, Dan. *fatte = catch*). Briefly, therefore, we may say that there is more than a 95% safety margin for concluding that an Anglo-American word beginning with V, if not obviously of remotely alien origin or derived from a proper name, is from Latin or its descendants.

To the above, all of which refer to *sonants* (i.e. consonantal sounds), we may add two rules relating to vowels:

(a) the sound represented by OY in *boy* or OI in *boil* is nearly always a signpost of French origin;

(b) the sound represented by OW (Germ. AU) in *cow* is nearly always a signpost of native origin, having displaced what persists in Scandinavian and in Scots dialect (e.g. *a wee hus*) as that of OO in *fool*.

We now turn to what indications of word origin we can derive from different spelling conventions for one and the same sound, and here we may best dispose of Greek at the outset.

D. GREEK ONLY

Several Greek consonant combinations have been ironed out in pronunciation on all fours with KN (=*kn* to *n*) in *knight*, and are all in scholarly (mostly medical and biological) terms, notably:*

(i) RH (p. 86) as in *rheostat* and *diarrhoea* (once for HR of O.E., Teutonic but now extinct);

(ii) MN- as in *mnemonic, amnesia*;

(iii) PS- as in *psaltery, psychology*;

(iv) PT- as in *Pterodactyl*;

(v) CH- for the *k*-sound as in *chromium* and *chrysalis*;

(vi) PH- for the *f*-sound as in *phonograph* and *photo*;

(vii) Y with the sound value of German EI in Einstein (e.g. *lyre* and *pyre*).

---

* The hyphen following (ii)-(vi) signifies that we interpret them as signposts of Greek only when they occur at the *beginning* of a word, or of a root of a word.

E. TEUTONIC ONLY

(i) words beginning with TH except as indicated for *B*(i) above;

(ii) words in which CH stands for the *tsh*-sound in *child* and *chap*;

(iii) words in which SH stands for the *sh*-sound in *ship* if either at the beginning of a word (as in *shine*) or at the end of a monosyllable as in *ash, wish, fish* (exceptions *cash* and *push*);

(iv) words beginning with WR-, WH-, W-;

(v) words containing -GHT (exceptions *delight, haughty, sprightly*).

F. FRENCH or LATIN

(i) words in which TI, SI or SSI (e.g. *nation, fusion, passion*), represent the *sh*-sound of the modern Teutonic *ship* (=O.E. SCIP);

(ii) polysyllabic verbs (e.g. *finish*) which end in SH with the same value;*

(iii) words in which CH has the same (*sh-*) value such as *chef, chassis, chamois, chauffeur* and *chemise*;

(iv) words in which C has the *s*-value, as in *cease, cede, censure, circle, celibate, ceiling*. Apparent exceptions, other than those already mentioned as overdue for censorship, are *cycle* and *cylinder*, from Greek through Latin;

(v) words in which G has the *zh*-value of *rouge* and *beige*, or of *dzh* as in *plunge*.

It should now be sufficiently clear to the reader that the intention of this chapter, which deals with how an Anglo-American may exploit the vagaries of English spelling as an aid to learning a foreign language, has nothing directly to do with what difficulties the learner whose native speech is not English encounters when confronted with its inconsistencies. However, it is here relevant to contrast the advantage of using more than one sign consistently for one sound in contradistinction to the use of only one sign for each sound. If one concedes the now-manifest advantage Anglo-Americans (and learners brought up to speak its sister languages) derive from reform of the first kind, i.e. directed to iron out inconsistencies such as *delight* and *pence*, there are two other objections to reform of the second kind. One is akin to the considerations for a limited programme of reform implicit in what has gone before, e.g. we should conceal the ancestral connexion (see Exhibit on p. 179) between *two, twin, twain* and *twice* if we spelt in the same way *two* and *too* (not to say *to* also). What is more important arises from the fact that Anglo-American is immensely rich in such homophones, whence innumerable sources of misunderstanding.

Since we pronounce members of such pairs in the same way, reformers who follow Bernard Shaw would persuade us to spell in the same way *bier* and *beer, sun* and *son*

---

* Nearly all these (e.g. *abolish, finish, embellish, ravish, demolish, garnish*) conform in the original to the *finir* pattern with an augmented stem (e.g. FINISS-).

and *boy* and *buoy*. If so, we should have no clue to whether the event occurred at the grave of Lazarus or at the wedding in Cana, when *Jesus stood beside the bier*; whether the first word of the hymn *Sun of my soul* replaces *Sonny Boy*, or whether the *woman diver who clasped the buoy desperately* had at last found her soul mate. Such examples are not far to seek. An enthusiastic crossword addict should not find it difficult to assemble a hundred pairs like the following: *pane—pain, hair—hare, pail—pale, flea—flee, peel—peal, meat—meet, tier—tear, foul—fowl, so—sow—sew*, etc. No useful rule dictates the spelling of such alternatives. To some extent they arise from diversification of English vowel sounds throughout the Middle and Tudor periods; and to some extent the impact of French may have encouraged a retreat from a simpler native pattern more akin to that of Swedish or Spanish. Since the English-speaking community spread first into the western hemisphere and later over the five continents, there has ceased to be any one standard of the spoken word acceptable as such to educated people.

THE ROMAN AND GREEK ALPHABETS

	1	2	3	4	5	6	7	8	9	10	11	12	13
(i)	A	B	C	D	E	F	..	H	..	I	..	L	M
(ii)	𐌀	𐌁	ᐸ	▷	𐤄	Ⴈ	Z	𐌇	⊕	ꟾ	K	ᐯ	᙭
(iii)	*A*	*B*	*Γ*	*Δ*	*E*	..	*Z*	*H*	*Θ*	*I*	*K*	*Λ*	*M*
(iv)	*α*	*β*	*γ*	*δ*	*ε*	..	*ζ*	*η*	*θ*	*ι*	*κ*	*λ*	*μ*

	14	15	16	17	18	19	20	21	22	23	24	25	26
(i)	N	..	O	P	Q	R	S	T	V	..	X	..	..
(ii)	ᴎ	𐌗	O	Γ	9	ᖇ	Ƨ	†	Y	Φ	X	Ψ	..
(iii)	*N*	*Ξ*	*O*	*Π*	..	*P*	*Σ*	*T*	*Υ*	*Φ*	*X*	*Ψ*	*Ω*
(iv)	*ν*	*ξ*	*ο*	*π*	..	*ρ*	*σ,ς*	*τ*	*υ*	*φ*	*χ*	*ψ*	*ω*

(i) Latin alphabet in Caesar's boyhood, excluding G (see notes).
(ii) An early common form of letters used by Latin- and Greek-speaking peoples.
(iii) and (iv) Classical Greek letters (capitals above, small below).

Notes on the Alphabets of p. 102:

1. The signs of the alphabet which peoples speaking Indo-European languages in the Mediterranean acquired from the Semitic Phoenicians about 800 B.C. have come down to us in a definite order (here shown as 1-26), perhaps because the later Greeks, like the Hebrews, used them also as signs for numbers.

2. Some of them are easily recognisable in the Greek script of Plato's time (about 350 B.C.) and the Roman script of Caesar's (about 50 B.C.). These are A, B, E, I, K, M, N, O, T, V (Y) and X, of which the last corresponds in Greek to the sound represented by CH in Scots *loch*.

Fig. 13. Icelandic Newspaper showing Þ and ð signs.

3. Others, such as C—Γ, D—Δ, and L—Λ, are easily recognisable if we recall the fact that there was no fixed convention of writing left to right, right to left or top to bottom and *vice versa* in the earliest inscriptions. The equivalent forms of P—Π, R—P and S—Σ are easily recognisable as such if we know the earliest shape they took.

4. Partly because different languages lack sounds which others possess, and partly because sounds used by a speech community change in the course of time, there are some discrepancies:

(a) in Greek script 6 and 18 eventually drop out; and in Roman 7, 9, 11, 15, 23 and 25 drop out;

(b) the sound values of 2, 8 and 24 are different in the Greek of Plato and the Roman of Caesar;

(c) the sign 26 for the long O in Greek is a new letter, possibly formed by modification of 16.

5. In early Latin there seems to have been no clear distinction between the sound

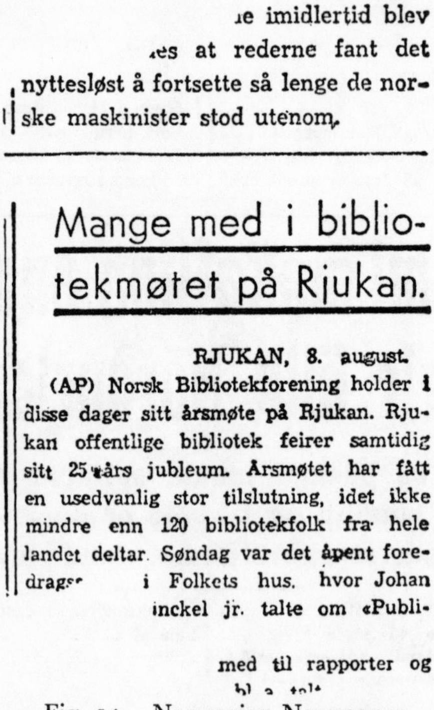

ıe imidlertid blev
ıes at rederne fant det
nyttesløst å fortsette så lenge de nor-
ske maskinister stod utenom,

Mange med i biblio-
tekmøtet på Rjukan.

RJUKAN, 8. august.
(AP) Norsk Bibliotekforening holder i disse dager sitt årsmøte på Rjukan. Rjukan offentlige bibliotek feirer samtidig sitt 25 års jubleum. Arsmøtet har fått en usedvanlig stor tilslutning, idet ikke mindre enn 120 bibliotekfolk fra hele landet deltar. Søndag var det åpent foredrag- i Folkets hus. hvor Johan inckel jr. talte om «Publi-

med til rapporter og
bl a tale

Fig. 14.   Norwegian Newspaper.

represented by Greek K as in *coat* and Greek Γ as in *goat*. Thus 11 dropped out in favour of 3, but when there was later a need for distinguishing the two sounds, two forms of 3 took shape, C for the Greek K and G for the Greek Γ.

6. Originally 8 had the same value as in Latin. This sound (as in *hat*) dropped out early in Eastern Greek dialects (as in late Latin), and came to stand for the long E as in *élite*. Classical Greek retained the rough breathing sound. In late Greek spelling it was customary to write *oh, am, ell* as ώ, ἀμ, ἐλ and *hoe, ham, hell* as ὡ, ἁμ, ἑλ. Similarly the Welsh *rh* sound is ῥ́, in contradistinction to ῥ for English *r*.

7. Probably the sound value of 15 in Greek was that which Latin gave to 24.

8. Besides G, not shown above, what we now call the Roman alphabet has J, K, W, Y and Z. Of these K, Y and Z came into use after Latin had begun to assimilate Greek words—from Caesar's time onwards. Latin itself had only the pure S of *sign*. It lacked the impure S of *pins* and *Zion*. The actual sound value of the Greek Z was probably more like DS in *cads* (cf. Modern German Z for *ts* sound).

9. Till quite late the Romans used only capital letters, and V stood for the sound we represent by OO before a consonant or by W before a vowel. The sign U appeared as an alternative to V like the small Greek v (pronounced as in Scots *gude*), and remained to represent the vowel, when the *w* sound before a consonant at the end of the Empire changed to *v* as in *virtue*. Teutonic scribes introduced VV for the original *w*- sound of V, whence W.

DAGBANE. N. Gold Coast.

A kul ni dʒɛm la a-Duɩɩma Naawuni, kulla o ko
ka a ni dʒɛm. 1935

Fig. 15. International Phonetic Symbols in Missionary Bibles.

10. In Latin as in Greek, 10 had the same value as in *élite*, but could also have the value of *y* in *yam*. Mediaeval scholars sometimes wrote II, ii as IJ, ij at the end of a word or numeral (such as xij), and eventually the J sign took over for the *y*-sound as used today in Swedish or German.

11. Latin had no sound corresponding to 9, 23 and 24 in Greek. In words taken from Greek writers, they represented 23 (as originally pronounced) by PH. Towards the end of the Empire it had the sound we represent as *f*. For Greek 9 in words of Greek origin, they used TH as in *thin*. They represented the vowels thus:

o or $\omega = $ O	$a\iota = $ AE
$\epsilon = $ E	$o\iota = $ OE
$\iota = $ I	$ov = $ U
$a = $ A	$v = $ Y
$\eta = $ A or E	

12. It is thus often possible to detect whether a word is of Greek or Latin origin. Only Latin words contain F. (See p. 100 for signposts of Greek origin).

13. The Greeks used γ for Welsh NG in *singer* (not *n-g* as in *finger*). This occurs only before γ, κ, ξ and χ. Before these, Latin authors represent it by N, so that

$$\gamma\gamma = \text{NG}; \ \gamma\xi = \text{NX}; \ \gamma\kappa = \text{NK or NC}; \ \gamma\chi = \text{NCH}$$

14. Note that the sound represented by B in classical Greek now stands, in modern Greek, for *v* (in *vest*), just as ϕ came to stand for the *f*- sound. Both changes

of pronunciation had occurred when Greek monks adapted their alphabet to the uses of Slavonic peoples, whence the similarity of the Russian symbol for *v* in *Soviet* to B and the Russian ϕ for *f*.

INTRODUCTORY NOTE ON QUIZ I (on page 107)

1. In the transliteration of a very large number of Greek words absorbed into their language, Latin authors commonly used the following conventions:

$K, \kappa = $C; $\Theta, \theta = $TH; $\Xi, \xi = $X; $X, \chi = $CH; $\Phi, \phi = $PH; $\Psi, \psi = $PS; O, o or $\Omega, \omega = $O; $H, \eta = $E or A; $o\iota = $OE; $o\upsilon = $U; $a\iota = $AE.

2. Some of the earliest Greek scripts assign to H the same value as in Latin; but H, η came to stand for a long E probably somewhat like E in *élite*. At the end of a word, A often replaces H, η in a Latin word assimilated from Greek.

3. In classical Greek writing, an apostrophe written thus ' indicates rough breathing (our H, h). At the beginning of a word which starts with a vowel the same sign in reverse (') indicates that there is *no* aspirate. Thus $\dot{\omega} = $HO and $\dot{\omega} = $O.

4. In the time of Julius Caesar, Latin authors sometimes restored K and Y, υ in words of Greek origin. We now use Y for the Greek Y, υ but U for $OY, o\upsilon$ in words of Greek origin.

5. Late Latin authors used CH for X, χ, but after the revival of Greek learning some authors inconsistently used K. This practice continues in some scientific terms, e.g. *kilogram, kilometer*.

6. Greek *OI* rendered by Latin OE often becomes E in English words of Greek origin. American writers also shorten AE for Greek *AI* to E in scientific terms.

QUIZ CORNER 3

Quiz 1

Names of Persons and Places in the History of the Greek-speaking civilisation

GREEK	OUR SPELLING	GREEK	OUR SPELLING
1. Πλατων	......	26. Βαβυλωνια	......
2. Περικλης	......	27. Ἑλληνες	......
3. Ἀλεξανδρος	......	28. Σπαρτη	......
4. Ἀριστοτελης	......	29. Εὐφρατης	......
5. Δημοκρατης	......	30. Ἑλλησποντος	......
6. Ἀναξαγορας	......	31. Τιγρης	......
7. Κροισος	......	32. Κορινθος	......
8. Σοφοκλης	......	33. Ἀθηναι	......
9. Εὐριπιδης	......	34. Αἰγυπτος	......
10. Ἀριστοφανης	......	35. Δελφοι	......
11. Ἐρατοσθενης	......	36. Μαραθων	......
12. Ἱππαρχος	......	37. Πειραιευς	......
13. Ἀρχιμηδης	......	38. Πελοποννησος	......
14. Ἐμπεδοκλης	......	39. Σαλαμις	......
15. Φιλιππος	......	40. Τροια	......
16. Θαλης	......	41. Ναζαρεθ	......
17. Πυθαγορας	......	42. Βηθλεεμ	......
18. Εὐκλειδης	......	43. Ἱερουσαλημ	......
19. Σωκρατης	......	44. Βηθσαιδα	......
20. Ξενοφων	......	45. Ἀντιοχεια	......
21. Ζηνων	......	46. Σαμαρια	......
22. Ἡροδοτος	......	47. Δαμασκος	......
23. Σαπφω	......	48. Μεσοποταμια	......
24. Σολων	......	49. Καππαδοκια	......
25. Ἐπικουρος	......	50. Βηθανια	......

Quiz 2

Names from the Greek Myths

GREEK	OUR SPELLING	GREEK	OUR SPELLING
1. *Ζευς*	. . . . .	26. *Μεδουσα*	. . . . .
2. *Κερβερος*	. . . . .	27. *Ἀπολλων*	. . . . .
3. *Μηδεια*	. . . . .	28. *Ἡρακλης*	. . . . .
4. *Περσεφονη*	. . . . .	29. *Κυκλωψ*	. . . . .
5. *Ἑρμης*	. . . . .	30. *Χαρων*	. . . . .
6. *Ὑδρα*	. . . . .	31. *Ἑκτωρ*	. . . . .
7. *Γοργω*	. . . . .	32. *Ἀχιλλευς*	. . . . .
8. *Νεκταρ*	. . . . .	33. *Ἀνδρομαχη*	. . . . .
9. *Ὀλυμπος*	. . . . .	34. *Ἑλενη*	. . . . .
10. *Ἀδωνις*	. . . . .	35. *Κασσανδρα*	. . . . .
11. *Ἀθηνη*	. . . . .	36. *Μιδας*	. . . . .
12. *Τιταν*	. . . . .	37. *Τριτων*	. . . . .
13. *Νεμεσις*	. . . . .	38. *Ἀγαμεμνων*	. . . . .
14. *Ἀνδρομεδα*	. . . . .	39. *Πλουτων*	. . . . .
15. *Μορφευς*	. . . . .	40. *Οἰδιπους*	. . . . .
16. *Ποσειδων*	. . . . .	41. *Ὀδυσσευς*	. . . . .
17. *Ἡρα*	. . . . .	42. *Ἀφροδιτη*	. . . . .
18. *Ἀργοναυτης*	. . . . .	43. *Πριαμος*	. . . . .
19. *Πηνελοπη*	. . . . .	44. *Ἰασων*	. . . . .
20. *Στυξ*	. . . . .	45. *Ἑκαβη*	. . . . .
21. *Δρυας*	. . . . .	46. *Ἀγχισης*	. . . . .
22. *Ἑσπεριδες*	. . . . .	47. *Δημητηρ*	. . . . .
23. *Περσευς*	. . . . .	48. *Θησευς*	. . . . .
24. *Ὀρφευς*	. . . . .	49. *Εὐρυδικη*	. . . . .
25. *Κιρκη*	. . . . .	50. *Καλυψω*	. . . . .

Quiz 3

Medical terms which have come over into our spelling with little or no change otherwise

	GREEK	OUR SPELLING		GREEK	OUR SPELLING
1.	ἀρθριτις	. . . . .	19.	σπασμος	. . . . .
2.	ἀποπληξια	. . . . .	20.	στομαχος	. . . . .
3.	ἀσθμα	. . . . .	21.	συμπτωμα	. . . . .
4.	διαρροια	. . . . .	22.	ἀορτη	. . . . .
5.	δυσεντερια	. . . . .	23.	ἀρτηρια	. . . . .
6.	ἐπιληψις	. . . . .	24.	ἐμβρυον	. . . . .
7.	γαγγραινα	. . . . .	25.	λαρυγξ	. . . . .
8.	θωραξ	. . . . .	26.	οἰσοφαγος	. . . . .
9.	καθαρσις	. . . . .	27.	σπλην	. . . . .
10.	καταρροος	. . . . .	28.	τραχεια	. . . . .
11.	νεφριτις	. . . . .	29.	φαλαγξ	. . . . .
12.	παραλυσις	. . . . .	30.	φαρυγξ	. . . . .
13.	προβοσκις	. . . . .	31.	φθισις	. . . . .
14.	ῥευματισμος	. . . . .	32.	ναυσια	. . . . .
15.	φλεβοτομια	. . . . .	33.	ὑμην	. . . . .
16.	λεπρα	. . . . .	34.	τενδον	. . . . .
17.	ψωρα	. . . . .	35.	ταρσος	. . . . .
18.	μανια	. . . . .	36.	πλευρα	. . . . .

Quiz 4

Some non-technical Greek words assimilated into English with little or no change

	GREEK	OUR SPELLING		GREEK	OUR SPELLING
1.	αἰνιγμα	. . . . .	7.	δραμα	. . . . .
2.	ἀκμη	. . . . .	8.	θεμα	. . . . .
3.	ἀσβεστος	. . . . .	9.	θεατρον	. . . . .
4.	βασις	. . . . .	10.	εἰκων	. . . . .
5.	δαιμων	. . . . .	11.	ἐμφασις	. . . . .
6.	δογμα	. . . . .	12.	ἠχω	. . . . .

GREEK	OUR SPELLING	GREEK	OUR SPELLING
13. ἰδεα	......	37. τυραννος	......
14. κριτηριον	......	38. φαλλος	......
15. κυδος	......	39. ἐλεφας	......
16. ὁριζων	......	40. κροκοδειλος	......
17. πανακεια	......	41. ἀσπαραγος	......
18. στιγμα	......	42. ἀνεμωνη	......
19. συνταξις	......	43. θυμος	......
20. ὑφεν	......	44. ἑλλεβορος	......
21. φαντασια	......	45. ναρκισσος	......
22. χαρακτηρ	......	46. ὀρχις	......
23. χαος	......	47. πεπερι	......
24. γενος	......	48. ὑσσωπος	......
25. μεθοδος	......	49. ζεφυρος	......
26. ἱστορια	......	50. δισκος	......
27. κυκλος	......	51. ζωνη	......
28. κυβος	......	52. παπυρος	......
29. κυλινδρος	......	53. ῥητορικη	......
30. προβλημα	......	54. συλλαβη	......
31. πυραμιδος	......	55. ὑμνος	......
32. ῥυθμος	......	56. χορος	......
33. σφαιρα	......	57. ψαλμος	......
34. σχημα	......	58. λυρα	......
35. ψυχη	......	59. σιφων	......
36. σχολη	......	60. καταστροφη	......

Quiz 5

Fill in an English word derived from each of the following

GREEK	MEANING	DERIVATIVE
1. ἐλεγος	lament	......
2. ἐπος	speech	......
3. ἱστορια	narrative	......
4. κανων	ruler	......

GREEK	MEANING	DERIVATIVE
5. καθεδρα	chair	. . . . . .
6. κλινη	bed	. . . . . .
7. κοτυλη	small cup	. . . . . .
8. κρατηρ	bowl	. . . . . .
9. μιτρα	girdle	. . . . . .
10. πλινθος	tile	. . . . . .
11. στηλη	pillar	. . . . . .
12. συριγξ	shepherd's pipe	
13. στυλος	pillar	. . . . . .
14. ταπης	carpet	. . . . . .
15. τραπεζα	table	. . . . . .
16. ἀνθραξ	coal	. . . . . .
17. ἠλεκτρον	amber	. . . . . .
18. κεραμος	clay	. . . . . .
19. κολλα	glue	. . . . . .
20. μαγνης	lodestone	. . . . . .
21. μαργαριτης	pearl	. . . . . .
22. μεταλλον	mine	. . . . . .
23. νιτρον	saltpetre	. . . . . .
24. πυριτης	flint	. . . . . .
25. βουκολος	herdsman	. . . . . .
26. δυναστης	ruler	. . . . . .
27. μαγος	magician	. . . . . .
28. οἰκονομος	steward	. . . . . .
29. προφητης	interpreter	. . . . . .
30. ἀγγελος	messenger	. . . . . .
31. εἰδωλον	image	. . . . . .
32. ἐπισκοπος	bishop	. . . . . .
33. μυστηριον	secret	. . . . . .
34. χριστος	anointed	. . . . . .
35. μανια	frenzy	. . . . . .
36. ἡρως	demigod	. . . . . .
37. θωραξ	breastplate	. . . . . .
38. θυρεος	shield	. . . . . .
39. πολεμος	war	. . . . . .
40. στρατηγος	commander	. . . . . .

GREEK	MEANING	DERIVATIVE
41. ἀσυλον	sanctuary	. . . . . .
42. ἀδην	glandule	. . . . . .
43. γονη	womb	. . . . . .
44. γυρος	ring	. . . . . .
45. δυναμις	power	. . . . . .
46. ἐλεημοσυνη	pity	. . . . . .
47. θαυμα	marvel	. . . . . .
48. θεραπεια	care, tending	. . . . . .
49. θεωρια	speculation	. . . . . .
50. κωμος	revel	. . . . . .
51. μαθημα	learning	. . . . . .
52. κινναβαρι	vermilion	. . . . . .
53. μιμησις	imitation	. . . . . .
54. ἀξων	shaft	. . . . . .
55. μουσικη	art of the muses	. . . . . .
56. ἐκκλησια	church	. . . . . .
57. ὀργια	secret rite	. . . . . .
58. βουτυρον	butter	. . . . . .
59. πραγμα	fact	. . . . . .
60. σαρκασμος	mockery	. . . . . .
61. σημα	symbol, sign	. . . . . .
62. σκανδαλον	offence	. . . . . .
63. στιγμα	mark, puncture	. . . . . .
64. ὀργανον	tool	. . . . . .
65. γεωργος	farmer	. . . . . .
66. λαος	people	. . . . . .
67. πολιτης	citizen	. . . . . .
68. ὑποκριτης	actor	. . . . . .
69. διαιτα	regimen	. . . . . .
70. ἐμετος	vomiting	. . . . . .
71. ἡπαρ, ἡπατος	liver	. . . . . .
72. ναρκη	numbness	. . . . . .
73. τραυμα	wound	. . . . . .
74. ὑγιεια	health	. . . . . .
75. ὑμην	membrane	. . . . . .
76. φαρμακον	drug	. . . . . .

GREEK	MEANING	DERIVATIVE
77. ζωνη	belt	. . . . . .
78. βοτανη	herb	. . . . . .
79. ουρα	tail	. . . . . .
80. ανεμος	wind	. . . . . .

Quiz 6

Some Russian words in the news of the day

Places

1. Россия	. . . . . .
2. Волга	. . . . . .
3. Ленинград	. . . . . .
4. Сталинград	. . . . . .
5. Урал	. . . . . .
6. Киев	. . . . . .
7. Украйна	. . . . . .
8. Кремль	. . . . . .
9. Москва	. . . . . .
10. Дон	. . . . . .

Persons

11. Ленин	. . . . . .
12. Сталин	. . . . . .
13. Иван	. . . . . .

14. Нехов	. . . . . .
15. Толстой	. . . . . .

Other Words

16. царь	. . . . . .
17. комиссар	. . . . . .
18. водка	. . . . . .
19. степь	. . . . . .
20. тройка	. . . . . .
21. икона	. . . . . .
22. совет	. . . . . .
23. мужик	. . . . . .
24. самовар	. . . . . .
25. комсомол	. . . . . .

Quiz 7

The GH Family

In Scots dialect we hear a hard breathing sound, somewhat like CH of *Loch Lomond*, in English words which now have a silent GH. In German this old Teutonic sound persists, spelt CH. In O.E., for lack of a sign for the sound, scribes wrote H for it at the end of a word or before another consonant.

Now fill in:

SCOTS   MODERN ENGLISH

1. Yon man is a bonnie fechter   . . . .
2. It's a bra brecht munlicht necht the necht   . . . .

Fill in the Modern English equivalents of the following, bearing in mind:

(a) that the dictionary forms of the O.E. and German verbs respectively end in -AN and -EN;

(b) that the prefix GE- has disappeared in Modern English.

MODERN ENGLISH	OLD ENGLISH	GERMAN
3.	FLYHT	FLUCHT
4.	LEOHT	LICHT
5.	MIHT	MACHT
6.	NIHT	NACHT
7.	PLIHT	PFLICHT
8.	RIHT	RECHT
9.	GESIHTH	GESICHT
10.	EAHTA	ACHT
11.	THOHTE	DACHTE
12.	SOHTE	SUCHTE
13.	BROHTE	BRACHTE
14.	NOWIHT	NICHTS
15.	HEAH	HOCH
16.	NEAH	NAHE
17.	PLOH	PFLUG
18.	RUH	RAUH
19.	TOH	ZÄHE
20.	FEOHTAN	FECHTEN
21.	HLEHHAN	LACHEN
22.	FORHT	FURCHT
23.	GENOH	GENUG
24.	DAH	TEIG

Quiz 8

The SH-sound

I. The *sk*-sound, spelt SC in O.E., began to change at an early date to the pure sound represented in the international phonetic script by ʃ. For this the Norman scribes used the combination SH as in *shall*, for which the Swedish is *skall*. This is a trademark of native origin whenever it occurs at the beginning of an English word. The same shift took place in the evolution of German where the spelling is SCH. The SCH in corresponding Dutch words now stands for a sound more like *sg*. The dictionary form of the O.E. verb ends in -AN, that of the Dutch in -EN. With these clues fill in the following:

MODERN ENGLISH	OLD ENGLISH	DUTCH
1.	SCEADU	SCHADUW
2.	SCAMU	SCHAAMTE
3.	SCEAP	SCHAAP
4.	SCEARP	SCHERP
5.	SCAFAN	SCHAVEN
6.	SCERAN	SCHEREN
7.	WASCAN	WASSEN
8.	SCYLL	SCHEL
9.	SCELD	SCHILD
10.	SCILLING	SCHELLING
11.	SCIN	SCHEEN
12.	SCINAN	SCHIJNEN
13.	SCIP	SCHIP
14.	SCEOH	SCHOEN
15.	SCEOTAN	SCHIETEN
16.	SCRINCAN	SCHRINKEN
17.	SCULDOR	SCHOUDER
18.	SCEATH	SCHEDE
19.	SCEAFT	SCHACHT
20.	SCUFAN	SCHUIVEN

II. In French spelling the sign for the sound we represent by SH at the beginning of a native word is CH as in the class of words of French origin to which belong:

chic	*chemise*	*champagne*	*chassis*	*chiffon*
chivalry	*chef*	*chamois*	*charabanc*	*charade*

III. In the middle of a word of French or Latin origin the signs CI, SS or TI may stand for the *sh*-sound, as in:

A	B	C
precious	*pressure*	*nation*
gracious	*fissure*	*addition*
efficient	*passion*	*completion*
capricious	*fission*	*ration*

Give one example of each of the above:

21A. ......   22B. ......   23C. ......

IV. Though SH at the beginning of a word is a trademark of native origin, it is nearly always a trademark of French origin when it stands for the same sound at the end of a *verb* and mostly of the class whose dictionary form ends in -IR. Find the French equivalents for the following:

24. abolish	......	38. languish	......
25. accomplish	......	39. nourish	......
26. banish	......	40. perish	......
27. blemish	......	41. polish	......
28. brandish	......	42. publish	......
29. burnish	......	43. punish	......
30. cherish	......	44. push	......
31. demolish	......	45. ravish	......
32. embellish	......	46. relinquish	......
33. astonish	......	47. replenish	......
34. finish	......	48. splash	......
35. establish	......	49. tarnish	......
36. furnish	......	50. relish	......
37. garnish	......	51. crash	......

V. Besides this large class of verbs, **SH** represents the same sound in *fashion* (French *façon*) and at the end of a small class of nouns of French origin. Find the French equivalent for:

52. anguish	. . . . . .	54. cash	. . . . . .
53. parish	. . . . . .	55. radish	. . . . . .

Quiz 9

The Letter G

I. In Teutonic languages, G originally stood for the hard sound in *gear*. It still does in German, Dutch and Danish; but in Swedish and Norwegian, G followed by the back vowels (E and I) now represents the *y*-sound in *year*. There is some evidence that this replacement of the hard *g*-sound began very early, long before Norman scribes replaced GE by Y at the beginning of a native word. For this *y*-sound which occurs at the beginning of some old Teutonic words, all the Teutonic languages other than English employ the sign J which does not exist in the Celtic alphabet. That we find GE instead suggests that GE already stood for a *y*-sound which had replaced the hard *g*-sound in many English words.

FILL IN	OLD ENGLISH	GERMAN
1.	GEA	JA
2.	GEAR	JAHR
3.	GEOLU	GELB
4.	GEONG	JUNG
5.	GEOSTRAN-	GESTERN
6.	GEARD	GARTEN

Clues: day before, back of house, sun's cycle, whom the Gods love, affirmation, what about GEOLCA?

II. At the end of a word there is often a dummy Y or W for the O.E. G, which has also passed out in the middle of some words, often without any gravestone in our spelling. This has happened in Norwegian where the Y represents the *y*- sound of *yes* between two vowels, but otherwise is pronounced as in *fully*.

FILL IN	OLD ENGLISH	GERMAN	SWEDISH	NORWEGIAN
7.	EAGE	AUGE	ÖGA	ØYE
8.	FLEAG	FLOG	FLÖG	FLØY

III. At the end of some words we now find a dummy Y for the old G preserved in Dutch and German.

FILL IN	OLD ENGLISH	DUTCH
9.	DÆG	DAG
10.	WEG	WEG
11.	MÆG	MAG

IV. In the middle of many O.E. words all trace of the *g*-sound has disappeared both in speech and in spelling, though we often find an irrelevant W in its place.

FILL IN	OLD ENGLISH	DUTCH	GERMAN
12.	FUGEL	VOGEL	VOGEL
13.	LAGU	RECHT	RECHT
14.	SUGU	ZEUG	SAU

Clue: It is against the rules of nature for pigs to fly.

V. Sometimes the G sign is a dummy in Modern English, because it had lost its distinctive Latin sound in Norman French before N, as in:

FILL IN	FRENCH
15.	RÈGNE
16.	SIGNE
17.	ALIGNER

VI. In modern French the old hard Roman G keeps its original value before A, O, U, but before E or I has a different value represented in many French words by the sign J. For this sound, which we may label *zh*, we have no special sign, but it occurs in a few words, all of French origin, such as:

A	B	C
pleasure	*division*	*prestige*
measure	*fusion*	*régime*
enclosure	*erosion*	*concierge*

Give three other English examples of each class:

18A. ....
19B. ....
20C. ....

VII. Where the French J (*zh*) sound occurs in Modern French words, English has another sound sometimes now represented by J or by G as in *jam* or *gentle*. This sound occurs only in a few words of truly English origin, in all of which DG replaces a sound represented by the signs CG at the end of an O.E. word. The outstanding exceptions to the rule that DG stands for the English J sound in native words only are *judge* (French *juge,* from Latin *judice*) and *pledge* (Old French *plege*). Here the D, like the B in *debt,* is a scholarly error.

	FILL IN	OLD ENGLISH
21.	......	BRYCG
22.	......	MYCG
23.	......	HRYCG
24.	......	WECG
25.	......	ECG

VIII. Where the English J sound of *jelly* and *gelatine* occurs otherwise, the word is of foreign origin, occasionally Semitic as in *Jehovah* and *jackal,* but nearly always French or replacing the Latin I at the beginning of a word.

A	B	C	D
general	danger	cage	jolly
gentle	plunge	rage	journey
gelatine	strange	sage	joy

Give two examples of each class:

26A. ....
27B. ....
28C. ....
29D. ....

IX. The Modern English combination NG may stand for the sound *n-g* in *finger*, *n-j* as in *ranger* and as always in Welsh (except in compounds such as *Bangor*) for the sound we may label *ng* as in *singer*. This *ng*-sound is the usual value of the combined sign NG in Teutonic languages and is accordingly a trademark of truly English origin, except as the terminal -ING added to any verb as in *deceiving* or *ceasing*.

	FILL IN	OLD ENGLISH	GERMAN
30.	......	BRINGAN	BRINGEN
31.	......	LANG	LANG
32.	......	LUNGEN	LUNGE
33.	......	HRING	RING
34.	......	SINGAN	SINGEN
35.	......	SPRINGAN	SPRINGEN
36.	......	THING	DING
37.	......	WRINGAN	RINGEN
38.	......	SWINGAN	SCHWINGEN

Quiz 10

The Letter C

I. In the Roman alphabet C stood for the *k*-sound in *coat* or *came*. Teutonic languages other than O.E. use the Greek K, O.E. almost always the Latin C. By the time Roman legions finally left Britain, the *k*-sound in different Latin-speaking parts of the Empire had given place to another sound before E and I. Before E and I in French it came to represent the *s*-sound in *cellar* and *circus*. At some date in O.E. C for the *k*-sound before E or I was giving place to our CH sound in *chief*. Examples of this change are: *ilk* for ÆLC (*each*) and *mickle* or *muckle* for MYCEL (*much*) in Scots dialect, *chicken* (CICEN), *ditch* (DIC) and *child* (CILD).

FILL IN	OLD ENGLISH	GERMAN
1.	CESE	KÄSE
2.	CEOWAN	KAUEN
3.	CEST	KISTE
4.	CIN	KINN
5.	RICE	REICH

Clue: No rich man's food nor heavy on the breast, no need to masticate.

II. The use of the sign C for the *s*-sound is Norman French, but it imposed itself on a few native words: *ice, since, mice, lice, fleece, pence, once, twice, thrice, hence, thence, whence.* Otherwise, it is a signpost of French origin, as in the following:

A	B	C	D	E
cease	face	deceive	scenery	access
cell	chance	recess	science	excess

Fill in other examples of each class:

6A.	......	......
7B.	......	......
8C.	......	......
9D.	E.	

III. When the Latin of Gaul was taking shape as Old French, the *k*-sound before Roman A and O softened to make way for the sound represented by CH in French *chef*. In some English words of French origin CH stands for this sound. More often English assimilated such words to the pattern CHILD. Compare the following words of French origin.

A	B
chivalry	chase
champagne	chaste

	A		B
	chalet		chain
	chassis		chair
	chauvinism		champion

Give three other examples of (B):

10. ....

IV. In Greek the *kh*-sound of Scots *loch* occurs in many words with the sign χ for which Roman scribes used CH. Where CH has a hard sound, the word is of Greek origin, as in *chasm*.

Give three other examples of the Greek CH:

11. ....

V. At the beginning of a word the sound *kn* was fairly common in the old Teutonic languages and in Greek. It occurs in the name of the famous king *Knut*, Frenchified as *Canute*, the sound in this position being foreign to Latin and to all its descendants. In English words beginning with KN, the K (always reliable otherwise) is now silent. It is a signpost of a native English word or word of Teutonic origin.

FILL IN	OLD ENGLISH	GERMAN
12.	CNEDAN	KNETEN
13.	CNAFA	KNABE
14.	CNEO	KNIE
15.	CNIHT	KNECHT

Give three other examples of such Teutonic words:

16. ....

VI. In its modern descendants, the *k*-sound replaces the Latin *kw*-sound represented by QU, though French spelling retains QU where the *kw*-sound occurred. We pronounce QU as *kw* in words of Latin or French origin, and follow the Norman scribes who replaced the CW of native words by QU. Words in which QU occurs are the only words of Latin or French origin containing the *w*-sound. In native words the *w*-sound may occur after and in combination with the *d*-, *s*- and *t*- as well as the *k*-sound.

MODERN ENGLISH	OLD ENGLISH	DUTCH	GERMAN	SWEDISH	DANISH
17.	SWELGAN	ZWELGEN	(VERSCHLIN-GEN)	(SLUKA)	(SLUGE)
18.	SWEALEWE	ZWALUW	SCHWALBE	SVALA	SVALE
19.	SWAN	ZWAAN	SCHWAN	SVAN	SVANE
20.	SWEARM	ZWERM	SCHWARM	SVÄRM	SVÆRM
21.	SWERIAN	ZWEREN	SCHWÖREN	SVÄRA	SVÆRGE
22.	SWAT	ZWEET	SCHWEISS	SVETT	SVED
23.	SWAPAN	(VEGEN)	(FEGEN)	SOPA	(FEJE)
24.	SWETE	ZOET	SÜSS	SÖT	SØD
25.	SWELLAN	ZWELLEN	SCHWELLEN	SVALLA	SVULME
26.	SWIMMAN	ZWEMMEN	SCHWIMMEN	SIMMA	SVØMME
27.	SWINGAN	(ZWAAIEN)	SCHWINGEN	SVINGA	SVINGE (*or* SVAJE)
28.	SWEORD	ZWAARD	SCHWERT	SVÄRD	SVÆRD
29.	DWEORH	DWERG	ZWERG	DVÄRG	DVÆRG
30.	DWELLAN	(WONEN)	(WOHNEN)	DVÄLJAS	DVÆLE
31.	TWIG	TWIJG	ZWEIG		(KVIST)
32.	TWIN	TWEELING	ZWILLING	TVILLING	TVILLING
33.	TWA	TWEE	ZWEI	TVÅ	TO
34.	TWELF	TWAALF	ZWÖLF	TOLV	TOLV
35.	TWENTIG	TWINTIG	ZWANZIG	TJUGO	TYVE

VII. For the *kw*-sound of QV or QU in Latin, the O.E. scribes used HW. French retains QU for the hard *k*-sound. At the beginning of a word this is a sign-post of Latin or French origin. The Celtic languages lost the *p*-sound. In words which originally had the *kw*-sound, the *p*-sound has come back in the Brythonic languages. Fill in:

	OLD ENGLISH	FRENCH	LATIN	GAELIC	WELSH
36.	HWA?	QUI	QUIS	CO	PWY
37.	HWÆT?	QUE	QUOD	CIOD	PA
38.	HWONNE?	QUAND	QUANDO	CUIN	PAN

	SWEDISH	CORNISH	GAELIC
39.	SON	MAP	MAC

Quiz 11

The Letter W

I. In Latin the signs U and V were interchangeable. At the beginning of a word and between vowels, Latin V stands for the *w*-sound in *wet*, elsewhere for a vowel as in *full*. The *w*-sound represented by V in Latin has made way for the *v*-sound of *virile* in all its modern descendants, whence we may suppose by the time when writing was in common use among the Teutons. The *w*-sound is common before a vowel at the beginning of a word in all the Old Teutonic languages, and scribes represented it by UU or VV, whence its name and form. It persists in English speech. In other Teutonic languages it has made way for the *v*-sound in *vile*, represented in Swedish or Danish by V, but still by W in Dutch and German.

	OLD ENGLISH	DUTCH	SWEDISH
1.	WÆS	WAS	VAR
2.	WACIETH	WAKT	VAKER
3.	WEARM	WARM	VARM
4.	WÆTER	WATER	VATTEN
5.	WEG	WEG	VÄG
6.	WEAX	WAS	VAX
7.	WEDER	WEDER	VÄDER
8.	WEL	WEL	VÄL
9.	WEBB	WEB	VÄV
10.	WICU	WEEK	VECKA
11.	WILDE	WILD	VILD
12.	WILLE	WIL	VILJA
13.	WIN	WIJN	VIN
14.	WIND	WIND	VIND
15.	WUDU	(HOUT)	VED

II. In many O.E. words the *w*-sound occurs at the beginning of a word before R, but the W sign is now silent.

	FILL IN	OLD ENGLISH
16.		WRENNA
17.		WRINGAN

	FILL IN	OLD ENGLISH
18.	......	WRITAN
19.	......	WRECAN
20.	......	WRENCAN
21.	......	WRANG
22.	......	WRATH

III. At the beginning of many O.E. words we find HW where we now use WH. The H was a hard breathing sound, in the North of Britain close to the *kh*-sound represented by the now silent GH, whence in old Scots chronicles we find QU for WH in Modern English. Danish spelling preserves this silent H in its original position.

	FILL IN	OLD ENGLISH	DANISH
23.	......	HWÆL	HVAL
24.	......	HWÆT?	HVAD?
25.	......	HWÆTE	HVEDE
26.	......	HWÆR	HVOR
27.	......	HWILC	HVILKEN
28.	......	HWIT	HVID
29.	......	HWA?	HVEM?

IV. In a few modern words WH has the *h*-sound through an error of the later scribes, as in:

	FILL IN	OLD ENGLISH
30.	......	HAL
31.	......	HORE

V. The sound *w* disappeared early in the spoken Latin of Gaul, but the Teutonic Franks left a few words in the language with the old Teutonic sound, and French scribes represented it by GU before A or I as in *Guillaume* for *Wilhelm* or *William*. When these came back into English they sometimes reverted to type.

	FILL IN (W-word)	FRENCH
32.	......	GUERRE, GUERRIER
33.	......	GUARDIEN (Old French)
		=GARDIEN (Mod. French)

VI. The combination GU was sometimes used by Norman scribes to signify that the G before E or I at the beginning of an O.E. word still stood for the hard sound in *goat*.

FILL IN	OLD ENGLISH
34.	GILD
35.	GYLT
	DUTCH
36.	GAST
37.	GISSEN

Quiz 12

The Two TH-sounds

I. In all the Old Teutonic languages, as in Welsh, there were two sounds we now represent by TH. Both were foreign to Latin and both are foreign to French. One, represented by TH in Welsh, is the sound in *thin*. The other, represented by DD in Welsh, is the sound in *this*, which we shall label as *dh*. These sounds have made way for T and D in German, Dutch and Swedish—and, except for the trace of the *dh* sound represented by D in some words, in Danish also. They have survived in English and in Icelandic. Icelandic still differs little from the Old Norse of the Viking conquerors of the half of England over which CNUT (*Canute*) ruled. Its spelling employs two Runic signs, þ for TH and ð for DH. The þ sound, represented by θ in Greek, came into some words which Latin borrowed; and the Roman scribes, having no sign for it, represented it by TH. English scribes used TH for both the TH sounds before A.D. 900. Later ones used þ and ð, as did mediaeval Welsh scribes. The Norman scribes scrapped these two useful signs, and sometimes used Y as in YE OLDE TEA SHOPPE. The usual pronunciation of Y in this advertisement is as much out of character as the drink.

II. The Greek words in which we meet the *th*-sound are all scholarly, such as:

THEME, THEATRE, THEOLOGY, THERMOSTAT, ORTHOGRAPHY, THESIS, NEOLITHIC, AESTHETIC.

Give three other examples:

1. . . . . . .   2. . . . . . .   3. . . . . . .

III. Otherwise the *th*-sound is almost always the trademark of a genuine native English word, *faith* from the Old French *feid*, Latin *fides* being an outstanding exception.

FILL IN	OLD ENGLISH	DUTCH	GERMAN
4.	THICCE	DIK	DICK
5.	THYNNE	DUN	DÜNN
6.	THENCETH	DENKT	DENKT
7.	THING	DING	DING
8.	THRI	DRIE	DREI
9.	THUNOR	DONDER	DONNER
10.	THUMA	DUIM	DAUMEN
11.	BÆTH	BAD	BAD
12.	BENEOTHAN	BENEDEN	HIENIEDEN
13.	DEATH	DOOD	TOD
14.	EORTHE	AARDE	ERDE
15.	MOTHTHE	MOT	MOTTE
16.	TOTH	TAND	ZAHN

IV. The *dh*-sound is exclusively a Teutonic trademark.

FILL IN	OLD ENGLISH	DUTCH	GERMAN
17.	THÆT	DAT	DAS
18.	THÆNNE	DAN	DANN
19.	THÆR	DAAR	DA
20.	BATHIETH	BADT	BADT
21.	FETHER	VEDER	FEDER
22.	LETHER	LEDER	LEDER

Quiz 13

Mixed Quiz on Spelling

I. First note what sound or sounds for which the old Roman alphabet had no symbol occurs in each word, using Y, W, and the combinations *th, dh, sh, zh, tsh, dzh, nh* to label them.

1. telepathy	2. lithograph	3. rash	4. ward	5. orthodox
6. collusion	7. jewellery	8. shear	9. sedge	10. wither
11. chassis	12. yoke	13. birch	14. amnesia	15. subtraction
16. weight	17. father	18. knife	19. genius	20. window
21. singe	22. Chevrolet	23. blithe	24. rouge	25. tether
26. anther	27. guard	28. emission	29. winter	30. spring
31. blight	32. knoll	33. birth	34. expression	35. journal
36. flesh	37. wing	38. wealth	39. reception	40. wheat
41. Xenophon	42. recite	43. other	44. luscious	45. circus
46. chaos	47. ought	48. judge	49. anxious	50. wish
51. string	52. recede	53. such	54. charm	55. know
56. rather	57. psychology	58. xylem	59. city	60. genuflect
61. further	62. character	63. cloth	64. jocular	65. psaltery
66. kneel	67. pyre	68. derision	69. jelly	70. xenophobia
71. fling	72. chorus	73. wreck	74. juxta-position	75. philately
76. gaol	77. wise	78. genteel	79. yonder	80. missionary
81. connexion	82. yawn	83. foreign	84. gather	85. fleece
86. leisure	87. gauge	88. Frank	89. extrusion	90. whither
91. empyrean	92. yeast	93. wonder	94. jealousy	95. amphibious
96. juvenile	97. engine	98. shoulder	99. thorough	100. chef

II. Now score each word as T (*Teutonic*), L (*Latin or French*), G (*Greek*).

1.	2.	3.	4.	5. ....
6.	7.	8.	9.	10. ....
11.	12.	13.	14.	15. ....
16.	17.	18.	19.	20. ....
21.	22.	23.	24.	25. ....

26.	27.	28.	29.	30. ....
31.	32.	33.	34.	35. ....
36.	37.	38.	39.	40. ....
41.	42.	43.	44.	45. ....
46.	47.	48.	49.	50. ....
51.	52.	53.	54.	55. ....
56.	57.	58.	59.	60. ....
61.	62.	63.	64.	65. ....
66.	67.	68.	69.	70. ....
71.	72.	73.	74.	75. ....
76.	77.	78.	79.	80. ....
81.	82.	83.	84.	85. ....
86.	87.	88.	89.	90. ....
91.	92.	93.	94.	95. ....
96.	97.	98.	99.	100. ....

4

Family Likeness among Languages

In previous chapters, there have been several references to the Teutonic and Latin clans within the Indo-European family. To designate groups of languages in such a way implies that they share to a greater or less degree common characteristics which betoken family likeness. Nowadays, most experts in the comparative study of languages interpret such similarity in terms of a common ancestry. In other words, we deem contemporary languages to be closely related if the ancestors of those who now speak them were at one time intelligible to one another. This is certainly true of French, Portuguese, Catalan, Spanish, Italian and Roumanian. All these are traceable to the speech of Roman soldiers who could converse with one another intelligibly at least as late as A.D. 400.

To discuss informatively the process which entails evolution of speech communities no longer able, as is true of the French and the Roumanians, to communicate with one another without an interpreter, we need to distinguish between two uses of the word *dialect*, i.e. as used by most of us in everyday life and as used by experts. Either way, we assume a high measure of *inter-communicability* among people who use local variants of a recognisably common pattern of speech. In popular usage, we speak of such variants as languages, if equipped with an official script with unique spelling conventions. Thus Swedish, Danish and Norwegian each have their own conventions; for the sounds of AW in *paw* and OR in *worker*, Swedish has Å, å, Danish AA, aa, or Å, å, Norwegian Å, å for the first, and for the second Swedish has Ö, ö, but Danish and Norwegian Ø, ø. For a sound like E in *pet* Swedish has Ä, ä, Danish Æ and æ and Norwegian E, e.

Actually, spoken differences between the three last-named so-called languages are no greater than the differences in the British Isles between the speech of rural Somerset and that of rural Aberdeenshire. Accordingly, a philologist whose criterion is intercommunicability would speak of the three official Scandinavian languages mentioned above as dialects of one speech community embracing (as does Anglo-American) different national and intra-national varieties. Needless to say, there is no absolute criterion of intercommunicability. There is a greater common measure of communication between a Brazilian (Portuguese-speaking) and an Argentinian (Spanish-speaking) than between either and an Italian. There is probably a higher common denominator of mutual understanding between a Spaniard and an Italian than between either and a Frenchman.

We have direct evidence of relationship of languages in the past only through the medium of the written word, and only if written words convey their sounds. This limits the landscape in our remote past to speech communities which have a

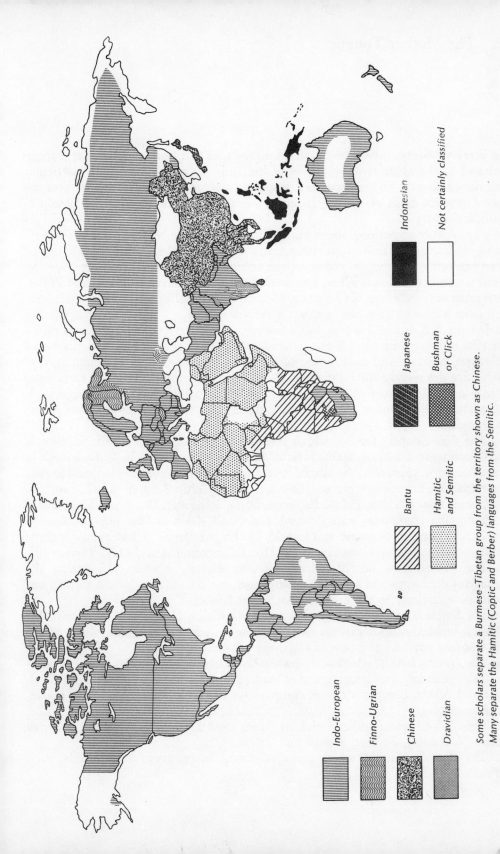

Indonesian

Not certainly classified

Japanese

Bushman
or Click

Bantu

Hamitic
and Semitic

Indo-European

Finno-Ugrian

Chinese

Dravidian

Some scholars separate a Burmese-Tibetan group from the territory shown as Chinese.
Many separate the Hamitic (Coptic and Berber) languages from the Semitic.

Fig. 16 Map of the Main Language Families of the World in the 20th Century.

long literary history, indeed to Semitic languages of the Jewish and Moslem scriptures and to the older representatives of the Indo-European family, in particular Sanskrit and Greek. So we may here properly pause to take stock of what progress experts have made in classifying languages in terms consistent with the notion of common ancestry.

We know little or nothing about many languages used in remote parts of Oceania and in other regions far from Western civilisation. Thus the work of classifying all the recognisably different languages of the world is still far from complete. Nor can we put a number to them. When Elizabeth I became queen of England and Wales, the number of translations of Christian, Moslem and Buddhist scriptures was scarcely more than a dozen. Two and a quarter centuries later, in 1804, Thomas Charles founded the British and Foreign Bible Society. There were then translations of the Christian scriptures in seventy-two languages. In 1938 the Society had promoted translation, printing and distribution of the Bible or parts of it in 734 languages, of which some are merely official dialects. A considerable proportion of the remainder fall into a small number of classes, the members of which have an unmistakable family likeness in terms of what one may distinguish as *word material, sound pattern* and *grammar*:

1. The *Indo-European* family, which includes most languages of Europe, that of Persia (adulterated with Arabic), most of the languages spoken in India except in the southernmost third of it, the official first language of bilingual Ceylon, and in Asia Minor *Armenian*. European representatives include the Celtic, Teutonic and Latin clans, the Slavonic clan (*Russian, Polish, Bulgarian, Czech, Ukrainian, Slovak* and *Serbo-Croat*), the Baltic clan (*Lithuanian* and *Latvian*), *Greek* and *Albanian* (the last adulterated with Turkish, Arabic, Slavonic and Greek). In this *galère*, many scholars now include also the long-since-extinct language of the Hittites, mentioned in the Old Testament.

2. The *Finno-Ugrian* family, which includes *Finnish, Estonian, Hungarian*, the language of the Lapps and some other languages, e.g. *Mordvinian*, spoken throughout an extensive territory in the north of the Soviet Union.

3. The *Semitic* family, which includes *Arabic, Abyssinian, Hebrew*, and the vernacular of Malta, besides various extinct tongues such as *Aramaic* (in which much of the Bible was first written) and that of Carthage (*Phoenician*).

4. The *Hamitic* family, which includes the *Coptic* of a considerable peasant population in Egypt and various languages of nomadic people (Berbers) in North and French Equatorial Africa. Some students of comparative linguistics place this with 3 above, in one assemblage.

5. The *Indo-Chinese* family, which includes South Chinese (*Cantonese*), North Chinese (*Mandarin*), *Burmese, Siamese* and *Tibetan*.

6. The *Dravidian* family, which includes several languages of South India, such as *Tamil*.

7. The *Bantu* family, which includes the languages spoken by the majority of Africans south of the Equator and some of the people of East Equatorial Africa. Such are *Swahili, Congolese, Herero* and *Xosa* (of South Africa).

8. The *Malayo-Polynesian* family, which includes languages spoken in various islands of Oceania (Fiji, Tahiti), that of the Maoris in New Zealand and *Malayan.*

9. The *Turco-Tartar* family, which includes *Turkish* and some languages spoken in the South of Soviet Asia. Some authorities place 2 and 9 with *Korean* and *Mongolian* in one *Uro-Altaic* family.

10. The various dialects spoken of as *Japanese* are a family with no clear relation to any others.

One language of Europe falls out of step with any group here mentioned. This is *Basque,* spoken in a small region of North Spain and South France at the western end of the Pyrenees. Some think it is the remains of a language spoken widely over Europe before tribes speaking primitive Indo-European tongues settled there. It may be related to the extinct Italian language called *Etruscan,* and possibly to a group of Caucasian languages such as *Georgian.* Outside the Soviet Union, few scholars have studied the last-named.

For many centuries, Jewish scholars had recognised the noticeable common characteristics of languages assigned to the Semitic family. Otherwise European scholars paid little attention to the comparative study of languages till William Jones, an outstanding Oriental scholar appointed (1783) as Judge of the Supreme Court in Calcutta, took up the study of Sanskrit and drew attention to the many resemblances between Sanskrit and Greek. Foremost among those who followed up this important clue was one of the brothers Grimm (1785-1863), better known as the authors of fairy stories originally intended as an anthology of Indo-European folklore. Grimm's great contribution was to recognise one very remarkable way in which pronunciation of words may change locally. Thus there comes the day when sounds we associate with what people mean in different localities are no longer recognisably alike.

To make clear what Grimm's conception of *sound-shifting* implies, let us look at a change which has occurred in the history of English. O.E. shares with Swedish many words with the sound represented by U in Scandinavian and O.E., but by OO in Anglo-American spelling. In corresponding words we still hear the same sound in the speech of the countryside of North Scotland. Here are examples:

OLD ENGLISH	HUND	HUS	MUS	LUS	SUR	THU
SWEDISH	HUND	HUS	MUS	LUS	SUR	DU

In Anglo-American dialects we now find in all descendants of these words the sound represented by OW in *howl* or OU in *foul.* So the reader can easily identify them without any previous acquaintance with Swedish or O.E. We see therefore that a single sound may in time replace another in a multitude of words. Indeed we might choose a very large number of words which illustrate a second sound-shifting disclosed by the couplet THU—DU. Where such local changes affect only the class of words we call vowels (e.g. U), they do not greatly impede communicability. When they involve consonants (e.g. D) they may eventually result in total lack

LYCKAD LANDNING FÖR KOSMONAUTERNA JÄTTEPARAD VÄNTAR

Turkije in gisting (slot*)

Ordening van de staat blijkt een moeilijk gewetensprobleem

Afstand tot het Westen inlopen

Wird Prozeß gegen Rothaar vertagt?

Gegensätzliche Auffassungen der medizinischen Sachverständigen / Der Verteidiger verlangt ein Obergutachten

Fig. 17. Newspaper Headlines in Teutonic Languages (Swedish, Dutch, German).

of reciprocal understanding between local speech-communities; and only by careful study may it then be possible to identify the common ancestry of words.

To recognise in writing such regular sound-shifts which conceal the ancestral pattern, we have to remind ourselves that speech communities which use the same alphabet do not necessarily use all the signs in the same way. As emphasised in Chapter 3, some consonant signs among those who use the so-called Roman alphabet are very reliable, and B, D, K, L, M, N, P, Q, R and T each have nearly always recognisably like values in different scripts. We have also seen that C, G, F, H, J, S, V, X and Z are less reliable. For what immediately follows, the reader will need to recall the vagaries of F and V, S and Z. Thus, Welsh uses F for the *v*-sound, as in *of*, and FF for our *f*-sound, as in *off*. Contrariwise, V in Dutch and in German words, such as *Vater*, has the *f*-sound as in *father*. In English spelling S may have the *s*-sound in *caps* or *sin*, or the *z*-sound in *cabs* and *arise*; but Z always stands for the latter, as in *zebra*. In German SS stands for the pure *s*-sound of *sin*. Before a vowel, a single S in German stands for the *z*-sound in *lose*, but Z stands for a sound like *ts* in *hats*. Hence the written form of a word may both conceal sound similarities which do exist and tempt us to infer similarities which do not. We have to pronounce OVE as Caesar would have pronounced it, and EWE as Alfred the Great would have done so, if we want to detect their common ancestry.

Since T is, from this viewpoint, one of the most reliable consonant signs of the Roman alphabet, it will be instructive to show how it is possible to recognise the common stock-in-trade of words which have undergone sound change in related languages. No such change has happened to the *t*-sound in native English words with the same ancestry as corresponding words in Dutch or in Swedish. So you may guess correctly the meaning of the following triplets:

DUTCH	OLD ENGLISH	SWEDISH
TONG	TUNGE	TUNGA
VOET	FOT	FOT
TIEN	TEN	TIO

Next look at these words:

ENGLISH	GERMAN		ENGLISH	GERMAN
tin	ZINN		foot	FUSS
ten	ZEHN		great	GROSS
toll	ZOLL		better	BESSER
tongue	ZUNGE		water	WASSER

We here see that the old *t*-sound of English, Dutch and Swedish words becomes the *ts*-sound represented by Z at the beginning of a German word and the pure *s*-sound represented by SS in the middle or at the end. When the divergence of dialects is not great, we find few such changes, and it is easy to detect them. Here is an easy example of a correspondence you will be able to recognise in a very large class of words listed in our Language Museum (pp. 155-160):

WELSH	DOD *or* DYFOD	MYNED	GWELED	CLYWED	CAFOD	CYMRYD
BRETON	DEVET	MONT	GWELET	CLEWET	KAVOUT	KEMERET
CORNISH	DOS	MONES	GWELES	CLEWES	CAFOS	KEMERES
ENGLISH	coming	going	seeing	hearing	getting	taking

The separation of Teutonic dialects cannot have been very sharp in Caesar's time when there was one Latin language where we now hear French, Italian, Portuguese, Spanish or Roumanian. So English and Dutch share an enormous number of words which we can recognise as such, if we consistently replace one sound by another. Contrariwise, we may be certain that the parent of the Teutonic languages and the earliest form of Latin were already very different in 1000 B.C. So the common stock of Latin and of Dutch or of O.E. words which we can readily recognise in this way is not very large. None the less, it is large enough to testify to a common ancestor of the two. Here are examples of one class of words which fall into line when we hold the clue:

LATE LATIN	PEDE*	PATER	PISCE	PLAT-	PLENO	* See note, p. 31.
ENGLISH	foot	father	fish	flat	full	
SWEDISH	FOT	FADER	FISK	FLAT	FULL	

Many Greek words are recognisably like Latin words if we replace the *s*-sound we find in Latin (or in Sanskrit) by the *h*-sound, as in

LATIN	SEMI	SEX	SEPTEM	SUDOR	SUPER	SUB
GREEK	HEMI	HEX	HEPTA	HUDOR	HYPER	HYPO
ENGLISH	half	six	seven	moisture, sweat	over	under

We meet the same shift in Welsh, but sometimes less abruptly from *s* to another hard-breathing sound as represented in Scots *loch* by CH.

LATIN	SENE	SALICE	SUS	SOROR	SEX
WELSH	HEN	HELYG	HWCH	CHWAER	CHWECH
ENGLISH	old	willow	pig	sister	six

The couplets *helium—solar* and *halogen—saline* recall two examples which show how the same sound-shift occurred both in Greek and in Welsh:

	LATIN	GREEK	WELSH
salt	SAL	HALS	HALEN
sun	SOL	HELI-	HAUL

When we have no written relics of the earliest form of a language, the best we can do is what a zoologist does when there are no fossils to disclose the story of evolution. If we find a family likeness among words, we may guess what the word in the parent language was most probably like; but we cannot be quite certain. Languages and animals have this in common, that the same changes may go on in the life story of different stocks. Thus the zoologist tells us that one-toed horses evolved from three-toed ancestors both in the Old World (where they survived) and in America, where they became extinct before white men arrived there. We have already seen that the *oo*-sound represented by U in O.E. or Old Norse as in Scots *hus*, becomes the OU of *house* in Modern English. The same change has occurred in many German words, where AU is equivalent to English OU or OW, as in *Haus*, *Maus* and *sauer*. Another parallel change of this sort has taken place both in English and in German. Many Modern English words begin with SH and many Modern German words begin with SCH, which respectively stand for the same sound in *shilling* and *schilling*. In corresponding words of Old Norse, as in O.E. in its earliest phase, we find instead the sound we represent by SK in *skate* or (in O.E.) by SC as, in *scarf*. Here are a few examples:

ICELANDIC	OLD ENGLISH	SWEDISH	GERMAN	ANGLO-AMERICAN
SKAFT	SCEAFT	SKAFT	SCHAFT	shaft
SKAMM	SCAMU	SKAM	SCHAM	shame
SKARP-	SCEARP	SKARP	SCHARF	sharp
SKAPA	SCIEPPAN	SKAPA	SCHAFFEN	shape
SKOFLA	SCEOFL	SKOVEL	SCHAUFEL	shovel

If our knowledge of the written language did not go back beyond A.D. 1200, it might be equally plausible to argue that the *sh*-sound common to German and English has made way for the *sk*-sound of the Scandinavian dialects or *vice versa*. Since we do know something about the fossil history of the Teutonic family, we can be confident that the *sh*-sound is the newcomer. Needless to say, no one who takes the study of language seriously would draw conclusions from so few examples. The ones here chosen illustrate a single sound-shift; and it is not easy to find pairs of words containing the same *single* outstanding sound difference, when languages have long been far apart. None the less, we have seen enough to understand one way in which scholars can recognise whether languages share a large common stock of word material. So now for an example nearer to the bone than *hemi* and *semi*. Grimm first pointed it out.

In other members of the Indo-European group, we commonly find the *p*-sound where we find the *f*-sound in the Teutonic clan. Since many of its F-words are of Franco-Latin (or Greek) origin, our hybrid Anglo-American does not furnish the best case-material to exhibit this sound-shift; and we shall here confine ourselves to examples which illustrate the *p* to *f* sound change at the beginning of a native English word, contrasted with that of a Sanskrit, Latin or Greek one of the same or related meaning. Any such example may illustrate a different sound-shift, e.g. Latin *t* to *d* in some other part of the word. None the less, the following are examples based on native words, all of which have patently recognisable equivalents in our sister Teutonic languages:

FATHER   Latin and Greek PATER, Sanskrit PITER.

FERN   Sanskrit PARNA (*feather* or *leaf*), probably from the same source as Latin PENNA (*feather*), whence *pen* (=goose feather) and *pennon*.

FEW   French PEU from Latin PAUCUS (*few*), PAULLUS (*small*), Greek PAUROS (*small*).

FIRE   Greek PYR- (as in *pyrex, pyre, pyrotechnics*).

FISH   (O.E. FISC), Latin PISCE.

FIVE   (German FÜNF), Greek PENT- (as in *pentagon*).

FLAT   Late Latin PLAT- as in *platitude* (=flat saying), and Greek PLATY-, as in duck-billed *Platypus* (=flat foot).

FLAX   Latin PLECTO and Greek PLEKO (=I weave).

FLAY   Greek PLESSO (= I strike).

FOOT   Latin PEDE (as in *pedal* and *centipede*), Greek POD- (as in *Arthropoda* and many other zoological names).

FULL   Latin PLENO (cf. pp. 148-9).

Transparently equivalent pairs of words which involve only a single sound-shift are hard to come by, if (as is especially true of the Teutonic clan in the context of the Language Common Market) several sound shifts commonly conspire to conceal their affinity. As inferred by comparative studies, the primitive Teutonic sound-pattern differs from that of the more remote ancestor of all the Indo-European family with respect to the following consonant values:

> *p* has become *f* (cf. *foot* with Latin *ped-*, Greek *pod-*, as above)
> *t* has become θ = *th* (cf. English *three* with Greek - Latin *tri-*)
> *k* has become *h* (cf. *heart* and *horn* with Latin *card-* and *corn-*)
> *b* has become *p* (cf. *deep* and Lithuanian *dubus*)
> *d* has become *t* (cf. *foot* and *heart*, above)
> *g* has become *k* (cf. *knee* and Latin *genu*, Greek *gon-*, p. 149)

The discerning reader may here ask how it is that *b, d* and *g* exist side by side in primitive Teutonic with *p, t* and *k*. The commonly accepted view is that the stock-in-trade of ancestral Indo-European speech included aspirated consonants which we may write *bh, dh, gh*; and these in the Teutonic stem replaced the transmuted *b, d, g* which had become *p, t, k*.

To exploit these clues adequately when learning any one of its sister Teutonic languages, we need to know both how English has deviated from the ancestral sound-pattern to which Gothic is nearest, and what changes have happened *pari passu* in the other groups. English itself has some conservative features, in particular survival of the *w*-sound which (except in some dialects) has made way for the *v*-sound in all other Teutonic languages, including Old Norse. Scandinavian languages use no W symbol. The fact that German and Dutch W has the sound value *v* suggests that the *w* to *v* sound shift happened later in the West Germanic group. Alone with Icelandic, English retains the voiceless TH (= θ) of *thin*, represented by þ in Icelandic script. In many English, and in fewer Icelandic, words this has

LAS REVISTAS ILUS-TRADAS AMERICANAS, HACIA UNA CRISIS
EN NUEVA YORK SE PREGUNTAN SI LLEGARAN A DESAPARECER LOS "MAGAZINES"

Les cérémonies commémoratives de la libération de Paris
Stationnement et circulation interdites samedi soir dans plusieurs quartiers

SI INAUGURA OGGI IN CAMPIDOGLIO LA PRIMA CONFERENZA MONDIALE SUL TURISMO
Riuniti i rappresentanti di 119 paesi per definire la figura del turista

Fig. 18.   Newspaper Headlines in Romance Languages (Spanish, French, Italian).

made way for the voiced equivalent of TH (our *dh*) of *then*. For the latter, the international phonetic alphabet uses the Icelandic symbol ð, of which the capital equivalent is Ð. There is a trace of this sound in Danish, but without a special symbol. Where we find TH with either sound value in English, we find in Swedish and Norwegian, as in Dutch, the *d*-sound appropriately labelled (D) as such.

Three outstanding changes which occurred late, if at all, in the sister languages began very early in English and were probably complete, except in northern Britain, even earlier than the Norman Conquest. Before a front vowel (E or I):

      (a) *k* becomes the *ch* (=tʃ) sound in *much*;
      (b) *g* becomes the *y*-sound in *yes*;
      (c) *sk* becomes the *sh* (=ʃ) sound in *ship*.

In Scots dialect, two common O.E. words have resisted the first of these three changes, possibly through the influence of Norse invaders and settlers. One is O.E. MYCEL, Scots *mickle* or *muckle*, Icelandic *mikill* and Modern English *much*. The other is CIRCE, Scots and Scandinavian *kirk* and Modern English *church*. Icelandic and Danish have been more resistant to these changes than either Swedish or Norwegian, both of which retain SK in script for the *sh*-sound where it occurs as in *skip* (Norw.), *skepp* (Swed.) for O.E. SCIP (=ship). The corresponding Dutch and German words are respectively *schip* and *Schiff*. In the latter, German SCH has the same sound value as our SH; and scribes of early Middle English used the same convention. Dutch SCH is ambiguous, having the sound value *sg* at the beginning and *s* at the end of a word. In the life history of many English words, transformation of *g* to *y* goes further, owing to fusion of *y*- with the vowel following. The new union produces a diphthong leaving no trace of the *y* (cf. in *fowl*, p. 27) or, if any, only in script (cf. *eye*, p. 22). The O.E. prefix GE- before a consonant is useful, and merits special comment in this connexion. As in Dutch and German, it is the hallmark of the so-called past participle of a verb. As such, it lingered into late Middle English, and in poetry (e.g. Spenser and Milton) into a later period, in the guise of Y- (long *i* as in *élite*); we meet it in the folk song SUMMER IS Y-CUMIN (in German, *Sommer ist gekommen*). However, the same prefix (as in German) tacks itself on to many verbs in *all* their forms. Thus the O.E. parent of *hear* is GE-HIERAN, as in Matt. vii. 24 of the Anglo-Saxon Gospels: ÆLC THÆRA THE THAS MINE WORD GEHIERTH (each of those that these mine words heareth). In such compound verbs, e.g. GE-BRINGAN (=bring), the prefix has left no trace in speech or in writing. The same is true of many O.E. collective nouns such as GEBROTHRU from which comes *brethren*.

One very characteristic feature of the Modern English sound-pattern is the fate of R (=*r*). At the beginning of a word, it replaces a hard breathing HR- (p. 93) in native words, and the Middle English speaker doubtless made a trilled sound, much as the French do. This is still true of some (especially Scots) dialects of Anglo-American; but far more often it is not so. With the same few exceptions, the R of writing is now merely a dummy in the terminal position (e.g. in *fear, far, for, fair*). In a medial position, Anglo-American speakers may retain it as in *arrow* or *perish*, or dispense with it as in *iron*. Fortunately for students of chemistry, there are recognisably different words for the two *ions* of *iron*, the *ferric* and the *ferrous*.

Little more need be said about Icelandic, except that the *v* (=V) replaces the *w* sound, as is true of the other Scandinavian languages, in all of which *d* replaces the two TH sounds of English and the parent θ (=þ) of Gothic. In Danish, we commonly find the voiced sounds *b, d, g* where we find in O.E., Swedish and Norwegian *p, t, k*. The pronunciation of Modern German merits more detailed comment. The High German of Germany, Austria and Switzerland differs not only from English and from the Scandinavian languages, but equally from Low German

(Dutch, Flemish and dialects of North Germany) on account of a group of highly characteristic changes sometimes referred to collectively as the *second sound-shift*. They are as follows:

(1) *þ* (=P) becomes *pf* (=PF) at the beginning of a word, elsewhere *f* (=FF); compare *pepper* with *Pfeffer*.
(2) *t* (=T) becomes *ts* (=Z) at the beginning of a word and either *ts* (=Z) or *s* (=SS) elsewhere, unless preceded or followed by another consonant; compare *tongue* and *foot* with *Zunge* and *Fuss*.
(3) *d* (=D) becomes *t* (=T); compare *daughter* with *Tochter*.
(4) *v* (=V) becomes *b* (=B) between vowels; compare *have* with *haben*, and *knave* with *Knabe*.

Our outline of consonant sound-shifts within the Teutonic clan will be incomplete if we fail to face up to one question which many readers will wish to ask, i.e. how do we know the shifts *k-* to *ch-*, *sk-* to *sh-* and *g* to *y* occurred early in the history of O.E.? If we concentrate illustratively on the last, it will be necessary to remind the reader that J in all the sister Teutonic languages has the sound value we here represent by *y* as in *year*, and that *g* retains its hard value in Low and High German. With these facts in mind, let us look at the comparatively few words in which the consonantal *y*-sound appeared at the beginning of a word from earliest times. O.E. GEAR (=*year*) clearly corresponds to Gothic *jer*, German *Jahr*, Dutch *jaar*. O.E. GEA (=*yea*) clearly corresponds to Gothic *jai*, and to *ja* both in German and in the Scandinavian languages. O.E. GEOC (=*yoke*) corresponds to Gothic *juk*, Dutch *juk*, German *Joch* and Latin *jug-* (in *subjugate*). O.E. GEONG (=*young*) corresponds to Gothic *juggs*, Dutch *jong*, German *jung*. Finally O.E. GEOL(-TID) =*yule*(*tide*) corresponds to *jul*(*tid*) in Swedish, *jul*(*e-tid*) in Danish and Norwegian, *jol*(*tid*) in Old Norse.

From the foregoing examples, it appears that we should not regard E after initial G in front of a back vowel (A, O, U) as part of a diphthong. Seemingly, it is a dummy in the sense that GE- does the work of J (=our initial Y) in the sister languages. Where it replaces German, Dutch or Scandinavian G (=*g*) before a back vowel, we may regard it as an arbitrary device to sidestep the lack of a special symbol for the consonantal *y*-sound in the form of the Roman alphabet which Celtic monks transmitted to their English converts. With due regard to the fate of the following vowel, we may regard initial CE and SCE as comparable conventions to represent the sounds *ch* (=tʃ) and *sh* (=ʃ).

Having thus surveyed the consonant sound-shifts which distinguish members of the Teutonic clan from other Indo-European languages and those which distinguish members of the same clan from one another, let us now briefly turn to another aspect of what we may call the Teutonic sound-pattern, i.e. to some initial consonant combinations highly characteristic of Teutonic languages. Of such we are already familiar (p. 24) with *kn* as in *knave, knife* and *knight*, and *hw* spelt HW in O.E. but WH in Middle English script. The aspiration, retained in Scots dialects, disappeared early in Dutch and German where we now find W, e.g. *wat* (Du.), *was* (Germ.) for *what*. In Scandinavian languages *hw* became *hv*, as in *hval* (*whale*) in Danish and Norwegian for O.E. HWÆL. Till late in the nineteenth century, Swedish preserved in writing its epitaph (HV) where we now read V (=*v*); but words with the same parentage as those of the English WH-class are recognisable by initial HV in the other modern Scandinavian languages. In O.E., as in Gothic, we meet three other aspirated initial consonants spelt HN, HL and HR. Their pronunciation ceased to be distinguishable from the usual sound values of N, L, R long before HW ceased to be distinguishable from W. Accordingly, they left no impress on Tudor English spelling. As examples, O.E. has HLAF, Gothic *hlaifs* for *loaf*; O.E. has HNUTU for Dutch *noot*, German *Nuss*, Modern English *nut*; O.E. has HROF, Old Frisian *rhoof* for later English *roof*. The aspirate leaves no trace in the spelling of Dutch, German, or modern Scandinavian languages other than Icelandic. Thus the Icelandic word for *horse* is *hross*. In older Teutonic languages we also meet an initial combination WR, now pronounced as *r*. Anglo-American spelling as in *write* and *wrong* still honours its memory.

By applying eight rules, we are now ready to change Anglo-Saxon—which we know only as a written language—to a bearing less unfamiliar to the eye of a contemporary whose native language is Anglo-American:*

(1) Where initial GE- occurs before a vowel, substitute Y;
(2) When initial GE- occurs before a consonant, cut it out;
(3) Where -G occurs as a terminal, substitute Y;
(4) For CE- and -CE substitute CH;
(5) For initial HW-, write WH-;
(6) For H before T (e.g. *niht—night*) or terminally (e.g., *neah—nigh*), substitute GH;
(7) For initial CN- and CW-, substitute KN- and QU-;
(8) For initial HL-, HN-, HR-, write L, N, R.

We shall later see how changes of pronunciation, other than those we associate with the name of Grimm, obscure even more than what we call sound-shifts the

---

* Owing to grammatical changes in the evolution of English, we can also sharpen the visual image of the filial likeness by elimination of a host of terminals such as -EN, -AN, -NA, -RA, -U and -UM; but we can fully appreciate why and which only after a glance at the grammar of O.E. This part of our story is the theme of the next chapter.

parental pattern of the Latin word in those of its descendants. In all of the latter, the symbol H is a dummy, being the epitaph of an *h*-sound which had disappeared from plebeian speech long before the Western Empire broke up. By that date, we may assume that several changes parallel to what occurred in the Teutonic languages

DIWEDD YMPRYD
EMYR Ll. JONES

Gwrthod bwyd am
bum niwrnod

ꝼꞃeaꞃꞃa Saꞃaiꞃꞇ

An Ró-ḃaoꞃal
ꝺ'áꞃ ꞃcꞃeiꝺeaṁ?

ꞃeanmóin ꞃaeḃilꞃe í
ꞃeo a ꞇuꞃ an ꞇaꞇaiꞃ ꞇ.
mac ꞃeinín. m.a., aꞃ
coláiꞃꞇe iaꞃꝼlaiꞇe
naoṁꞇa, ꞇuaim, uaiḋ aꞃ
cꞃuaic ꝼáꝺꞃaiꞃ, ꝺia
ꝺoṁnaiꞃ.

An Creid Thu So?

GWELL EO BRUD VAD
DA BEB HINI
EVID MADOU
LEUN AN TI

Fig. 19. Newspaper Headlines in Celtic languages (Welsh, Erse, Gaelic, Breton).

were beginning or had begun. First, the initial consonantal *w*-sound, represented by a symbol written (p. 24) alternatively as U or V, had made way for the *v*-sound represented as V in all modern descendants of Latin. At the same time, the g ($=$G) and k ($=$C) sounds were beginning to undergo displacement by others in different regions when preceding a front vowel. What we have already seen (p. 92) to be so of French is also true of all the daughter languages. The letters G and C have each come to have two different values, i.e. their original value (in *goat* and *coat*) remained before a back vowel (represented by A, O or U), and a new one before a front vowel (represented by E or I):

	FRENCH	ITALIAN	SPANISH
G	*zh* ($=$ ʒ) as in *measure*	*dzh* as in *gem*	*kh* ($=$χ) as in *loch*
C	*s* as in *cell*	*ch* ($=t\int$) as in *chop*	*th* ($=\theta$) as in *thin*
SC	*s* as in *science*	*sh* ($=\int$) as in *shop*	—

We see from this table that the secondary value of G in French is the same as that of French J, and the Italian secondary value of G is that of the English J, both being different from that of the Teutonic and Italian J ($=$our Y). Where G retains its original hard value before a front vowel, the Spanish convention is to replace it by GU, the Italian to replace it by GH. Where C has its secondary value before a back vowel, the French convention is to mark the C with a *cedilla* (as in *ça*, a contraction of *cela*), and the Italian convention replaces C by CI (as in Count Ciano). In both French and Spanish, *kw* becomes *k* but retains the Latin symbol (QU). Where this change occurs in Italian, we find CH for *k*. Otherwise QU retains its Latin value *kw*. Be it here said that Q, from Q in the Phoenician and earliest Greek alphabets, was not redundant in Latin, while U or V could still stand either for a consonantal sound (*w*) or short and long vowel sounds like OO in *book* and *boot* respectively. Roman writers introduced the convention that C before U stands for the *k*-sound in *coo*, and U after Q ($=k$) stands for the *w*-sound. This makes the distinction between words such as QUI and CUI.

The sound-shift from Latin *w* to the *v* of its modern descendants had started in the half century before the beginning of the Christian era. In the first century another change was on the way. Between vowels the *v*-sound replaced *b* as in Portuguese, Italian and French (cf. Italian *avere*, French *avoir* for Latin *habere*=*have*). The Spanish equivalent of *habere* is *haber*. Here the spelling recalls that the change was less complete in the Iberian peninsula. Contemporaneously in the early history of the Empire *s* between vowels became *z*; but Latin writers of this and of later periods used Greek Z only in words borrowed from Greek, whence the French convention mentioned in the next paragraph.

A comparison of sound-shifts or other changes of pronunciation within the modern

Latin family is intelligible only if we remind ourselves about its very diverse spelling conventions. In French, S answers for the voiced *z*-sound of *his* and SS for the voiceless *s*-sound of *hiss*. In Italian, S commonly has its voiced value (as in *his*) between two consonants, otherwise the voiceless (as in *this*). Spanish has no voiced *z*-sound, and S always stands for the *s*-sound. Other major differences concern J, CH and Z. As regards J, which replaces I before a vowel at the beginning of a Latin word, e.g. in the modern spelling of *Jove* and *Jupiter*, Italian retains the ancestral value of the sign it replaces, i.e. Latin I before a vowel at the beginning of a word had the value of Y in *yes*. This initial I acquired its peculiar values in French after the break-up of the Western Empire.

	FRENCH	ITALIAN	SPANISH
CH	*sh* (=ʃ) as in *chivalry*	*k* as in *character*	*ch* (=tʃ) as in *much*
J	*zh* (= ʒ) as in *measure*	like Y in *yes*	*kh* as in *loch*
Z	*z* or (if terminal) usually silent	*ts* as in German *Zunge*	*th* (= θ) as in *thin*
GN		—Like GN in *mignonette*—	(The symbol for the sound equivalent to GN in French and Italian is Ñ with the diacritic mark called *tilde*.)

Having now surveyed the same or different changes which affected the same Latin consonant in modern descendants of the parent speech, little need be said about French. We have dealt elsewhere (p. 31) with a highly characteristic consonantal French sound-shift, i.e. *k* (=C) to *sh* (CH), (e.g. *chien* and *cheval* from Latin *cane* and *caballo*). The new value of Latin *gn* appears in the above table. Where LL occurs in the middle of a word, e.g. *billet* (=*ticket*), it has commonly come to resemble the *y*-sound in *yes* or the I in *junior*. IL at the end of a word as in

MUSEUM EXHIBIT—THE MISSING *f*-SOUND OF OLD SPANISH

ANGLO-AMERICAN	LATIN	ITALIAN	FRENCH	PORTUGUESE	SPANISH
bean	faba	fava	fève	fava	HABA
to make	facere	fare	faire	fazer	HACER
falcon	falcone	falcone	faucon	falcão	HALCON
hunger	fame	fame	faim	fome	HAMBRE
flour	farina	farina	farine	farinha	HARINA

ANGLO-AMERICAN	LATIN	ITALIAN	FRENCH	PORTUGUESE	SPANISH
to split	findere	fendere	fendre	fender	HENDER
hay	faeno	fieno	foin	feno	HENO
fervour	fervore	fervore	ferveur	fervor	HERVOR
iron	ferro	ferro	fer	ferro	HIERRO
fig	fico	fico	figue	figo	HIGO
son	filio	figlio	fils	filho	HIJO
daughter	filia	figlia	fille	filha	HIJA
thread	filo	filo	fil	fio	HILO
leaf	folia	foglia	feuille	fôlha	HOJA
fork	furca	forca	fourche	fôrca	HORCA
form	forma	forma	forme	forma	HORMA
ant	formica	formica	fourmi	formiga	HORMIGA
to flee	fugere	fuggire	fuir	fugir	HUIR
smoke	fumo	fumo	fumée	fumo	HUMO
liver	ficato	fegato	foie	fígado	HÍGADO

MUSEUM EXHIBIT

A. Simplification of the initial sounds of *cl*, *fl*, *pl* in modern descendants of Latin.

ANGLO-AMERICAN	LATIN	ITALIAN	SPANISH	PORTUGUESE	FRENCH
key	CLAVE	chiave	llave	chave	clef
said	DICTO	detto	dicho	dito	dit
flame	FLAMMA	fiamma	llama	chama	flamme
milk	LACTE	latte	leche	leite	lait
bed	LECTO	letto	lecho	leito	lit
night	NOCTE	notte	noche	noite	nuit
eight	OCTO	otto	ocho	oito	huit
full	PLENO	pieno	lleno	cheio	plein
to rain	PLUERE	piovere	llover	chover	pleuvoir
roof	TECTO	tetto	techo	teto	toit

B. The Late Latin E- before SC, SP, SQ, ST.

ANGLO-AMERICAN	FRENCH	SPANISH	ANGLO-AMERICAN	FRENCH	SPANISH
scald	échauder	escaldar	spine	épine	espina
scarlet	écarlate	escarlata	sponge	éponge	esponja

ANGLO-AMERICAN	FRENCH	SPANISH	ANGLO-AMERICAN	FRENCH	SPANISH
school	école	escuela	spouse	époux	esposo
scripture	écriture	escritura	stamp	étampe	estampa
scum	écume	espuma	standard	étendard	estandarte
slave	esclave	esclavo	state	état	estado
space	espace	espacio	stomach	estomac	estómago
scale (v.)	escalader	escalar	strange	étrange	extraño
Spain	Espagne	España	study (v.)	étudier	estudiar
spice	épice	especia	stuff	étoffe	estofa

C. Effacement of Medial or Final Consonants from the Parental Image.

ANGLO-AMERICAN	FRENCH	SPANISH	PORTUGUESE	ITALIAN	LATIN
foot	pied	pie	pé	piede	PEDE
stone	pierre	piedra	pedra	pietra	PETRA
holds (v.)	tient	tiene	tem	tiene	TENET
ten	dix	diez	dez	dieci	DECEM
dies (v.)	meurt	muere	morre	muore	MORITUR
can (v.)	peut	puede	pode	può	POTEST
new	neuf	nuevo	novo	nuovo	NOVO
fire	feu	fuego	fogo	fuoco	FOCO

soleil (*sun*) and *travail* (*work*) is roughly like I in *élite*. Terminal Latin T and X are silent when the next word begins with a consonant. Terminal X in numerals and adjectives has the *s*-sound when the next word begins with a vowel. The T of Latin -TION of abstract nouns (e.g. *nation*) also has the value *s*. What is characteristic of the French sound-pattern as a whole is that its vowel values have departed radically from those of Spanish and Italian, which we may infer to have retained those of parental Latin. No French vowel precisely corresponds to any English vowel.

In Spanish script, the Latin LL has the sound value *l-y* of LLI in *billiards* and in *million*. Where this sound shift occurs in Italian, as occasionally before I, the spelling convention is GLI. The equivalent Portuguese convention is LH. A medial Latin L becomes in Spanish *kh* represented by J as in the table p. 145. What is most characteristic of the pattern of native Spanish words is that initial Latin *f* has ceased to have any sound value before a vowel. Instead a dummy H marks its absence. Thus the parents of Spanish *haba, hembra* and *hacer* are Latin *faba* (*bean*), *femina* (*woman*) and *facere* (*make*). The second members of these triads illustrate a peculiar intrusion of an alien B (= *b*) after M in some Spanish words, as in *hembra* above, *hombre* for Latin *homine* (*man*), *hambre* for Latin *fame* (*hunger*), *legumbre* for Latin *legumine* (French *légume*, Italian *legume*, meaning *vegetable*), *sembrar* for Latin *seminare* (*to sow*). One explanation for the frequent disappearance in Old Spanish words of the parental F is that there is no such sound in Basque, supposedly the language of the Iberian peninsula before the Romans annexed it. Against this we have to weigh the fact that Portuguese has not lost it.

If Portuguese were merely the language of Portugal, we might dismiss it along with Catalan, spoken in and around Barcelona, as a minor Iberian dialect. It is, however, the official language of Brazil, and as such merits comment in this context. Aside from other changes, which we shall next discuss, Portuguese differs from Spanish especially because vowels preceding the parental *nasal* consonant sounds *m* and *n* themselves become nasal, and disappear. However, the so-called *tilde* honours their memory in script, e.g.:

SPANISH	PORTUGUESE	ANGLO-AMERICAN
cristiano	cristão	christian
lana	lã	wool (cf. *lanolin*)
pan	pão	bread (cf. *pantry*)

It would be easier to recognise the common ancestry of pairs of words in different languages, if regular sound-shifts such as those last discussed were the only way in which divergence of pronunciation occurs. In fact, the habit of slurring, i.e. failure to articulate all sound components of a word, often makes it impossible to recognise at sight or by ear the common ancestry of two contemporary words unless we can invoke the evidence of a fossil language nearer than either to the common ancestor of both. Slurring may take several forms, in particular dropping: (a) a middle consonant or vowel in a word of two syllables; (b) a terminal syllable or consonant; (c) one component of a consonant pair or triplet.

As an example of the first process, let us compare Anglo-American *world* with German *Welt*. In the first, the *r* of O.E. WORULD is now silent, except in a few dialects; but it was fully articulate throughout England in Chaucer's time. From this viewpoint, its Dutch equivalent *wereld* preserves the ancestral form in spelling, though the W of modern Dutch and German in most dialects now stands for the *v*- which has displaced the ancestral *w*-sound. As we have seen, the terminal *t* for *d* is one of the sound-shifts characteristic of High German.

Elimination of a vowel, as in *world* from WORULD, may result in creating a consonant cluster. Thus our modern *knee*, O.E. CNEO, Dutch and German *Knie*,

Danish *knæ* and Swedish *knä*, with Gothic *kniu*, are not words whose common ancestor is peculiar to the Teutonic family. Where we find the *k-* in a Teutonic language, we find the *g*-sound in Latin and Greek; but in *truly* Latin words we rarely (if at all) meet the initial consonant-cluster *gn*. If Latin shares a common ancestor with the *kniu* of Gothic, etc., we might thus expect it to have the shape *g.n.* (in which the dots stand for vowel sounds). Actually the Latin word is *genu*, which has become *genou* in French. Here, the conservatism of the written word conceals a sound-shift in the French word, i.e. replacement of the hard Latin *g-* by the *zh*-sound of *s* in *measure* before a front vowel. The corresponding Greek root is *gon-*.

En passant, we may notice that borrowed words with an initial consonant-cluster alien to the speech of the borrower reverse the process last illustrated. Thus French *canif* is not a word of Latin ancestry, being of Teutonic origin like its English equivalent *knife* and Scandinavian *kniv*. In the same way, Norman scribes wrote the name of King *Knut* as *Canute*. Kingship provides us with examples of slurring in both the terminal and medial positions. The Icelandic word for *king* is *konungur*. By dropping the last syllable, we recognise it as equivalent to the O.E. form CYNING, itself recognisably equivalent to Dutch *koning*. Danish *konge* has retained a terminal, but dropped the middle consonant. German *König* has retained the middle, but dropped one component of the final consonant. In Swedish *kung* we have a simple monosyllable like its Modern English equivalent.

Elimination of medial consonants obscures the parental image of many French, Portuguese and Spanish words. This is true especially of *d* in all three. In Portuguese the ancestral Latin *l* also disappears commonly between vowels, as illustrated in the following examples:

A-A	LATIN	ITALIAN	SPANISH	PORTUGUESE	FRENCH
hear	audire	udire	oir	ouvir	ouïr
fall	cadere	cadere	caer	cair	échoir
sky	caelo	cielo	cielo	céu	ciel
colour	colore	colore	color	côr	couleur
believe	credere	credere	creer	crer	croire
health	salute	salute	salud	saúde	salut
fly	volare	volare	volar	voar	voler

In EAGE (=*eye*), we have already met one example of how elimination of a medial consonant conceals the ancestral pattern of an English word. Two others are worthy of mention in the same setting. Dutch has *hoofd*, Danish *hoved* and Swedish *huvud* for *head*. The ancestral O.E. is HEAFOD, in which F (as in *of*) has the *v*-sound value. With a comparable tale to tell is the O.E. word HLAFORD. The first part (HLAF) has become *loaf*; and the compound itself literally means *bread-keeper*. By elimination of medial F, so privileged a person becomes a *lord* in Modern English. As an example of the elimination of one or other component of a consonant pair, we may first compare Swedish *mun* with O.E. MUTH (=*mouth*). In Danish and German *Mund*, as in Dutch *mond*, the *th* (= θ) sound of primitive Teutonic retained in English and Icelandic gives way to *d*. A fossil specimen now comes to our aid. The Gothic equivalent is *munths*. If we eliminate from this *th* and *s*, we arrive at the Swedish, and if we eliminate *n* and *s*, we arrive at the English form, which might seem to have no *prima facie* connexion with its cousins.

Among modern descendants of Latin, there has been extensive simplification of consonant clusters. The couplets CT (=*kt*) and PT (=*pt*) which occur in a medial position in ancestral Latin but terminally also in its descendants, undergo simplification by dropping the C (=*k*) and P (=*p*) in French, Italian and Portuguese. The same is true of *pt* in Spanish; but Latin CT (=*kt*) in the latter gives place to the complex sound we represent by CH as in *much*, and with the same spelling convention. As regards the first of these couplets, one may cite: Latin *facto* (*fact*), French *fait*, Italian *fatto*, Spanish *hecho* (cf. *haba*, *hembra*, *hacer* above); Latin *lacte* (*milk*), French *lait*, Italian *latte*, Spanish *leche*. The Latin numeral *septem* illustrates the elimination of *p* before *t*: Italian *sette*, Spanish *siete*. The P in French *sept* (pronounced like Anglo-American *set*) is a paper fiction attributable to bogus scholarship. In an initial position, French has retained CL (=*kl*), FL (=*fl*) and PL (=*pl*); but in Italian, Spanish and Portuguese, one or other of the consonants of each pair sometimes disappears thus:

LATIN AND FRENCH	ITALIAN	SPANISH	PORTUGUESE
PL	PI (like *pea*)	LL (as in *million*)	CH
CL	CHI (as in *chin*)	LL	
FL	FI (like *fee*)		

Our Museum Exhibit on p. 155-160 shows examples of a number of these and another departure from the parental plan. First, however, we may take stock of a simplification from the *st* of Latin and Old French to *t* in Modern French words. That this change occurred after the Middle period when English was borrowing so many words of French origin is evident from the following French-English couplets: *bâtard*—*bastard*, *bête*—*beast*, *cloître*—*cloister*, *côte*—*coast*, *coûter*—*cost*, *fête*—*feast*, *île*—*isle*, *huître*—*oyster*. In all such French words a circumflex (^) accent over the vowel preceding T signalises the loss of the *s*-sound. In Late Latin, words beginning with ST-, SC-, SP- and SQ- tacked on an initial E bequeathed to some English words of French origin (e.g. *estate*, *esquire*, *espouse*, *especially*). Modern French (as É), Spanish and Portuguese retain it; but we do not meet it in Italian. Commonly, but not invariably in French, the *s*-sound of such words drops out. The lower half of our Museum Exhibit on p. 146 exhibits this.

With reference to all foregoing simplifications in the modern descendants of Latin, it is important to remember that they refer only to *native* words, i.e. the local stock of corrupt Latin current in Gaul, Italy and the Iberian peninsula during the centuries of the great Teutonic migrations after the collapse of the Western Roman Empire. French, Italian and to a lesser degree Spanish and Portuguese later assimilated through ecclesiastical, legal and (at a later date) scientific scholarship a very considerable battery of words from the Latin of classical writers. Accordingly, as mentioned (p. 42) earlier, we find in all these languages pairs of words with many comparable examples in English, e.g. from Latin *fragile* directly, *fragile* in both French and English, but *frail* from late Gallic Latin (i.e. Old French) *fraile*, whence in Modern French *frêle*.

Another way in which pronunciation changes, though comparatively rare, is here worthy of mention. We have already illustrated it (p. 27) by the change from O.E. BRIDD or BRID to *bird*. Another is from THRIDDA to *third*. The O.E. form of the latter at once connects it with *tredje* (Swed. and Dan.) or *dritte* (Germ.). As an extreme example of the way in which different processes of sound-change conspire to conceal the common ancestry of two words, let us consider Modern English *tooth* and its French equivalent *dent*. Like *dente* (Italian) and *diente* (Spanish), the French one is a descendant of a Latin word whose genitive singular case form is DENTIS. Now we have seen that Teutonic *t-* replaces the more primitive *d-*, and Teutonic *th* ($= \theta$) replaces the more primitive *t*-sound of the common Indo-European word stock. Thus we might expect to find in the earliest Teutonic a form *t.nth.s*. This indeed tallies with the Gothic genitive singular case form *tunthaus*. By loss of the *n*-sound this becomes *t.th.s*; and this is recognisably the O.E. genitive singular TOTHES, which has shed its genitive -*s* terminal in its modern descendant. Alternatively, by losing the *th* component, we derive the Norwegian *tanns*; and additionally by the sound shift from *t* to *ts* ($=Z$), we derive the German genitive *Zahnes*. Only Icelandic and English now preserve the *th* of primitive Teutonic. The subsequent shift of *th* to *d* yields Danish *tandes* and Swedish *tands*. Dutch *tand* has lost all trace of the genitive terminal which persists in a small category of English words (e.g. *day's* and *man's*) where the apostrophe is the death knell of a formerly intervening vowel.

Against the preceding background the reader will now be ready with a few hints to recognise a family likeness in Indo-European interrogatives equivalent to *who*, *when*, *what*, etc. We have seen that ancestral *k* becomes *h*, whence *kw* ($=Q$) becomes *hw* ($=$HW or WH) in the Teutonic group. Old Irish retains *kw* but this becomes *k* ($=C$) in Modern Erse and Scots Gaelic. In the Brythonic group (p. 51) *kw* becomes *p* (*b* at the end of a word in Modern Welsh), whence we label two branches of the same clan as P-Celtic and Q-Celtic, easily remembered by the word for *son*: *mac* (from earlier *maqui*) in Modern Gaelic and *mab* (from earlier *map*) in Modern Welsh. Note also: (a) W in Welsh is equivalent to OO in English unless at the beginning of a word; (b) Ṫ (with a dot) in Erse script stands for *h*:

OLD ENGLISH	LATIN	ERSE	WELSH
HWA	QUIS	CIA	PWY
HWONNE	QUANDO	CAṪAIN	PAN
HWÆT	QUOD	CA	PA

Key Words in the Mother Tongue

FOR OUR LANGUAGE MUSEUM

---

1. AN 2. TWA 3. THRI 4. FEOWER 5. FIF 6. SIX 7. SEOFON
8. EAHTA 9. NIGON 10. TEN

---

11. HWIT 12. SWEART or BLÆC 13. READ 14. GEOLU 15. GRENE
16. BLÆW 17. GRÆG 18. BRUN

---

19. HEOFON 20. SUNNE 21. MONA 22. STEORRA 23. EORTHE
or WORULD 24. GRUND 25. TIMA or TID 26. DÆG 27. NIHT
28. WICU 29. MONATH 30. GEAR

---

31. EORTHE 32. LYFT 33. FYR 34. WÆTER

---

35. MANN 36. WIMMAN 37. WIF 38. CILD or BEARN 39. FÆDER
40. MODOR 41. SUNU 42. DOHTOR 43. BROTHOR 44. SWEOSTOR

---

45. REGN 46. WIND 47. SNAW 48. IS

---

49. ÆG 50. BREAD 51. MILC 52. CESE 53. SEALT 54. METE
55. HUNIG

---

56. HEAFOD 57. HÆR 58. NOSU 59. MUTH 60. LIPPE 61. TUNGE
62. EAGE 63. EARE 64. TOTH 65. EARM 66. HAND 67. FINGER
68. SCANCA 69. CNEO 70. FOT 71. TA 72. BREOST 73. HEORTE
74. FLÆSC 75. BAN 76. BLOD

---

77. CATT 78. HUND or DOCGA 79. SCEAP 80. LAMB 81. GAT
82. STEOR 83. CU 84. CEALF 85. HORS or MERE 86. SWIN
87. HENN 88. COCC or HANA 89. MUS 90. CONNIN 91. WULF
92. BRIDD or FUGEL 93. FISC 94. BEO

---

95. LENCTEN 96. SUMOR 97. HÆRFEST 98. WINTER

---

99. NORTH 100. EAST 101. WEST 102. SUTH

103. MERSC 104. MOR 105. HYLL 106. DÆL 107. MERE
108. STREAM 109. BROC 110. BRYCG 111. SÆ 112. SCIP *or* BAT
113. FELD 114. GEAT

115. WYRT 116. BLOSTMA 117. SÆD 118. THORN 119. RISC
120. TREO *or* BEAM 121. WUDU 122. ÆSC 123. AC 124. BECE
125. BEORC 126. ELM 127. HÆSEL 128. HOLEGN 129. WELIG *or*
SEAJ H

130. GREAT 131. LYTEL *or* SMÆL 132. EALD 133. GEONG 134. NIWE
135. GOD 136. YFEL 137. THICCE 138. THYNNE 139. HEFIG
140. TREOWE 141. STRANG 142. WAC 143. HEAH 144. LAH
145. CWIC 146. DEAD 147. CROOKED 148. BLIND 149. DEAF
150. FULL

	DUTCH	GERMAN	SWEDISH	DANISH
1.	een	eins	en	en
2.	twee	zwei	tvä	to
3.	drie	drei	tre	tre
4.	vier	vier	fyra	fire
5.	vijf	fünf	fem	fem
6.	zes	sechs	sex	seks
7.	zeven	sieben	sju	syv
8.	acht	acht	åtta	otte
9.	negen	neun	nio	ni
10.	tien	zehn	tio	ti
11.	wit	weiss	vit	hvid
12.	zwart	schwarz	svart	sort
13.	rood	rot	röd	rød
14.	geel	gelb	gul	gul
15.	groen	grün	grön	grøn
16.	blauw	blau	blå	blå
17.	grijs	grau	grå	grå
18.	bruin	braun	brun	brun
19.	hemel	himmel	himmel	himmel
20.	zon	sonne	sol	sol
21.	maan	mond	måne	måne
22.	ster	stern	stjärna	stjerne
23.	wereld	welt	värld	verden
24.	aarde	erde	jord	jord
25.	tijd	zeit	tid	tid

	FRENCH	PORTUGUESE	SPANISH	ITALIAN
1.	un	um	uno	uno
2.	deux	dois	dos	due
3.	trois	três	tres	tre
4.	quatre	quatro	cuatro	quattro
5.	cinq	cinco	cinco	cinque
6.	six	seis	seis	sei
7.	sept	sete	siete	sette
8.	huit	oito	ocho	otto
9.	neuf	nove	nueve	nove
10.	dix	dez	diez	dieci
11.	blanc	branco	blanco	bianco
12.	noir	prêto or negro	negro	nero
13.	rouge	vermelho	rojo	rosso
14.	jaune	amarelo	amarillo	giallo
15.	vert	verde	verde	verde
16.	bleu	azul	azul	azzurro
17.	gris	cinzento	gris	grigio
18.	brun	castanho	castaño	bruno
19.	ciel	céu	cielo	cielo
20.	soleil	sol	sol	sole
21.	lune	lua	luna	luna
22.	étoile	estréla	estrella	stella
23.	monde	mundo	mundo	mondo
24.	terre	terra	tierra	terra
25.	temps	tempo	tiempo	tempo

	WELSH	CORNISH	BRETON	GAELIC
1.	un	un	unan	aon
2.	dau	deu	deu	da
3.	tri	try	tri	tri
4.	pedwar	peswar	pear	ceithir
5.	pump	pymp	pemp	cóig
6.	chwech	whegh	hueh	se
7.	saith	seyth	seih	seachd
8.	wyth	eth	eih	ochd
9.	naw	naw	nau	naoi
10.	deg	dek	dek	deich
11.	gwyn	gwyn	guen	geal or fionn
12.	du	du	du	dubh
13.	coch	cough or ruth	ru	ruadh or dearg
14.	melyn	melen	melen	buidhe
15.	glas or gwyrdd	glas or gwer	gwer	glas or gorm
16.	glas	glas	glas	gorm or liath
17.	llwyd	los	louet	liath or glas
18.	llwyd	teual	gell	donn
19.	nef	nef	nenv	neamh
20.	haul	houl	heol	grian
21.	lloer	lor	loar	gealach or re
22.	seren	steren	stered	reul
23.	daear	dor	bed	cruinne
24.	llawr	lur	leur	talamh
25.	amser or pryd	prys	amzer	am or aimsir

#	DUTCH	GERMAN	SWEDISH	DANISH	FRENCH	PORTUGUESE	SPANISH	ITALIAN	WELSH	CORNISH	BRETON	GAELIC
26.	dag	tag	dag	dag	jour	dia	dia	giorno	dydd	deth	dez	latha
27.	nacht	nacht	natt	nat	nuit	noite	noche	notte	nos	nos	noz	oidche
28.	week	woche	vecka	uge	semaine	semana	semana	settimana	wythnos	seythen	sizun	seachdain
29.	maand	monat	månad	måned	mois	mês	mes	mese	mis	mys	miz	mios
30.	jaar	jahr	år	år	an	ano	año	anno	blwyddyn	bledhen	bloaz	bliadhna
31.	aarde	erde	jord	jord	terre	terra	tierra	terra	daear	dor	doar	talamh
32.	lucht	luft	luft	luft	air	ar	aire	aria	aer	ayr	aer	adhar
33.	vuur	feuer	eld	ild	feu	fogo	fuego	fuoco	tan	tan	tan	teine
34.	water	wasser	vatten	vand	eau	agua	agua	acqua	dwr	dour	dour	uisge
35.	man	mann	man	mand	homme	homem	hombre	uomo	dyn or gwr	den or gur	den	duine or fear
36.	vrouw	frau	kvinna	kvinde	femme	mulher	mujer	donna	benyw	benen	maouez	bean
37.	vrouw	frau	hustru	hustru	épouse	espôsa	esposa	sposa or moglie	gwraig	gwrec	gwreg	ceile
38.	kind	kind	barn	barn	enfant	menino	niño	fanciullo	plentyn	flo or bearn	bugel	leanabh
39.	vader	vater	fader	fader	père	pai	padre	padre	tad	tas	tad	athair
40.	moeder	mutter	moder	moder	mère	mãe	madre	madre	mam	mam	mamm	mathair
41.	zoon	sohn	son	søn	fils	filho	hijo	figlio	mab	mab	mab	mac
42.	dochter	tochter	dotter	datter	fille	filha	hija	figlia	merch	myrch	merc'h	nighean
43.	broeder	bruder	broder	broder	frère	irmão	hermano	fratello	brawd	braud	breur	brathair
44.	zuster	schwester	syster	søster	sœur	irmã	hermana	sorella	chwaer	choar	c'hoar	piuthar*
45.	regen	regen	regn	regn	pluie	chuva	lluvia	pioggia	glaw	glaw	glao	fras
46.	wind	wind	vind	vind	vent	vento	viento	vento	gwynt	gwyns	gwent	gaoth
47.	sneeuw	schnee	snö	sne	neige	neve	nieve	neve	eira	ergh	erc'h	sneachda
48.	ijs	eis	is	is	glace	gêlo	hielo	ghiaccio	rhew	rew	skourn	eigh
49.	ei	ei	ägg	æg	œuf	ôvo	huevo	uovo	wy	oy	ui	ugh
50.	brood	brot	bröd	brød	pain	pão	pan	pane	bara	bara	bara	aran
51.	melk	milch	mjölk	mælk	lait	leite	leche	latte	llaeth	leth	laez	bainne
52.	kaas	käse	ost	ost	fromage	queijo	queso	formaggio	caws	kes	keuz	cais
53.	zout	salz	salt	salt	sel	sal	sal	sale	halen	halen	halen	salann
54.	vlees	fleisch	kött	kød	viande	carne	carne	carne	cig	kyk	kig	feoil
55.	honing	honig	honung	honning	miel	mel	miel	miele	mel	mel	mel	mil
56.	hoofd	kopf	huvud	hoved	tête	cabeça	cabeza	testa	pen	pen	pen	ceann
57.	haar	haar	hår	hår	cheveu	cabelo	cabello	capelli	gwallt or blew	gwalht or blew	bleo	falt

#	DUTCH	GERMAN	SWEDISH	DANISH	FRENCH	PORTUGUESE	SPANISH	ITALIAN	WELSH	CORNISH	BRETON	GAELIC
58.	neus	nase	näsa	næse	nez	nariz	nariz	naso	trwyn	tron	fri	sron
59.	mond	mund	mun	mund	bouche	bôca	boca	bocca	ceg	ganow or min	genou	beul
60.	lip	lippe	läpp	læbe	lèvre	labio	labio	labbro	gwefus or min	gweus or min	gweuz	liob
61.	tong	zunge	tunga	tunge	langue	lingua	lengua	lingua	tafod	tavos	teod	teanga
62.	oog	auge	öga	öje	œil	ôlho	ojo	occhio	llygad	lagat	lagad	suil
63.	oor	ohr	öra	øre	oreille	orelha	oreja	orecchio	clust	scovarn	skouarn	cluas
64.	tand	zahn	tand	tand	dent	dente	diente	dente	dant	dans	dant	deud
65.	arm	arm	arm	arm	bras	braço	brazo	braccio	braich	bregh	brec'h	gairdean
66.	hand	hand	hand	hånd	main	mão	mano	mano	llaw	luf or dorn	dourn	lamh
67.	vinger	finger	finger	finger	doigt	dedo	dedo	dito	bys	bys	biz	meur
68.	been	bein	ben	ben	jambe	perna	pierna	gamba	coes	gar	gar	cas or lurga
69.	knie	knie	knä	knæ	genou	joelho	rodilla	ginocchio	penglin	penclin	glin	glun
70.	voet	fuss	fot	fod	pied	pe	pie	piede	troed	tros	troad	cas
71.	teen	zehe	tå	tå	orteil	dedo do (pé)	dedo del pie	dito del piede	bys-troed	bis-truit	biz-troad	ordag
72.	borst	brust	bröst	bryst	sein	seio	seno	seno	bron	bron	bronn	uchd or com
73.	hart	herz	hjärta	hjerte	cœur	coração	corazón	cuore	calon	colon	kalon	cridhe
74.	vlees	fleisch	kött	kød	chair	carne	carne	carne	cnawd or cig	kyk	kig	feoil
75.	been	knochen	ben	knokkel	os	osso	hueso	osso	asgwrn	ascorn	askorn	cnaimh
76.	bloed	blut	blod	blod	sang	sangue	sangre	sangue	gwaed	gos	gwad	fuil
77.	kat	katze	katt	kat	chat	gato	gato	gatto	cath	cath	kaz	cat
78.	hond	hund	hund	hund	chien	cão	perro	cane	ci	ci	ki	cu
79.	schaap	schaf	får	får	mouton	ovelha	oveja	pecora	dafad	davas	davad	caora
80.	lam	lamm	lamm	lam	agneau	cordeiro	cordero	agnello	oen	on	oan	uan
81.	geit	ziege	get	ged	chèvre	cabra	cabra	capra	gafr	gaver	gavr	gobhar
82.	stier	stier	tjur	tyr	taureau	touro	toro	toro	tarw	tarow	taro	tarbh
83.	koe	kuh	ko	ko	vache	vaca	vaca	vacca	buwch	buch	buoh	bo
84.	kalf	kalb	kalv	kalv	veau	vitela	ternero	vitello	llo	loch	leue	laogh
85.	paard	pferd	häst	hest	cheval	cavalo	caballo	cavallo	march or ceffyl	margh	marc'h	each

No.	DUTCH	GERMAN	SWEDISH	DANISH	FRENCH	PORTUGUESE	SPANISH	ITALIAN	WELSH	CORNISH	BRETON	GAELIC
86.	varken	schwein	svin	svin	cochon	porco	puerco or cerdo	porco	mochyn	moch	moc'h	muc or uircean
87.	kip/hen	henne	höna	høne	poule	galinha	gallina	gallina	iar	yar	yar	cearc
88.	haan	hahn	tupp	hane	coq	galo	gallo	gallo	ceiliog	celioc	kilhog	coileach
89.	muis	maus	mus	mus	souris	rato	ratón	sorcio or topo	llygoden	logoden	logoden	luch
90.	konijn	kaninchen	kanin	kanin	lapin	coelho	conejo	coniglio	cwningen	cynin	konikl	coinean
91.	wolf	wolf	varg	ulv	loup	lôbo	lobo	lupo	blaidd	blaidh	bleiz	faol
92.	vogel	vogel	fågel	fugl	oiseau	passaro	pájaro or ave	uccello	aderyn	edhen	evn or labous	eun
93.	vis	fisch	fisk	fisk	poisson	peixe	pez	pesce	pysgodyn	pesc	pesk	iasg
94.	bij	biene	bi	bi	abeille	abelha	abeja	ape	gwenynen	gwenen	gwenan	beach
95.	lente	frühling	vår	forår	printemps	primavera	primavera	primavera	gwanwyn	gwainten	nevez-amzer	earrach
96.	zomer	sommer	sommar	sommer	été	verão or estio	verano or estio	estate	haf	haf	hanv	samhradh
97.	herfst	herbst	höst	efterår	automne	outono	otoño	autunno	hydref	kyniaf	dilost-hanv	foghar
98.	winter	winter	vinter	vinter	hiver	inverno	invierno	inverno	gaeaf	gwaf	goanv	geamhradh
99.	noord	norden	norr	nord	nord	norte	norte	nord	gogledd	cleth	hanternoz	tuath
100.	oost	osten	öst	øst	est	este	este	est	dwyrain	howl-drehevel	reter or sav-heol	ear
101.	west	westen	väst	vest	ouest	oeste	oeste	ovest	gorllewin	howl-sedhas	kornog	iar
102.	zuid	süden	söder	syd	sud	sul	sur	sud	dehau	dyghow	kreisteiz	deas
103.	moeras	morast	moras	marsk	marais	pantano	pantano	pantano	cors	kersek	palud	lon or boglach
104.	heide	heide	hed	hede	lande	lande	llano	landa	gwaun	gun	lann	monadh or sliabh
105.	heuvel	hügel	kulle	bakke	colline	colina	colina	collina	bryn	bron	krec'h	torr or cnoc
106.	vallei or dal	tal	dal	dal	vallée	vale	valle	valle	glyn or dyffryn	glyn or nans	traonienn	dail or gleann
107.	meer	see	sjö	sø	lac	lago	lago	lago	llyn	lyn	lenn or loc'h	loch

	DUTCH	GERMAN	SWEDISH	DANISH	FRENCH	PORTUGUESE	SPANISH	ITALIAN	WELSH	CORNISH	BRETON	GAELIC
108.	rivier	fluss	flod	flod	fleuve	rio	río	fiume or riviera	afon	avon	aven or ster	abhainn
109.	beek	bach	bäck	bæk	ruisseau	riacho or arroio	arroyo	ruscello	nant	gover	gwaz	allt or caochan
110.	brug	brücke	bro	bro	pont	ponte	puente	ponte	pont	pons	pont	drochaid
111.	zee	see/meer	hav	hav	mer	mar	mar	mare	mor	mor	mor	muir
112.	boot or schip	boot or schiff	båt or skepp	båd or skib	bateau or navire	barco or navio	barco or barca	barca or bastimento	bad or llong	gorhel	bag or lestr	bata or long
113.	veld	feld	fält	mark	champ	campo	campo	campo	cae	kew	park	machair
114.	poort	pforte or tor	port	port	porte	portão	puerta	porta	clwyd	yet	dor	dorus or geata
115.	kruid	kraut	ört	urt	herbe	erva	hierba	erba	llysieuyn	losowen	louzou	luibh
116.	bloem	blume	blomma	blomst	fleur	flor	flor	fiore	blodeuyn	blejan	bleunv	blath
117.	zaad	saat	säd	sæd	graine	semente	semilla	seme	had	has	had	siol
118.	doorn	dorn	törne	torn	épine	espinho	espina	spina	draen	dren	draen or spern	droigheann or dris
119.	bies	binse	säv	siv	jonc	junco	junco	giunco	brwynen	bronnen	broenn	luachair
120.	boom	baum	träd	træ	arbre	arvore	árbol	albero	pren	pren or gwedhen	gwezenn	crann
121.	hout	holz	trä	træ	bois	madeira	madera	legno	coed	pren	prenn	coill or fiodh
122.	essen	esche	ask	ask	frêne	freixo	fresno	frassino	onnen	onnen	onn	uinnseann
123.	eik	eiche	ek	eg	chêne	carvalho	roble	quercia	derwen	derowen	dero	darach
124.	beuk	buche	bok	bøg	hêtre	faia	haya	faggio	ffawydden	fawen	faoenn	faibhile
125.	berk	birke	björk	birk	bouleau	vidoeiro	abedul	betulla	bedwen	bedhewen	bezvenn	beithe
126.	olm	ulme	alm	elm	orme	olmo	olmo	olmo	llwyfen	elowen	evlec'henn	leamhan
127.	hazel	hasel	hassel	hassel	noisetier	aveleira	avellano	avellano	collen	knofen	gwezenn	calltuinn
128.	hulst	stechpalme	järnek	kristtorn	houx	azevinho	acebo	agrifoglio	celynnen	kelynnen	kelenn	cuileann
129.	wilg	weide	pil	pil	saule	salgueiro	sauce	salcio	helygen	helygen	halegen	seileach
130.	groot	gross	stor	stor	grand or large	grande	grande	grande or largo	mawr	mur	meur or bras	mor
131.	klein	klein	liten	lille	petit	pequeno	pequeño	piccolo	bach	boghes	bihan	beag
132.	oud	alt	gammal	gammel	vieux	velho	viejo	vecchio	hen	hen or coth	koz	sean

	DUTCH	GERMAN	SWEDISH	DANISH	FRENCH	PORTUGUESE	SPANISH	ITALIAN	WELSH	CORNISH	BRETON	GAELIC
133.	jong	jung	ung	ung	jeune	jovem	joven	giovane	ieuanc	yonk	yaouank	og
134.	nieuw	neu	ny	ny	nouveau	novo	nuevo	nuovo	newydd	noweth	nevez	nuadh
135.	goed	gut	god	god	bon	bom	bueno	buono	da	da	mat	math or deagh
136.	slecht	schlecht	dålig	dårlig	mal	mau	mal(o)	malvagio	drwg	drok	droug	droch
137.	dik	dick	tjock	tyk	épais	espêsso	espeso	spesso	tew	tew	teo	tiugh
138.	dun or mager	dünn or mager	tunn	tynd	maigre	magro or delgado	delgado	magro	tenau or main	tanow	treut	tana
139.	zwaar	schwer	tung	tung	lourd	pesado	pesado	pesante	trwm	pos	pounner	trom
140.	waar	wahr	sann	sand	vrai	verdadeiro	verdadero	vero	gwir	gwyr	gwir	fior
141.	sterk	stark	stark	stark	fort	forte	fuerte	forte	cryf	cref	krenv	laidir
142.	zwak	schwach	svag	svag	faible or débile	debil	débil	debole	gwan	gwan	gwan	fann
143.	hoog	hoch	hög	høj	haut	alto	alto	alto	uchel	ughel	uhel	uasal
144.	laag	niedrig	låg	lav	bas	baixo	bajo	basso	isel	ysel	izel	iosal
145.	levend	lebend	levande	levende	vivant	vivo	vivo	vivo	byw	bew	beo	beo
146.	dood	tot	död	død	mort	morto	muerto	morto	marw	marow	maro	marbh
147.	krom	krumm	krokig	krum or kroget	courbé or tordu	curvo or tortuoso	curvo	curvo or tortuoso	cam	cam	kamm	cam
148.	blind	blind	blind	blind	aveugle	cego	ciego	cieco	dall	dall	dall	dall
149.	doof	taub	döv	døv	sourd	surdo	sordo	sordo	byddar	bodhar	bouzar	bodhar
150.	vol	voll	full	fuld	plein	cheio	lleno or pleno	pieno	llawn	lun	leun	lan

* 44. Scots Gaelic *piuthar* is an intruder, not authentically Celtic. In modern Irish the word for *sister* is *deirfiúr*.

QUIZ CORNER 4

Quiz 1

The Language Museum

Because different languages have adapted to their native sounds the same Latin alphabet in different ways, we shall here use B, D, F, H, J, K, L, M, N, P, QU, R, T, V, W and Z for the sounds they stand for in English with very few exceptions such as *of* (with F for the *v*-sound), *lamb* or *thumb* (B silent), *honour, ghost* or *what* (H silent), *knight* or *knife* (K silent), *psalm* or *psychology* (P silent). In addition we here use:

S (as in Welsh, Breton and Dutch) as in *sin*
Y (German, Dutch, Scandinavian J) as in *yet*
G as in *get*
TH for TH in *thin*
DH (Welsh DD) for TH in *then*
CH as in *chin*
SH as in *shin*
ZH (French J or G before E and I) as in *fusion, measure, vision*
KH (CH *Welsh, German*; C'H *Breton*) for CH in Scots *loch*

Note also:

German: Z has the sound *ts*, as in *hats*, and SCH for SH above.
Teutonic and *Latin*: SS for S above, and S for English Z.
French: C before E or I for S, and CH for SH above.
French: QU now stands for K above.
Spanish: C before E or I for S above.
Italian: G before E or I for J above.
Welsh: FF for F, and F for V as above.
German and *Dutch*: W now stands for the *v*-sound.

Now answer the Quiz questions by the number attached to the key word the Language Museum, and/or by the sound sign as given above:

1. The SK-sound in O.E. becomes .... in Modern English as in ......

2. The G-sound in some O.E. words
(a) has made way for the ....-sound as in ......
(b) is now silent and represented by a dummy Y as in ......
(c) is silent and has left no trace as in ......

3. In native words the sign KN now stands for the ....-sound as in ......

4. In native words we find the J-sound represented by .... as in ......
The CH sound replaces the O.E. .... -sound represented by .... before E or I in ......

5. To the W-sound in O.E. corresponds in Swedish or Danish the .... -sound as in ......

6. To the TH-sound in O.E. corresponds in the Teutonic group the .... -sound as in ......

7. To the DH-sound in O.E. corresponds in the Teutonic group the .... -sound as in ......

8. To the ZH-sound in French corresponds .... in Modern English, as in ......

9. For the KH-sound represented by .... in O.E. we find the *dummy* sign .... in Modern English, but CH in German (and Scots) as in ......

10. To the K-sound before A in its Latin allies corresponds the French .... -sound as in ......

11. To the B-sound in Spanish (as in Latin) corresponds the .... -sound in its Latin allies.

12. OLD ENGLISH AND SWEDISH	GERMAN	
	(a) *Beginning of word*	(b) *Elsewhere*
T	.... -sound spelt	.... -sound spelt ....
as in: (a) .... (b)		
P	.... -sound spelt	.... -sound spelt ....
as in: (a) .... (b)		

OLD ENGLISH AND SWEDISH	GERMAN (a) *Beginning of word*	(b) *Elsewhere*
K	.... -sound spelt	.... -sound spelt ....
as in:		
(a)	....	
(b)	....	
D	.... -sound spelt	.... -sound spelt ....
as in:		
(a)	....	
(b)	....	

13. For C before A or O in Latin we now find in French the .... -sound represented by .... as in ......

14. C before E or I stands for the .... -sound as in the following English words derived from French words listed:

....

15. English has adapted from French the following words:

....

16. French adapted from the Teutonic *Franks:*

....

17. To the D- or T-sound at the end of a Welsh or Breton word or syllable corresponds the .... -sound in Cornish as in ......

18. To the TH- or DH-sound in Welsh corresponds .... in Breton as in ......

19. To the K-sound in Gaelic corresponds the .... -sound in Welsh as in ......

20. WELSH	GAELIC	
H	........sound as in..
GW	........sound as in..

21. Give O.E. words to which the following are clues:

Shanks's pony ....   *Swarthy blacksmith* ....
Hornbeam, whitebeam ....   *St. John's wort, Ragwort* ....
Steer ....   *Windermere* ....
Coney ....   *Luftwaffe, Lufthansa* ....

22. Against each of the following words of Classical Latin origin indicate its derivation by the number of the corresponding item in the Language Museum:

veracity	....	Nigeria	....	apiary	....
marine	....	paternal	....	sanguinary	....
annual	....	ovary	....	glacial	....
portal	....	seminal	....	digit	....
sorority	....	canine	....	fraternal	....
mundane	....	mellifluous	....	gallinaceous	....
dentist	....	osseous	....	soda	....
senile	....	altitude	....	oculist	....
vaccine	....	carnal	....	filial	....
stellar	....	linguistics	....	capillary	....
aquatic	....	celestial	....	vivisection	....
piscine	....	maternal	....	temporal	....
debility	....	labial	....	ventilator	....
manual	....	plenitude	....	plural	....
lactose	....	mortality	....	nocturnal	....
terrestrial	....	novel	....	pedal	....
lunar	....	octave	....		

Quiz 2

Dutch—Danish

(a) Sentences cited with the same number at the end of the quiz (p. 166-167) mean the same.

(b) In Dutch and Danish spelling, J stands for the *y*-sound in *yield*; in Dutch, V represents the *f*-sound in *field*; and in Danish, ø is pronounced like *or* in *work*.

(c) Before trying to translate, compare the Danish and Dutch sentences, word by word, noting carefully differences of word order.

(d) Ask yourself:
(i) which has more words recognisably like the English words of the same meaning, Dutch or Danish?
(ii) which of the two languages has the order of words in a sentence more like the English order?

I. Fill in the following blanks:

ENGLISH	W	WH	TH	SH
DUTCH	....	....	....	....
DANISH	....	....	....	....

II. Fill in the following blanks:

	I	MY	YOU or THOU	HE	HIM	COME
DUTCH	......	......	......	......	......	......
DANISH	......	......	......	......	......	......

	HER	IT	WE	TOO	WHERE	ALSO
DUTCH	......	......	......	......	......	......
DANISH	......	......	......	......	......	......

	ALREADY	AGAIN	NOT	YES	NO	KNOW
DUTCH	......	......	......	......	......	......
DANISH	......	......	......	......	......	......

Useful clues: (a) Luke ii, 49; (b) Chaucer's *eke* in Robert Burns' poem:

> "And now Yerl Galloway's sceptre broke,
> And eke my hangman's knife."

III. When you have filled in the above, translate the sentences shown below and on the next page.

1. ....
2. ....
3. ....
4. ....
5. ....
6. ....
7. ....
8. ....
9. ....
10. ....
11. ....
12. ....
13. ....
14. ....
15. ....
16. ....
17. ....
18. ....
19. ....
20. ....

DUTCH

1. Hoorde u de jonge man?
2. Wij hadden hem al gehoord. Hij zong goed.
3. Hij stond naast uw moeder. Is hij haar vriend?
4. Nee. Hij is haar zoon. Haar huis is in deze straat.
5. Dat wist ik niet. Hoe heet hij?
6. Jan. U zult hem weer zien.
7. Hier is mijn boek. Het is nieuw.
8. Is het een goed boek?
9. Nee; het is te dik.
10. Waar zullen wij nu naar toe gaan?
11. U moet bij mij thuis komen.
12. Ik wil niet alleen komen. Mag mijn broer mee komen?

13. Ja. Laat hem komen.
14. Mag ik mijn zuster ook mee brengen?
15. Is dit uw huis?
16. Nee. Mijn huis is wit. De deur is rood.
17. Zullen wij uw vader ontmoeten?
18. Ja. Ik hoop dat wij hem kunnen zien.
19. Hier is mijn huis. Laat mij de deur voor u openen.
20. Laat mijn zuster voorgaan.

DANISH

1. Hørte du den unge mand?
2. Vi havde hørt ham allerede. Han sang godt.
3. Han var ved siden af din moder. Er han hendes ven?
4. Nej. Han er hendes søn. Hendes hus er i denne gade.
5. Jeg vidste det ikke. Hvad er hans navn?
6. Jan. Du vil se ham igen.
7. Her er min bog. Den er ny.
8. Er det en god bog?
9. Nej; den er altfor lang.
10. Hvor skal vi nu gå hen?
11. Du må komme til mit hus.
12. Jeg vil ikke komme alene. Må min broder komme?
13. Ja. Lad ham komme.
14. Må jeg bringe min søster også?
15. Er dette dit hus?
16. Nej. Mit hus er hvidt. Døren er rød.
17. Skal vi møde din fader?
18. Ja. Jeg håber, at vi kan se ham.
19. Her er mit hus. Lad mig åbne døren for dig.
20. Lad min søster gå først.

Quiz 3

Dutch—Swedish

Study word by word the two versions below, pp. 169–170, one in Dutch, the other in Swedish.

I. In both languages you will find two words for our single word *the*, when no adjective (e.g. *green, old*) comes between *the* and the noun. Fill in the following:

		THE		*Delete one word*	IT
DUTCH	1.	2.		Before/After noun	......
SWEDISH	1.	2.		Before/After noun	......

II. In Swedish we find for *the* in front of an adjective:

      1. Followed by an *it*-noun   ......

      2. Followed by *any other* noun   ......

III. The words for *a, an* or *one* in Dutch and Swedish are:

	Before an *it*-noun	Before *any other* noun
DUTCH	......	......
SWEDISH	......	......

IV. Fill in the corresponding words in Dutch and Swedish for:

	NEAR	HER	NOT	AND	IT	ALREADY
DUTCH	......	......	......	......	......	......
SWEDISH	......	......	......	......	......	......

	ALSO	FOR	ON	CHILD	LAKE	HEAD
DUTCH	......	......	......	......	......	......
SWEDISH	......	......	......	......	......	......

	ROOM	SNORE	HEAR	SEE	WE	COULD
DUTCH	......	......	......	......	......	......
SWEDISH	......	......	......	......	......	......

	THROUGH	WANT	HIM	THEY	HIS	SHE
DUTCH	......	......	......	......	......	......
SWEDISH	......	......	......	......	......	......

V. Above the following English sentences you will find numbers. When you have studied them carefully, fill in A, C, D, E and F below to show typical word order in Dutch and Swedish—B has already been filled in, as an example:

	1	2	3	4	5	6
A.	WE	SAW	HIM	—	—	—
B.	THEY	WERE	NOT	THERE	—	—
C.	WE	CAN	SEE	HIM	AGAIN	—
D.	WE	SHALL	NOT	SEE	THEM	AGAIN
E.	WE	HAVE	SEEN	IT	ALREADY	—
F.	WE	HAVE	NOT	SEEN	IT	BEFORE

	DUTCH							SWEDISH				
A.	...	...	...	...	...	...	A.	...	...	...	...	...	...
B.	1	2	4	3	...	...	B.	1	2	3	4	...	...
C.	...	...	...	...	...	...	C.	...	...	...	...	...	...
D.	...	...	...	...	...	...	D.	...	...	...	...	...	...
E.	...	...	...	...	...	...	E.	...	...	...	...	...	...
F.	...	...	...	...	...	...	F.	...	...	...	...	...	...

VI. After looking back to the Dutch-Danish Quiz (2), fill in the following:

	MAG	LAG	DAG
DUTCH			
ENGLISH	......	......	......

VII. Translate paragraphs 1–4 below.

DUTCH

1. De dag was koud. Er was sneeuw op de grond. De zon scheen niet. Er was ijs op het meer. Er was een boot op het meer. Wij konden een groen grasblad in

het veld naast het huis niet zien. Vanaf de deur konden wij niet een man op straat zien.

2. Het huis was warm. Naast het vuur sliep een oude man. Hij had een rode kap op zijn hoofd en een lange witte baard. Wij kenden hem niet. Een hond zat naast hem op de vloer. De kat lag daar ook.

3. De moeder had een blauwe japon aan. Ze kookte vlees voor de oude man. Haar dochters hielpen haar. In de aangrenzende kamer konden wij een kind horen snurken.

4. Het was reeds te laat. Wij wilden de oude man niet wekken. Wij wilden het werk in het huis niet hinderen. Wij gingen voort in de straat.

SWEDISH

1. Dagen var kall. Det var snö på marken. Solen sken inte. Det var is på sjön. Det var en båt på sjön. Vi kunde inte se ett grönt gräs strå på fältet nära huset. Genom dörröppningen kunde vi inte se en människa på gatan.

2. Huset var varmt. Nära elden sov en gammal man. Han hade en röd mössa på huvudet och ett längt vitt skägg. Vi kände inte honom. En hund satt nära honom på golvet. Katten låg där också.

3. Modern hade en blå klänning. Hon kokade mat för den gamle mannen. Hennes döttrar hjälpte henne. I det nästa rummet kunde vi höra ett barn snarka.

4. Det var redan alltför sent. Vi ville inte väcka den gamle mannen. Vi ville inte hindra husets arbete. Vi gingo ut på gatan.

TRANSLATION

1. ....
....
....

2. ....
....
....

3. ....
....
....

4. ....
....
....

Quiz 4

Mixed Teutonic Test

I. Mark the sentences in IV below as *G* (German), *D* (Dutch), *d* (Danish) or *S* (Swedish):

1	2	3	4	5
a.	a.	a.	a.	a. ....
b.	b.	b.	b.	b. ....
c.	c.	c.	c.	c. ....

II. Fill in:

	STREET	TOWN	THROUGH	RAIN
DUTCH	......	......	......	......
GERMAN	......	......	......	......
SWEDISH	......	......	......	......
DANISH	,.....	......	......	......

III. What Viking relic do we find in:

Ramsgate, Margate ......   *Whitby, Grimsby* ......

IV. Translate the sentences below, each given in three different languages:

1. ....
2. ....
3. ....
4. ....
5. ....

1a. Vi hade gått ut genom den lilla dörren på en gata.
1b. Wir sind durch die kleine Tür in eine Strasse gegangen.
1c. Vi var gået ud på en gade igennem den lille dør.

2a. Hele byen sov.
2b. De gehele stad was in slaap.
2c. Die ganze Stadt schlief.

3a. Wij waren alleen onder de volle maan. Er was vorst op de grond.
3b. Vi var alene under fuldmånen. Der var frost i jorden.
3c. Vi voro ensamma under fullmånen. Det var frost på marken.

4a. Es begann zu regnen. Wir konnten unsere Freunde nicht finden.
4b. Het begon te regenen. Wij konden onze vriend niet vinden.
4c. Det begyndte at regne. Vi kunne ikke finde vor ven.

5a. Det var en isande vind. Jag stod där skälvande av köld.
5b. Es war ein grausamer Wind. Ich stand dort schauernd vor Kälte.
5c. Er was een ruwe wind. Ik stond daar te bibberen van de kou.

5

The Ancestral Pattern of Anglo-American Grammar

There is an authentically practical reason why some readers may find it worth while to know something about the grammatical peculiarities of O.E.. Persons brought up in the Anglo-American speech community are now at a peculiar disadvantage when starting to learn any western language of the great Indo-European family, including those of the Teutonic group and modern descendants of Latin. This is because of an idiosyncrasy which distinguishes Middle and later English both ·from O.E. and from each of the sister languages. In the period of transition from Old to Middle English, the Mother Tongue underwent a stupendous simplification of what grammarians call its system of *concord*. This is another way of saying that Old, unlike later, English was a highly *flexional* language like Latin, Greek or Sanskrit; and one may best clarify the meaning of *concord* by making clear that of *flexion*.

First it will be well to avoid vagueness by distinguishing *roots* common to clusters of what we ordinarily refer to as words, e.g. the root LOV in *love—loves—loved—loving—lovable—loveless—lovely*. In Anglo-American the two sets *he—him—his* and *man—man's—men—men's* illustrate clusters of flexional forms based on the same root, the first cluster classifiable in only one way, referred to as *case* flexion, and the second in two ways respectively as case flexion and *number* flexion. Thus the difference between *man* and *man's* or between *men* and *men's* involves only case flexion but the difference between *man—man's* on the one hand and *men—men's* on the other illustrates flexion of number. We speak of the first two members of the fourfold set as *singular* forms and of the second pair as *plural*. The second members of each pair (*man's* and *men's*) are what grammarians call *genitive* case forms. Since *his* can replace only *man's*, we speak of it as the genitive case form of the set *he—him—his*. No noun of late Middle (or later) English has more than two case forms, and no pronoun more than three. In O.E., however, a pronoun, noun or adjective might have four distinguishable case forms respectively labelled *nominative, accusative, genitive* and *dative*. The third needs no further comment. We shall distinguish between the other three at a later stage. Meantime, any reader with a smattering of French or German (or both) will sufficiently appreciate their uses from the table below:

CASE FORMS	OLD ENGLISH	GERMAN	FRENCH	ANGLO-AMERICAN
Nominative	HE	ER	IL	HE
Accusative	HINE	IHN	LE	HIM
Dative	HIM	IHM	LUI	HIM

In general, the term *concord* refers to what circumstances determine the choice of one or other flexional form of a cluster such as either of the foregoing. One criterion of concord is *replaceability*. For instance, *he* or *him* can replace *a man* but only *his* can replace *a man's*. Such is *case concord* between pronoun and noun. No member of this pronoun triplet can replace *men* and *men's*. Instead we have to use *they* or *them* and *their(s)*. This obligation illustrates number concord between pronoun and noun. The criterion of concord between the pronoun or noun and the verb or between demonstratives (*this—these, that—those*) and the noun that follows them illustrates a different criterion of concord, that of association, i.e. the company words keep. Though we must say *falls* after *he, she, it, one* or any singular noun, we have to say *fall* after *they* or any plural noun. Though we say *this* or *that* before *man*, we have to say *these* or *those* before *men*. The last two examples respectively illustrate number concord of verb with noun or pronoun, and of demonstrative with the noun.

Choice of the correct flexional form of the verb illustrates three other types of concord. One is concord of person. This implies classification of personal pronouns as first (*I—me—my* and *we—us—our*), second (*you—your*), and third (the several case forms of *he, she, it, one* and *they*). In O.E. all pronouns of the third person were flexional forms based on the same root as are *he, him, his, it* (HIT) and *her*. We shall later see (p. 211) that *she* (HEO) and *they—them—their* are intruders like *went* (p. 71) in the company of *go*. However, this need not bother us in this context. Concord of person between pronoun and verb, like concord of number between noun or pronoun and verb, has left only one trace in Anglo-American. After *I* or *you* (singular) we can say *fall*; but after *he, she, it* or *one* we have to say *falls*. Choice of flexional forms of the verb involves two other types of concord. The more familiar, illustrated by what can keep company respectively with *daily* (e.g. *wash* or *washes*) and *yesterday* (e.g. *washed*), one customarily refers to as *tense* concord.* The other, represented by the use of *were* instead of *was* after *if* (e.g. *if I were to do so*), we call concord of *mood*. The last example illustrates its only trace in Anglo-American other than the equivalent *be* for *is* in *if this be true*.

One other form of Anglo-American concord demands attention. We may call it *sex* concord, inasmuch as we replace *man—man's* by *he—him—his*, *lady—lady's* by *she—her*, and *snail* or *hat* by *it—its*. Here the rule is simple. One uses *he*, etc., for male names, *she*, etc., for female names, *it*, etc., for names of things and for creatures of unspecified sex. To be sure, sailors sometimes speak of a ship and poets sometimes speak of the moon as *she*, but such usage has no sanction in O.E.; SCIP was a HIT-word and MONA was a HE-word. O.E. concord of the sort illustrated

---

* For what we customarily call *tense* forms in English (and in the Teutonic languages), modern grammarians use the term *aspect*, emphasis being less on *time* (past, present or future) than on what is *habitual* or *continuing* and what is over and done with.

by these two had little to do with sex. Grammarians call it *gender* concord.

To be sure, we may put all O.E., like all Latin, Greek, Russian, German or Icelandic, names into three heaps called respectively masculine, feminine and neuter, since respectively replaceable by HE, HEO (*she*) and HIT. However, no simple sex rule serves to distinguish them as members of one or another of the three heaps. Admittedly, many HE-names are those of males, such as* COCC, FOX, MANN, FÆDER, SUNU, BROTHOR and CYNING (p. 153). HENN, FIXEN, MODOR, DOHTOR, SWEOSTOR and CWEN are names of females, and are also HEO names. Likewise, names of many inert things such as GLÆS, WÆTER, HUS, DOR, GEAT, and of many creatures of either sex, such as LAMB, CEALF, CILD or BEARN, are HIT-names. However exceptions to any such natural classification are more numerous than words which conform.

Thus WIMMAN (=WIF-MANN) is masculine and WIF is neuter. DURU, another name for the same part of a HUS as DOR, is feminine. Though WORD is neuter, BOC is feminine. Of two words for the same sort of plant, TREO is neuter, BEAM is masculine, and of particular names for the TREO-BEAM class, ÆSC, EOW are masculine, BEORC and BECE feminine. Regardless of sex, some creatures are masculine, e.g. FISC, WYRM, FROCGA, BERA, FLEA. Others, whether male or female, are feminine, e.g. CRAWE, MOTHTHE, BEO, MUS and GOS. While GAT is feminine, its near relation SCEAP is neuter. Some parts of the body are HE-words, such as FINGER, EARM, FOT, TOTH. Some are HEO-words, such as HAND, TUNGE, BRU. Others are HIT-words, such as EAGE, CNEO, HEAFOD, BREOST, THEOH. Whereas FETHER is feminine, ÆG is neuter. Among names of places, MOR, HYLL, CNOLL, STREAM are all HE-words. Whereas BAN (the hard material of the body) is neuter, STAN (the hard thing you should not throw out of glass houses) is masculine.

To use the pronouns of O.E. correctly, a Norman soldier would thus need to know the *gender* class (masculine, feminine, neuter) to which every noun belongs; but correct use of the pronouns would be the least of the difficulties with which gender would confront him. Only two Anglo-American words (*this* and *that*) give us a clue to them. As we all know, correct use of these involves number concord inasmuch as they have plural forms for use with plural nouns; but they involve no choice of the type implied by the terms *case concord* and *gender concord*. Contrariwise, in O.E., THES has different *case* forms, singular and plural; and the correct case form depends on the gender of the noun which follows. We require THES HUND, THISNE HUND, THISSUM HUNDE for *this hound*, THISSES HUNDES for *this hound's*, THAS HUNDAS and THISSUM HUNDUM for *these hounds* and

---

* The reader should be able to guess the modern equivalents of words here printed in capitals, and can check them by recourse to the *Concise Oxford Dictionary*.

THISSA HUNDA for *these hounds*'. HUND is a masculine noun; and the right case forms are different when we couple *this—these* with a feminine one. For *this queen* we need THEOS CWEN, THAS CWEN, THISSE CWENE, for *this queen's* THISSE CWENE, for *those queens* THAS CWENA, THISSUM CWENUM and for *those queens*' THISSA CWENA. To translate *this* and *these* correctly in Harold's English, the Norman invader would indeed need to know the gender of the following noun, and the case forms of THES, THEOS, etc., singular and plural for all three genders.

The Anglo-American demonstratives *this* and *that* are unique. Descriptive words such as *big*, *blue*, *bad*, *heavy*, *high* and *hearty* do not change like *this* or *that*; but corresponding words in all the sister languages do so. Icelandic and German apart, they do not have separate case forms; but they change in concord with both the number and the gender class of the noun, as illustrated by the behaviour of the Spanish words *candalero* (masc.) and *cortina* (fem.) as below:

el candalero blanco	*los candaleros blancos*
(the white candlestick)	(the white candlesticks)
la cortina blanca	*las cortinas blancas*
(the white curtain)	(the white curtains)

Nouns of the modern descendants of Latin, other than Roumanian, have only two forms, singular and plural. Those of German and Icelandic, like those of O.E., Latin, Greek and Russian, have also different case forms; and the adjective of such languages has forms the choice of which depends on the case, as well as on the number and on the gender, of the noun they qualify, and on whether a *determinative* word precedes them. If such a word, i.e. one equivalent to *the*, *this—these*, *that—those*, *my*, *his*, *their*, etc., comes before it, the O.E. adjective may appear in one of four forms, otherwise in as many as eight. Even the first three numerals AN, TWA, THRI (Museum Exhibit, p. 179) have several flexional forms.

We may thus say that O.E. words are classifiable as: (a) pronouns and nouns which exhibit case and number flexion; (b) verbs which exhibit flexion of number, person, tense and mood; (c) adjectives and demonstratives which exhibit flexion of case, number and gender; (d) particles (variously called adverbs, prepositions and conjunctions) which are flexionless. In Tudor English and in Anglo-American we find no trace of flexion in words which were ancestrally adjectives; and *gender*, in contradistinction to *sex*, concord has disappeared entirely owing to the adoption of a straightforward unexceptionable rule to prescribe which pronouns can replace a noun. The flexional system of the verb has also simplified greatly inasmuch as there is little trace left of mood or number; and case flexion has simplified in two ways. At most, nouns have only two case forms. Since we may substitute *of the*

All Welsh place names mean something. This village in Anglesey takes its name from two parishes respectively of Saint Mary and Saint Tysilio. The full translation is: Parish (of) Mary (in a) hollow (of) white hazels by the rapid whirlpool (and) parish (of) Tysilio (with the) red cave.

A page of the Codex Argenteus *and other famous versions of the Bible, from the frontispiece to* The Gothic and Anglo-Saxon Gospels, etc., *edited by Bosworth and Waring, 1874.*

Rosetta Stone (found during Napoleon's Egyptian campaign) shows: top third, ancient picture writing of Egyptian priesthood; middle, later form of Egyptian writing; bottom third, the Greek translation.

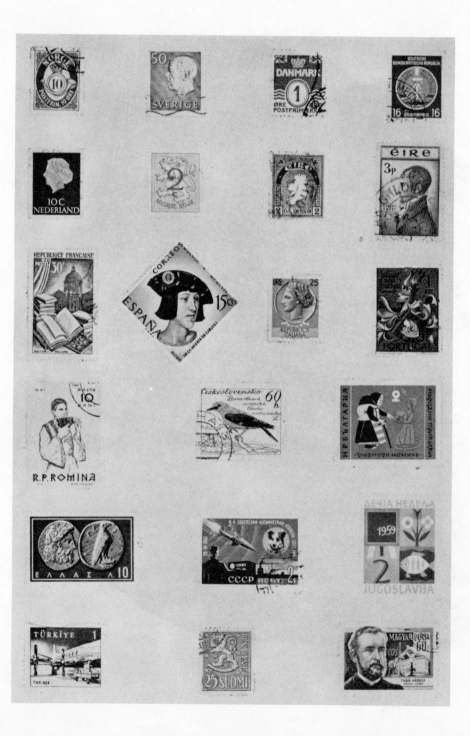

(a) *This specimen from an early twelfth-century version of the Anglo-Saxon Bible in the Wessex dialect exhibits the first few verses of the gospel of St. Luke. The reader will detect three signs which do not belong to the Celtic alphabet, ð and þ for the sounds represented by th in English and p for w, the last two being of runic origin, also the Greek Z. Otherwise their forms tally closely with those of the corresponding signs in the contemporary alphabet of Eire (see key, p. 152), the signs equivalent to g, r and s being especially different from our own, and difficult to distinguish.*

(b) *This whalebone panel, the front of the Franks Casket, dates from c. A.D. 700, and bears a runic inscription. The runic alphabet included the signs given below:*

(a)

(b)

f	u	ð	o	r	k	ꞏ	ȝ	w	h	n	i	j	th	p	lox

s	t	b	e	m	l	ng	d	œ	a	æ	ea	y

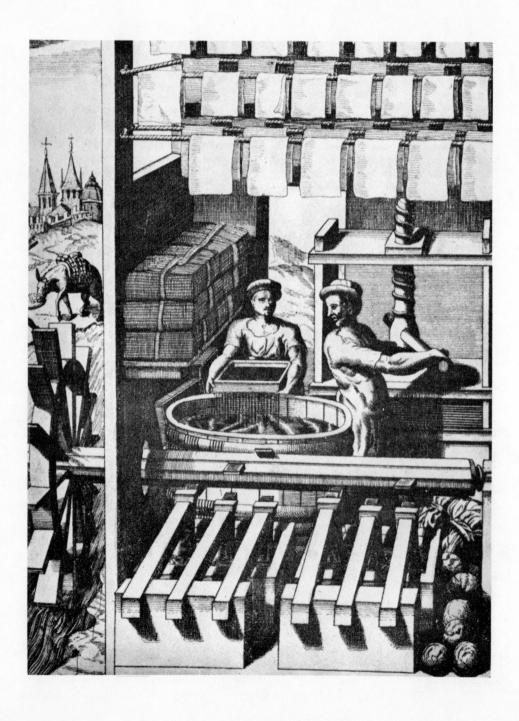

Playing Cards (Fifteenth-century.) Wood-block printing was used for playing cards a century or more before the Gutenberg Bible.

Specimen of William Caxton's books, taken from "Recuyell of the Histories of Troye", translated from the French original between 1469 and 1471, and printed about 1475.

In thefe two bokes precedent. we haue by the helpe
of god; tretyd; of the two firft deftrucyons of Troye
with the noble fuytes and; dedes of the ftronge and;
puiffant Hercules .that made and; dyd fo many mer-
vayllis that the engyne humayn of alle men oughte to
meruaylle. And; alfo how he flewe the kynge Laome
don bete doun and; put his cyte of troye to ruyne Now
in the thirde and; lafte book god; to fore . we fhall fate
how the fayd; cyte was by Priamus fone of the faid;
kynge laomedon rediffied and repayred more ftronge
and; more puyffante than euer hit was before . And;
afterward; how for the rauyffhement of dame Hela-
yne wyf of kynge Menelaus of grece . the fayd; cyte
was totally deftroyed; Priamus hector and; alle his
fones flayn with nobleffe wyth out nombre . as hit
fhall appere in the proces of the chapitres . .

How the kynge Priant rediffied the cyte of troye
more ftronge than euer hit was afore ſ of his fones
and; doughters . And; how after many councayllis he
fente Anthenor and; Polydamas in to grece for to ve
mande his fufter epione. that Apar mayntenyd; . .

FOR to entre than in to the matere . ye haue
herd; here to fore at the feconde deftruccion of
Troye how hercules had; taken pryfonner
Priamus ꝑ fone of kynge Laomedon. And
had; put hym in prifon. how be hit dares of frigie fayth
ꝑ his fader had; fente hym to meue warre in a ftrange

father for *the father's*, the genitive is never obligatory; and relatively few Anglo-American nouns have even an optional genitive. For instance, one cannot say *the house's roof* for *the roof of the house*. The modern pronoun has at most three distinguishable case forms. That of the O.E. pronoun, like that of the O.E. noun and adjective, might have four in each number—eight in all.

In this context, it should remove some of the mystification distilled by textbooks, to say that grammarians have been slow to make a distinction named by biologists as *homology* and *analogy*. One says that the legs of an insect and the jaws of a centipede are *homologous* because they develop in the same way on the same ancestral pattern regardless of function; but the *analogous* jaws of a shark and those of a lobster, though functionally similar (in the sense that they are masticatory organs), develop in a different way from different ancestral beginnings. Unhappily, traditional grammatical distinctions cut across considerations of *structure* (i.e. classification of flexional forms) and *function* (i.e. situations in which we use a word whether a particle or one or other flexional based on the same root). Thus there is structurally no clear-cut distinction in Anglo-American between *thing* (noun) and *it* (pronoun) or between *persons* (noun) and *they—them* (pronoun). The only essential distinction resides in the company they keep. For instance, we can put *a* in front of *thing* or *person*, and we can put a *determinative* (i.e. *the, this, that, my, our*, etc.) in front of *thing(s)* or *person(s)*; but we cannot do so before *it, they*, etc. Similarly, we are at liberty to call the distinction flexional between an adjective (now otherwise a particle) such as *happy* and a corresponding so-called adverb *happily*. However, this structural distinction (not applicable to the uses of *daily* or *soon*) is on a different level of classification from what we mean when we distinguish three such words with exactly the same meaning as: *meanwhile* (adverb), *during* (preposition), *while* (conjunction). Here the distinction has no reference to flexional variants based on a common root. It is merely one of context. This will be clear to the reader who compares the equivalent statements:

They knocked at the door. *Meanwhile* he was at dinner.
They knocked at the door *during* his dinner.
They knocked at the door, *while* he was dining.

Such distinctions as between verb and noun are meaningful only in terms of the flexions a dictionary leaves the grammar book to explain. For instance, two statements in headline idiom here convey exactly the same meaning by substitution of *marriage* (noun) and *marries* (verb): (a) *Marriage of heiress to lounge lizard*; (b) *Heiress marries lounge lizard*. To classify a word as an adjective in English merely means *either* that it is a word which entailed the characteristic dictates of adjectival concord in O.E. *or* that it is a word whose equivalent would conform to at least one such rule of concord in a foreign language. Many languages have no such rules. For words which correspond to Anglo-American nouns, Chinese has no different flexional forms, and what correspond to our verbs, like Anglo-American *must*, are changeless. We recognise *must* as a verb only if we know it as one ancestral member of a cluster of flexional forms based on the same root, or if we have to translate it into a language where it trails along the flexions characteristic of a verb, as in French *il doit* (he must), *il a du* (he had to), *il devra* (he will have to), *il devrait* (he would have to), etc.

Gender, in contradistinction to sex, concord is alien to Anglo-American, or indeed to Middle and Tudor English. So, likewise, is a case distinction common to nouns, pronouns and adjectives of Latin, of all the older Teutonic languages, of Modern German and of contemporary Icelandic. Though the adjective and the noun of modern descendants of Latin, other than Roumanian, have no separate case forms, they do preserve four forms of the pronoun corresponding to O.E. HE—HINE—HIM—HIS (p. 209). As stated, Tudor (and later) English has only an optional trace of case flexion with respect to the noun, Dutch none, Swedish, Danish and Norwegian only a separate genitive form corresponding to HIS, etc., use of which scarcely calls for comment; but anyone who wishes to learn German or Icelandic will find it useful to label the three remaining case forms of the noun or adjective corresponding to HE, HINE and HIM.

We have spoken of HE as the *nominative*, and it suffices to say that this is the so-called *subject*, i.e. the form which precedes the Anglo-American verb in a simple affirmative statement, such as *he saw the red light*. In Middle, Tudor or later English *him* may come after a verb or, as commonly (though not invariably) like HIM, after a preposition (e.g. *without him, by him*, etc.). To translate *him* into O.E., German, French, Spanish, Italian, etc., we need, however, to distinguish between two ways in which the Anglo-American *him* may immediately follow the verb in a simple affirmative statement. If *him* comes immediately after the verb we can sometimes replace it by *to him*; when we cannot do so, schoolbook grammar then calls *him* the *direct object* of the verb. This is the chief use of HINE, called the *accusative* case form, which actually lingers in some English hayseed dialects as *'un*. We may also use *him* after some verbs (*e.g. give, show, write, tell, promise, read*) in interchangeable constructions such as: (a) *I wrote him a letter*; (b) *I wrote a letter to him*. In such situations, the good books call *him* an *indirect object*, and one use of the so-called O.E. *dative* case form HIM was in this way. Being also the form used after most prepositions, it eventually ousted HINE.

Since we should now be clear about what we mean by case-concord of the noun, that of the pronoun which can replace it, and that of the adjective which keeps company with it, we are now ready to take a glance at the luxuriant overgrowth of word forms corresponding to one dictionary entry of an O.E. noun or adjective. The majority of O.E. nouns (Museum Exhibit, p. 179) conform to one of four patterns which we may respectively call *masculine*, *neuter* and *feminine*, in accordance with the gender class, and *weak*. The last named includes feminines such as SUNNE,

EORTHE (*earth*), HEORTE (*heart*), TUNGE (*tongue*), masculines such as NAMA (*name*), MONA (*moon*), FODA (*food*), MUTH (*mouth*), and a few neuters, notably EAGE (*eye*), EARE (*ear*). O.E. nouns had separate dative case forms, nearly always distinguished by the terminal -E if singular, and always by the terminal -UM if plural. The genitive plural terminal is either -A or -ENA. The nominative singular of a sizeable number of nouns of all three gender classes ends in -U. A miscellaneous class exhibits flexion by vowel change. In addition to the ancestral forms of *man, tooth, foot, goose, mouse*, etc., this class includes NIHT, BOC, BROTHOR, DOHTOR and FREOND, the meaning of which the reader may guess and check in the usual way.

MUSEUM EXHIBIT—THE NOUN AND NUMERALS OF ALFRED THE GREAT

	Masculine (*stone*)	Neuter (*house*)	Feminine (*week*)	Weak (*sun*)
Nom. Sing. Acc. Sing.	STAN	HUS	WICU	SUNNE
Gen. Sing.	STANES	HUSES	WICE	SUNNAN
Dat. Sing.	STANE	HUSE		
Nom. and Acc. Plur.	STANAS	HUS	WICA	SUNNAN
Gen. Plur.	STANA	HUSA	WICENA	SUNNENA
Dat. Plur.	STANUM	HUSUM	WICUM	SUNNUM

	M	N	F		M	N	F		M	N	F
Nom.		AN			TWEGEN	TWA			THRI	THREO	
Acc.	AENNE		ANE								
Gen.	ANES					TWEGRA				THREORA	
Dat.	ANE		ANRE			TWAM				THRIM	

MUSEUM EXHIBIT—THE ADJECTIVE OF ALFRED THE GREAT

	Strong Masc.	Strong Neuter	Strong Femin.	Weak Masc.	Weak Neuter	Weak Femin.
Nom. Sing.		GOD		GODA	GODE	
Acc. Sing.	GODNE		GODE			
Gen. Sing.	GODES		GODRE	GODAN		
Dat. Sing.	GODUM		GODRE	GODAN		
Nom. and Acc. Plur.	GODE	GOD	GODA	GODAN		
Gen. Plur.	GODRA					
Dat. Plur.	GODUM					

Notes:

1. Some adjectives have the terminal -U in the Strong Feminine Nominative Singular.

2. We may meet -E for -A in the Strong Feminine Nominative and Accusative Plural.

3. As for nouns, we may meet -ENA for -RA in the Weak Genitive Plural.

Each O.E. adjective had flexional forms which are classifiable in accordance with each one of the four major noun classes. In all, therefore, it had nine or ten forms. The weak forms were those which followed a *determinative* (p. 176). In the singular there was an additional case form usually called the *instrumental*. Its distinctive terminal was -E, and its use was comparable in one way with the ablative case form of Latin nouns, inasmuch as it conveys manner. Thus GLADE means *in a glad way*, i.e. *gladly*; and the instrumental terminal has the same force as -*ly* in adjectival adverbs of Modern English. The latter comes from the instrumental form LICE of LIC (*like*) and was originally an adjectival ending, as it still is in *manly, godly, cowardly, monthly, weekly*, etc.

Three outstanding features which distinguish flexional forms of the adjective from that of the noun are: (a) the strong masculine singular accusative which has the same (-NE) terminal as the pronoun (cf. HINE, THISNE); (b) the strong feminine genitive and dative terminal (-RE) which recalls HIRE (*her*); (c) the strong genitive plural terminal (-RA), recalling the O.E. equivalent of *their*. During the transitional period from Old to Middle English, all these terminals except -E disappeared. In the English of Chaucer and Wycliffe there was merely a trace of adjectival flexion, viz. the use of -E after a determinative or if the noun partner was plural. Thus we meet *a smal fowl on a gret sea* but *smale fowles on the grete sea*. The situation is much the same in Modern Dutch; but in Tudor English, that of Tyndale's Bible, the equivalent word was invariant.

We have already seen (p. 142) how to give a passage of O.E. a new look by certain changes of spelling conventions with due regard to changes of pronunciation. To these rules we may now add the following with the same end in view: eliminate the terminals -A, -AN, -NE, -RA, -RE, -U and -UM. More often than not, one can cut out -E. As we shall now see, we may also knock off the verb terminals -INNE, -EN and -ATH.

Two grammatical peculiarities are most characteristic of the Teutonic clan. A separate weak so-called declension of the adjective dictated by a preceding determinative is one; the other is a large class of verbs distinguished as *strong*. The latter are verbs whose flexional forms exhibit internal vowel change, as is true of *give—gave—given* or *know—knew—known*. The alternative and now dominant type, designated *weak*, has past forms distinguished by the terminal -ED (or -T) e.g. *hope—hoped*. In modern Teutonic languages we meet transitional types which illustrate the continuing process of conversion of the strong into the dominant pattern. In Tudor English (as in the Anglican Prayer Book and King James Bible), we find many examples (see below), and in the Scots dialect of *Annie Laurie* we meet *gied* for *gave*. Thus some English verbs which are now weak are traceable to strong ancestors, as is *climb* from CLIMBAN with past like BINDAN. Chaucer uses the older strong forms of *swell, climb, carve*. Milton uses *foughten*. *Inter alia*, the Bible of A.D. 1611 uses *holpen, baken, folden* where we should use *helped, baked, folded*:

> He hath holpen his servant Israel. (*Luke* i 54)
> A meat offering baken in the oven. (*Levit.* ii 4)
> They be folden together as thorns. (*Nahum* i 10)

Our next Museum Exhibit cites an example of each type of O.E. verb. Before we scrutinise them, it may be well to cite the meaning of our terms:

1. *Infinitive.* The -AN form followed an auxiliary (e.g. HE MIHTE RÆDAN (*he could read*) and certain other verbs, e.g. HE BEGANN RÆDAN (*he began reading*). It would be equally correct to write HE BEGANN TO RÆDENNE. The TO couplet did service to express suitability or to qualify an adjective, e.g. BREAD TO ETENNE, or THÆT WIN WÆS GOD TO DRINCENNE.

2. *Present Participle.* This was an adjective like *doting* in *doting mother*. It was fully

inflected and as such its use is comparable with the form of the verb with the corresponding terminal, -ANDE or -END(E), in other Teutonic languages. As we shall see, it left no descendant in Tudor or later English.

3. *Past Participle.* Only a few verbs in Tudor or later English have such a form distinct from the past tense, e.g. *risen, given* in contradistinction to *rose, gave.* Like its descendants, it had three functions: as an adjective (e.g. *risen Lord*); after *have* or *had* to form compound past tense forms, e.g. *had risen*; and after BE or WEORTHAN (p. 30) to form passive constructions comparable to *he was given.* Note that American *gotten* is nearer to O.E. in usage than modern British *got.*

4. *Present and Past Tense Forms.* The use of terms for the tenses tallies with contemporary usage; but each has alternative forms respectively called *indicative* and *subjunctive.* The former was for use in simple assertions, questions and negations, when no element of doubt is implicit. The latter had many uses of which a trace remains in such expressions as: *if I were* (not *was*) *to say, if it be true,* etc. In the accompanying Museum Exhibit of the verb of Alfred the Great (see below), the indicative precedes the subjunctive alternative.

If we contrast the O.E. verb with that of Tudor or later English, three features of the former are of special interest for one who is starting to learn Dutch or German, and two (iv-v) are important to anyone who is learning any of the sister languages (see Museum Exhibit on p. 79).

(i) As in German and Dutch the so-called past participle of O.E. had the prefix GE- unless the verb stem started with a prefix such as BE- or FOR-. As was true of not a few O.E. and is still of many German verbs, GE- itself was one such prefix.

MUSEUM EXHIBIT—THE VERB OF ALFRED THE GREAT

1. A STRONG VERB (*bind*)		2. A WEAK VERB (*hear*)	
Infinitive	bindan	*Infinitive*	hieran
	—to bindenne		—to hierenne
Present		*Present*	
Participle	bindende	*Participle*	hierende
Past		*Past*	
Participle	gebunden	*Participle*	gehiered
Present	ic binde	*Present*	ic hiere
	thu bindest *or* binde		thu hierst *or* hiere
	he (etc.) bindeth *or* binde		he (etc.) hierth *or* hiere
	we (etc.) bindath *or* binden		we (etc.) hierath *or* hieren
Past	ic band *or* bunde	*Past*	ic hierde
	thu bunde		thu hierdest *or* hierde
	he (etc.) band		he (etc.) hierde
	we (etc.) bundon *or* bunden		we (etc.) hierdon *or* hierden

During the transition from Old to Middle English, this had faded out into a vowel sound represented by Y, which disappeared in spoken English before the Tudor period. However, it lingered longer in poetry as a gimmick for scansion. Even Milton resorts to it at least once (*by heaven y-clept Euphrosyne*). This GE- prefix is a hallmark of the West Germanic group, being absent in the Scandinavian clan. This may be why its relic (Y-) disappeared earliest in the north of Britain where Scandinavian influence was strongest (Museum Exhibit, p. 184). In the Scandinavian clan the -EN form of the past participle (e.g. Swedish *given*) is an adjective used also to form a passive construction; but there is a special flexional form, the so-called *supine* (e.g. Swedish *givit*), for use after *have* (Swedish *hava*).

(ii) The so-called infinitive has the terminal -AN or -ENNE which became -EN in the transitional period as in German and Dutch. It has no terminal -N in Scandinavian languages, whence probably its disappearance was earliest in the north of Britain.

(iii) As in German and Dutch, both tense forms had a common terminal if the subject was plural (*we*, etc., or a plural noun). This common terminal -EN was the *subjunctive* plural of O.E. In the Midlands and south of Britain, it displaced the indicative alternatives (-ATH, -ON) early in the transitional period. The plural -EN, which lingered into early Tudor times in the south of Scotland, does not occur in the Scandinavian clan. Nor does the terminal -ATH which seems to have given place in North Britain to what one might frivolously call an *anti-lisp* sound-shift to -S.

(iv) The terminal -TH of the third person singular in the present tense (indicative), modified to -T in Dutch and German, is foreign to Scandinavian. In the north, we find that -S takes its place in the transitional period from Old to Middle English. By the end of the subsequent transitional period the -S had there disappeared as a plural terminal. Chaucer's Scottish contemporary William Dunbar retains it in the third person singular (e.g. *says*, *gives*) just as we use it today; but Midland and southern English (as in the Bible of King James) retained the -TH terminal (e.g. *saith*, *giveth*) till the end of the seventeenth century. Possibly, the exodus of Scots across the Border after the Union (1707) of the two parliaments expedited its displacement.

(v) The foregoing changes have illustrated the likelihood of Scandinavian influence during and after the later O.E. period. Another, which began in the extreme South, and was certainly not due to Norse settlement, puts the spotlight on a highly characteristic and puzzling feature of late Middle and subsequent English usage. The consonant core of the present participle of all other Teutonic languages, including O.E., is -ND-, corresponding to -NT- in Latin and its modern descendants, as in French *aimant*. Since we translate the latter by *loving*, many elementary textbooks refer to this very idiosyncratic English -ING derivative as a present participle. This is historically incorrect, and it is misleading to do so for another reason, i.e. its title to do the job of the Teutonic or Latin present participle, as when we speak

MUSEUM EXHIBIT—THE ENGLISH VERB OF A.D. 1300

NORTHERN	MIDLAND	SOUTHERN
to hope	to hope *or* to hopen	to hopen
hopende	hopende	hopinge
hoped	hoped *or* y-hoped	y-hoped
I hopes	I hope	Ich hope
thu hopes	thu hopes	thu hopest
he hopes	he hopeth	he hopeth
we hopes	we hopen	we hopeth
ye hopes	ye hopen	ye hopeth
they hopes	they hopen	hie hopeth
I hoped	I hopede	Ich hopede
thu hoped	thu hopedes	thu hopedest
he hoped	he hopede	he hopede
we hoped	we hopeden	we hopeden
ye hoped	ye hopeden	ye hopeden
they hoped	they hopeden	hie hopeden

of a *doting mother*, is the least important of its functions. Its variegated uses have their parallel only in the use of the Welsh so-called verb-noun. It is therefore worthwhile to examine its credentials closely.

Here is the story. All Teutonic languages have a suffix -ING or -UNG, as little meaningful as -dom, -ness, -hood, etc., in that it merely labels the word as abstract, like the French -age in *marriage*. Just as -NES attaches itself to adjectives as in RIHTWISNES (righteousness), -UNG or -ING attaches itself to verb stems, as does -age to *marri-*. O.E. had more than its fair share of such combinations which merely duplicated the use of the -AN form when it is a verb-noun, as when we say alternatively: (a) *it is difficult to read Arabic*; (b) *reading Arabic is difficult*. The territory of the -ING form increased during the transitional period to Middle English in the south of Britain, and it had established itself throughout the country before the end of the period as the hall-mark of the English verb. By then, it had supplanted the Teutonic present participle, and had begun to acquire a third function, possibly through its use in so-called *predicative* constructions trailing behind *be, was—were, have been, should be—would be, could be, might be* or *have been*, etc. This equipped English with far richer resources for conveying the notion of time than is possible with some 500 or more flexional forms of the Greek and of the Sanskrit verb.

The last remarks bring into focus how far English has moved from being a highly flexional language like Sanskrit, Latin and Greek, to becoming much nearer than its sisters and cousins to a language of the isolating type, as are Chinese or Nigerian Yoruba, i.e. languages in which all words are unchangeable particles like *good* and *must*. As stated, we speak of the latter meaningfully as a verb, partly because its equivalent in other flexional languages would be one of a constellation of words having flexional peculiarities characteristic of the verb, and partly because its ancestor in O.E. had indeed such peculiarities. Similarly, we speak correctly of *bad*, *beautiful* and *bleak* as adjectives because their equivalents in sister languages and their ancestral forms in O.E. or French have flexional forms characteristic of adjectival concord. From a different viewpoint, we might equally call them—or any other Anglo-American adjective so-called—nouns, as when we speak of *the Good*, *the True* or *the Beautiful*.

If we here take stock of some figures to illustrate the vast quantity of useless grammatical luggage which English had already off-loaded in the Tudor period, we must do so with the proviso that they refer to recognisably different *forms*, in contra-distinction to different *uses*. It is suitable to point this out because patterns set forth in textbooks convey at first sight an exaggerated impression. For instance, it is customary to exhibit classical Latin nouns in textbooks under six case-headings, both singular and plural. None the less, it is far from true to say that every (or indeed any) Latin noun has twelve distinguishable flexional forms. None has more than seven, the majority only six.*

The circumstance last mentioned helped not a little to make the British Empire what it was. For many generations before Arnold of Rugby unleashed his well-birched bright boys to bear the White Man's Burden, many others had tasted the birch in a fruitless endeavour to discover why: (a) MENSA (nominative) *a table*, spelt in the same way as MENSA (vocative) *Oh Table* were placeable as different case forms, even with the help of a table (of a different sort) to set them forth separately as such; (b) in what non-caneable circumstances one would address an article of furniture as *Oh Table*! Conceivably, the dilemma contributed to the ingenuity with which colonial experts trained in the same grammatical tradition approached the (as yet) intractable problems of culture contact where there exists a wealthy White Settler group in an unprivileged African milieu.

Such conundrums do not confront one who wishes to become a member of the

---

* Only a few names for males have a so-called *vocative* distinguishable from the *nominative* singular (*Dominus* Lord, *Domine*, Oh Lord), and no nouns have a distinctive vocative form in the plural. No Latin nouns have distinguishable *dative* and *ablative* case forms in the plural, and a sizeable proportion of masculine and neuter nouns have identical singular case forms for dative and ablative use. The comparative rarity of the distinction explains why Roman grammarians failed to recognise it till Julius Ceasar wrote a tract on the Ablative.

Anglo-American speech community. The definite article (*the*) of Middle and later English is invariant, like the adjective. Its Dutch equivalents are two (*het* neuter singular, otherwise *de*). Its French equivalents are three. Spanish and Italian have four (p. 207). German has recourse to six, as have Swedish and Danish. For the invariant Tudor and later English adjective, classical Latin prescribes fourteen forms; French, Italian and Spanish at least three, commonly four. Dutch, Danish and Swedish all prescribe three, German five, and Icelandic thirteen. Nouns of modern descendants of Latin in the West have only two forms (singular and plural) on account of the complete disappearance of case distinction. The same is true of Dutch nouns and of the overwhelming majority of Anglo-American nouns. A small class (p. 173) have a third optional (genitive singular*) form; but *man* and *woman* each with four forms in modern usage are pathological, since the genitive of no O.E. noun had the -ES terminal in the plural. Modern Danish and Swedish have four (-S) forms comparable to those of *man*. In German the flexional forms of a noun may be two, three, or four, singular *and* plural.

From a statistical point of view, perhaps the most remarkable contrast between the Teutonic and Latin clans emerges when we contrast the luxuriance of the flexional guises of the Romance verb in even one of the modern descendants of Latin compared with those of the oldest representatives of the Teutonic group. In what follows the figures treat as one what flexional forms a participle or verbal noun may have, and take no cognisance of auxiliaries (e.g. *shall, can, may, must*). If we cite the -ING form as a flexional form and deem *thou* to be archaic, Anglo-American weak (and most strong) verbs have only four forms (e.g. *hate—hating—hates—hated: find—finding—finds—found*), a few have five (e.g. *give, drink*) and a few (e.g. *cut, put,*) have only three. For Danish and Swedish the numbers are five and six respectively. In O.E., as in Modern German, a typical verb has only twelve forms. Owing to the fact that it has separate personal flexions in the plural, the number for the Icelandic verb is twenty. Partly for the same reason and also because the Gothic verb has a distinctive dual (p. 214) as well as singular and plural forms, the corresponding number for the oldest known Teutonic language is forty-three. However, this is appreciably less than the corresponding number (fifty-seven) for Modern Spanish and considerably less than half the figure for Latin (over 100).

In our next chapter there will be more to say about the ways in which Anglo-American differs from its sister and half-sister languages. Should our story so far have whetted the appetite of the reader to explore in the easiest way what O.E. was like, he or she will know (p. 32) why the best recipe is to start with the Anglo-Saxon Gospels, for which a crib is easily obtainable. If so, our outline of O.E. grammar is incomplete. It has dealt only with flexional forms; but one can read the O.E.

---

* The apostrophe which distinguishes *day's* and *days'* is merely a typographical figment.

version of the gospels only if one knows something about the uses of the particles, customarily classified as prepositions and conjunctions. Most of the native stock-in-trade of such words have survived but not their meanings.

Thus we often meet ON in Old English where we should now use *in*, and we meet OFER where we should now use *on*. OF has left twins. We now use it (so spelt) as an empty word where the O.E. writer used the genitive case form (*heaven's kingdom* for *kingdom of heaven*); but its earlier meaning (retained in *off*) was alternative to FRAM and *away*, as when *it fell off the table*. Likewise, WITHUTAN meant *outside*, as in the *green hill . . . without a city wall*; and BUTAN did service for *without* in its modern sense allied to *save = except* (both French intruders) as in *whence all but he had fled*. Where we now use *with*, the O.E. equivalents (MID and SAMOD) have disappeared. As in *withstand*, WITH itself originally meant *against*, the last mentioned being a pseudo-superlative corruption of ONGEAN. ÆR (which survives in literary usage as *ere*) was the more usual word for *before* in a temporal sense, and BEFORAN in a spatial sense (= *in front of*). HWONNE and HWÆR were interrogatives. For the corresponding conjunctions (*when* and *where*) the particles THONNE and THÆR did service, *as do the corresponding words in contemporary sister Teutonic languages.*

Among particles which have also left no survivors we have noted ÆC (p. 32). Others are: YMB (now replaced by the French intruder *around*), THY (now replaced by the hybrid Anglo-French *because*, written *by cause* as two words in the Wycliffe Bible), AC (*but*), THA (*when*), OTH (*until*). Other conjunctions were AND which has come down without change, GIF (*if*), HWÆTHER (*whether*), and ALLSWA or ALS (*as*). These are a few of the more important ones. Of those that have left descendants, nearly all are recognisable as such, as is GIF (*if*) with due allowance for the softening of G before a front vowel; but in many situations where we should now use a so-called adverbial conjunction, O.E. writers employed constructions invoking the relative O.E. particle THE. These are comparable to substituting for *while* the phrase *during the time that*. Among such, we may meet in the O.E. version of the gospels:

FOR THE	*because*
ÆFTER THÆM THE	*after* (that which)
ÆR THÆM THE	*before* (ere that which)
THA HWILE THE	*when* (the while that)
NU THE	*now that*
SITHAN THE	*since*

To get the feeling of the English Gospels in A.D. 1000, one must remember that the translators were accustomed to write in short sentences without relying on words such as *because, since, although*, to link parts of a long sentence together. Instead they used words equivalent to *then, thus, aforetime* at the beginning of a new one to link it to the last. For instance, here are sentences from Matt. vii 23-25:

THONNE CWETHE IC TO HIM THÆT IC EOW NÆFRE NE CUTHE .... EORNOSTLICE, ÆLC THÆRA THE THAS MINE WORD GE-HYRTH AND THA WYRCTH BITH GELIC THAM WISAN WERE, SE HIS HUS OFER STAN GETIMBRODE. THA COM THÆR REN AND MYCELE FLOD AND THÆR BLEOWUN WINDAS .... AND HIT NA NE FEOLL, SOTHLICE HIT WÆS OFER STAN GETIMBROD.

Then quoth I to him that I never nay could (=knew) you .... Earnestly, each of those that these mine words heareth and them worketh, beeth like the wise (one) who his house over stone timbered. Then came there rain and muckle flood and there blew winds .... and it fell not. Soothly (truly), it was over stone timbered.

Sometimes, recurrence of EORNOSTLICE, WITODLICE, SOTHLICE (*soothly*) and the like in the gospel story becomes a little tedious, as when people begin every other sentence with *frankly*; but the trick, carried over into the English Bible of A.D. 1611 as *verily, therefore, of a truth*, etc., has set a salutary pattern. It has preserved the written language as a means of lucid human communication, and prevented it from degenerating into a crossword puzzle of the sort one meets in a modern German scientific treatise. To know when to end a sentence with a full stop and to start the next with *So* or *Thus* is the A.B.C. of writing clear, forceful, informative English.

One item the last citation contains might at first fox the reader: CUTHE = *could*. In all Teutonic languages, there are two verbs which are equivalent to *know*:

OLD ENGLISH	DUTCH	GERMAN	SWEDISH	DANISH
WITAN	WETEN	WISSEN	VETA	VIDE
CUNNAN	KENNEN	KENNEN	KÄNNA	KENDE

O.E. also had CNAWAN. WITAN persisted throughout (*he wot, he wist*) as in the King James Bible, but has now made way for CNAWAN. The verb CUNNAN (IC CAN, IC CUTHE, etc.) has the sense of having the know-how, whence it has stayed on as *can—could*, but lingers in its original meaning *to con* in Scots *dinna ken*.* Between *kan* and *känner* in Swedish there is still common territory. Somewhat oddly, most languages of the Indo-European family have two words for *know* with the same somewhat different flavour as WITAN and CUNNAN, in French *savoir* (*know = understand*) and *connaître* (*know = be acquainted with*), in Welsh

---

* The original meaning of CAN—CUTHE also survives in the words *cunning* and *uncouth*.

gwybod (=*savoir*) and *adnabod* (=*connaître*). In O.E., the semantic equivalent of *can—could* was MÆG—MIHTE. The latter survive with a different meaning implying possibility (as in *it may, or might, happen*) or permissibility (as in *what may, or might, one say?*). Comparable changes of meaning of auxiliaries, as of the particles in all the Teutonic group, account for the fact that ancestrally equivalent words of these classes sometimes have very different meanings.

In this context, it is relevant to recall a usage common to Tudor, Middle and Old English *en rapport* with both that of French and that of Teutonic languages other than Anglo-Saxon. Anglo-American uses the verb *have* etc. to form past constructions with *all* verbs except other helpers; but the English of the King James Bible adheres to an earlier pattern which prescribes the use of *be* etc. in similar situations, if the verb denotes *motion*, as in: *when that which is perfect is come.*

QUIZ CORNER 5

Quiz 1

Study the O.E. (A.D. 1000) and Icelandic (like Old Norse) forms of *that—those—the ones* (above) and *he—it—she* (below):

A. OLD ENGLISH				B. ICELANDIC			
1. SE	5. THÆT	9. SEO		1. SA	5. THATH	9. SU	
2. THONE	6. THÆT	10. THA		2. THANN	6. THATH	10. THA	
3. THÆS	7. THÆS	11. THÆRE		3. THESS	7. THESS	11. THEIRRAR	
4. THAM	8. THAM	12. THÆRE		4. THEIM	8. THVI	12. THEIRRI	

13. THA		13. THEIR	15. THAU	19. THÆR	
14. THA		14. THA	16. THAU	20. THÆR	
15. THÆRA			17. THEIRRA		
16. THAM			18. THEIM		

A. OLD ENGLISH				B. ICELANDIC			
17. HE	21. HIT	25. HIO		21. HANN	25. THATH	29. HUN	
18. HINE	22. HIT	26. HIE		22. HANN	26. THATH	30. HANA	
19. HIS	23. HIS	27. HIRE		23. HANS	27. THESS	31. HENNAR	
20. HIM	24. HIM	28. HIRE		24. HONUM	28. THVI	32. HENNI	

29. HIE		33. THEIR	35. THAU	39. THÆR	
30. HIE		34. THA	36. THAU	40. THÆR	
31. HIRA			37. THEIRRA		
32. HIM			38. THEIM		

Now fill in as for HE, etc., what may have been the ancestors of:

WYCLIFFE (A.D. 1380)				TYNDALE (A.D. 1526)		
he 17A	it	she		he	it	she ......
him 20A	it	hire		him	it	her ......
his 19A	his	hire		his	his	her ......
him 20A	him	hire		him	him	her ......

THEI	THEY	THE ......
HEM	THEM	THAT ......
HIRE	THEIR	
HEM	THEM	

Now use the following code to fill in the meaning of each word below: 1. *whose?* 2. *what?* 3. *whom?* 4. *who?*

HWÆT (......)   HWA (......)   HWONE (......)
HWÆS (......)   HWÆM (......)

Quiz 2

Case

Study the simple sentences and phrases in O.E. given below. In each example ask yourself which personal pronoun of Modern English would replace THES HUND in its several disguises.

HE SEAH THISNE HUND : THES HUND SEAH HINE
HE SEAH THAS HUNDAS : THAS HUNDAS SAWON HINE

WE GEAFON THISSUM HUNDE : WE GEAFON THISSUM HUNDUM
BAN   WÆTER

THURH THISNE HUND : WITHUTAN THISSUM HUNDE
THURH THAS HUNDAS : WITHUTAN THISSUM HUNDUM

GEONDAN THISNE HUND : FRAM THISSUM HUNDE
GEONDAN THAS HUNDAS : FRAM THISSUM HUNDUM

UNDERNEOTHAN THISNE HUND : OFER THISSUM HUNDE
UNDERNEOTHAN THAS HUNDAS : OFER THISSUM HUNDUM

THISSES HUNDES EARE
THISSA HUNDA EARAN

You will now see that there are two forms of THES and HUND for which we can put *him* and two forms for which we can put *them*. For one of the *him*-forms we can also use *to him* and for one of the *them*-forms *to them*. This form is also the one used after nearly all prepositions, i.e. words such as *from, with, after* in Modern English. An exception is the O.E. equivalent for *through*. Now fill in:

1. HE   THES HUND   5. *they*   ....
2. HINE   ....   6. *them*   ....
3. HIS   ....   7. *theirs* ....
4. HIM   ....   8. *to them* ....

Quiz 3

Case and Gender

I. Quiz 1 shows you the singular and plural case forms of O.E. THÆT, etc. O.E. adjectives had in all nine case forms singular and plural, some used only after a pronoun such as THIS or THÆT, etc., and MIN, THIN, URE, IOWER, etc., others used in all other situations.

Remember that THURH (*through*) comes before HINE, FRAM before HIM. After studying the key sentences, fill in the blanks of the following by reference to the code on p. 193:

MODEL LAY-OUT			*After* THÆT, MIN, *etc.*				*Otherwise*	
HE	HIT	HEO	BLIND	......	......		BLIND	......	......
HINE	HIT	HIE	......	......	......	......	......	......
HIS	*its*	HIRE	......	......	......	......	......	......
HIM	*to it*	HIRE	......	......	......	......	......	......
	they			......			......	
	them			......			......	
	theirs			......			......	
	to them			......			......	

II. In O.E. the noun might appear in as many as six disguises where at most (*man, man's, men, men's*) we have four and usually (*house—houses*) two only. There are four main classes:

A. the typical masculine (*he*-word) such as HUND;
B. the typical feminine (*she*-word) such as HENN;
C. the typical neuter (*it*-word) such as SCEAP, WÆTER or BAN;
D. a so-called weak class including some masculine names (such as DOCGA), some feminine (such as TUNGE), and some neuter (such as EAGE). Fill in the pattern from the code below.

HUND	HENN	SCEAP	DOCGA
......	......	......	......
......	......	......	......
......	......	......	......

HUND	HENN	SCEAP	DOCGA
......	......	......	......
—	—	—	—
......	......	......	......
......	......	......	......
......	......	......	......
......	......	......	......

Code:

1. BLIND 2. BLINDE 3. BLINDA 4. BLINDNE 5. BLINDES 6. BLINDAN
7. BLINDUM 8. BLINDRE 9. BLINDRA

10. HUND 11. HUNDE 12. HUNDES 13. HUNDUM 14. HUNDA
15. HUNDAS

16. HENN 17. HENNE 18. HENNA 19. HENNUM

20. SCEAP 21. SCEAPE 22. SCEAPA 23. SCEAPUM

24. DOCGA 25. DOCGUM 26. DOCGENA 27. DOCGAN

SE HUND (*or* DOCGA) IS BLIND
SEO HENN WÆS BLIND
THÆT SCEAP IS BLIND

THA HUNDAS (*or* DOCGAN) SINT
  BLINDE
THA HENNA WÆRON BLINDA
THA SCEAP WÆRON BLIND

WE SAWON BLINDNE HUND (*or*
  DOCGAN)
WE SAWON BLINDE HENNE
WE SAWON BLIND SCEAP

WE SAWON SIX BLINDE HUNDAS
  (*or* DOCGA)
WE SAWON SIX BLINDA HENNA
WE SAWON SIX BLIND SCEAP

BLINDES HUNDES (*or* DOCGAN)
  BAN
BLINDRE HENNE TUNGE
BLINDES SCEAPES EAGE

SIX BLINDRA HUNDA (*or* DOC-
  GENA) BAN
SIX BLINDRA HENNA TUNGAN
SIX BLINDRA SCEAPA EAGAN

FRAM BLINDUM HUNDE

FRAM SIX BLINDUM HUNDUM
  (*or* DOCGUM)

FRAM BLINDRE HENNE
FRAM BLINDUM SCEAPE

FRAM SIX BLINDUM HENNUM
FRAM SIX BLINDUM SCEAPUM

SE BLINDA HUND (DOCGA) WÆS DEAF

THA BLINDAN HUNDAS (DOC-GAN) WÆRON HÆR

SEO BLINDE HENN WÆS EALD

THA BLINDAN HENNA WÆRON THÆR

THÆT BLINDE SCEAP WÆS DEAD

THA BLINDAN SCEAP WÆRON DEAD

WE SAWON THONE BLINDAN HUND (DOCGAN)

WE SAWON THA BLINDAN HUNDAS (DOCGAN)

WE SAWON THA BLINDAN HENNE

WE SAWON THA BLINDAN HENNA

WE SAWON THÆT BLINDE SCEAP

WE SAWON THA BLINDAN SCEAP

WE GEAFON THAM BLINDAN HUNDE (DOCGAN) BAN
WE GEAFON THAM BLINDUM HUNDUM (DOCGUM) BAN

WE GEAFON THÆRE BLINDAN HENNE WÆTER
WE GEAFON THAM BLINDUM HENNUM WÆTER

WE GEAFON THAM BLINDAN SCEAPE WÆTER
WE GEAFON THAM BLINDUM SCEAPUM WÆTER

THÆS BLINDAN HUNDES (DOCGAN) BAN
THÆRA BLINDRA HUNDA (DOCGENA) BAN

THÆRA BLINDAN HENNE EAGE
THÆRA BLINDRA HENNA EAGAN

THÆS BLINDAN SCEAPES TUNGE
THÆRA BLINDRA SCEAPA TUNGAN

Quiz 4

The English of Edward the Confessor

Clues: GE- before a consonant has disappeared, and final -G, now soundless, is Y in print.

1. Thæt hus is **geræde**. Hit is wearm mid tham the hit is ceald withut**an**, and we habbath mete til ur**um** giest**um**.

2. Min sweostor is **gecumen** mid hire freond, ac eower modor ne is hier giet.

3. Se freond hæfth **gebroht** lytelne hund se the is hwit and sweart. Hio hæfth æc hire hors.

4. Ic am glæd for the hio brohte thæt hors. Se weg to hire hame is lang. Hio ne wille faran thider ærlice to-niht.

5. Nu hiere ic eowere modor cumende. We will**ath** beginn**an** swa sona swa hio bith **geræde**.

6. Wilt thu sing**an** to us? Gea, thæt wille ic don. Thu canst tha word.

7. Ne far, sægde thæt mægden, ræst
Thin werigne heafod uppan thissum breoste.
Tear wæs in his beorhtan eagan.
Æfre andsweriode he sicende.
Ic wille upweard gan.

8. Sothlice, can ic tha word ac thes ne is ende. Ic hæbbe tha word in thære sangbec. Ic wille bringan hie.

9. Ic hæfde ne gesawen thas boc ær. Heo is god. Ic am glæd for the thu hie hæfst. Hwa wrat hie?

10. Ic ne wat. Min brothor hæfth othre. Gif thu wyscst, ber hie onweg. Thu meaht habban hie.

Quiz 5

The Anglo-Saxon Gospels (A.D. 950)

Fill in the chapter and verse of each of the following:

Note: The scribes were not consistent about spelling. In particular we may find Y for I and *vice versa* for one and the same word on the same page. Here we use I where I and Y were interchangeable. Contractions such as *nis* for *ne is* (=*isn't*) also occur in the text. The words are here in full.

1. God mann sothlice of godum gold-horde bringth god forth, and yfel mann of yfelum gold-horde bringth yfel forth.

   Sothlice ic secge eow thæt ælc idel word the menn sprecath, hi agyldath gescead be tham on domes dæge.

   Matt. .... Verses ......

2. Tha cwæth se Hælend to Simon Petre, Simon Johannis, lufast thu me swithor thonne thas? He cwæth to him, Gea Drihten, thu wast thæt ic the lufige. He cwæth to him, Heald mine lamb.

   He cwæth eft to him, Simon Johannis, lufast thu me? He cwæth to him, Gea Drihten, thu wast thæt ic the lufige.

   Tha cwæth he to him, Heald mine lamb.

   He cwæth thriddan sithe to him, Simon Johannis, lufast thu me? Tha wæs Petrus sarig fortham the he cwæth thriddan sithe to him, Lufast thu me, and he cwæth to him, Drihten, thu wast ealle thing. Thu wast thæt ic the lufige. Tha cwæth he to him, Heald mine sceap.

   John .... Verses ......

3. Ge gehyrdon thæt gecweden wæs, Lufa thinne nextan and hata thinne feond. Sothlice, ic secge eow, lufiath eowre find and doth wel tham the eow yfel doth. ...

   Matt. .... Verses ......

4. Tha sæde he him, Thæt tha thing the of tham men gath, tha hine besmitath. Innan, of manna heortan yfele gethancas cumath.

   Mark .... Verses ......

5. And swa ge willath thæt eow men don, doth him gelice. And hwilc thanc is eow, gif ge lufiath tha the eow lufiath? Sothlice sinfulle lufiath tha the hi lufiath.

   And gif ge wel doth tham the eow wel doth, hwilc thanc is eow? Witodlice, thaet doth sinfulle.

   Luke .... Verses ......

6. Sothlice, Johannes com ne etende ne drincende, and hi cwædun, He hæfth deoful-seocnysse.

   Mannes sunu com etende and drincende, and hi cwethath Her is ettul-man and win-drincende, manfulra and sinfulra freond. And wisdom is gerihtwisud fram heora bearnum.

   Matt. .... Verses ......

7. Ic arise and ic fare to minum fæder and ic secge him, Eala fæder, ic syngode on heofenas and beforan the.

Nu ic ne eom wyrthe thæt ic beo thin sunu genemned, do me swa anne of thinum hyrlingum.

And he aras tha and com to his fæder. And tha gyt tha he wæs feor, his fæder hine geseah and wearth mid mild-heortnesse astyrod.

Luke .... Verses ......

8. Thar wæron sume of tham bocerum sittende and on heora heortan thencende.

Hwi spicth thes thus? He dysegath, hwa mæg sinna forgifan buton God ana? Tha se Hælend thæt on his gaste oncneow thæt hi swa betwux him thohton, he cwæth to him, Hwi thence ge thas thing on eowrum heortum?

Hwæther is ethre to secgenne to tham laman, The sind thine sinna forgifene, hwæther the cwethan, Aris nim thin bed and ga?

Thæt ge sothlice witon thæt mannes sunu hæfth anweald on eorthan sinna to forgifanne, he cwæth to tham laman,

The ic secge, Aris, nim thin bed and ga to thinum huse.

Mark .... Verses ......

9. Tha genealæhte him an bocere and cwæth, Lareow, ic fylige the, swa hwæder swa thu færst.

Tha cwæth se Hælend to him, Foxas habbath holu, and heofenan fuglas nest, sothlice mannes sunu ne hæfth hwær he his heafod ahylde.

Tha cwæth to him other of his leorning-cnihtum, Drihten, alyfe me ærest to farenne and bebyrigean minne fæder.

Tha cwæth se Hælend to him, Fylig me and læt deade bebyrigean hira deadan. And he astah on scip and his leorning-cnihtas him fyligdon.

Matt. .... Verses ......

10. And tha he in-eode, he cwæth, Hwi sind ge gedrefede and wepath? Ne is this mæden na dead, ac heo slæpth.

Tha tældon hi hine. He tha, eallum ut-adrifenum, nam thæs mædenes moder, and tha the mid him wæron and inn-eodon suwiende, thar thæt mæden wæs. And hire hand nam and cwæth . . . Mæden, the ic secge, Aris. And heo sona aras and eode. Sothlice, heo wæs twelf wintre. And ealle hi wundredon mycelre wundrunge.

Mark .... Verses ......

11. Andswariath me and ic secge eow thonne on hwilcum anwealde ic this do.
Hwether wæs Johannes fulluht the of heofone, the of mannum? Andswariath me.
Tha thohton hi and cwædon betweox him, Gif we secgath of heofone, he segth
us, Hwi ne gelyfde ge him?
Gif we secgath of mannum, we ondrædath this folc.
Ealle hi hæfdon Johannem thæt he wære sothlice witega.
Tha andswaredon hi tham Hælende and cwædon, We ne witon. Tha cwæth
se Hælend. Ne ic eow ne secge on hwilcum anwealde ic thas thing do.

Mark .... Verses ......

12. Behealdath heofonan fuglas, fortham the hig ne sawath, ne hig ne ripath, ne hig
ne gadriath on berne, and eower heofonlica fæder hig fet.

Matt. .... Verses ......

13. Sona tha an wif, be him gehyrde, thære dohtor hæfde unclænne gast, heo
in-eode and to his fotum hi astrehte. Sothlice thæt wif wæs hæthen, Siro-
fenisces cynnes. And bæd hine, thæt he thone deofol of hire dehter adrife. Tha
sæde he hire, Læt ærest tha bearn beon gefilled.
Ne is na god thæt man nime thara bearna hlaf and hundum werpe.
Tha andswarode heo, and cwæth, Drihten thæt is soth.
Witodlice tha hwelpas etath under thære mysan of thara cilda cruman.

Mark .... Verse ......

14. Sume tha Pharisei cwædon, Ne is thes man of Gode the reste-dæg ne hylt.
Sume cwædon, Hu mæg sinful man thas tacn wyrcan? And hig fliton him
betweonan.
Hig cwædon eft to tham blindan, Hwæt segst thu be tham, the thine eagan
untynde. He cwæth, He is witega . . .
Tha clypedon hig eft thone man the ær blind wæs, and cwædon to him, Sege
Gode wuldor. We witon thæt he is sinful.
And he cwæth, Gif he sinful is, thæt ic ne wat. An thing ic wat, thæt ic wæs
blind and thæt ic nu geseo.

John .... Verses ......

15. Eagan ge habbath and ne geseoth, and earan and ne gehyrath. Ne ge ne
thencath.
Hwænne ic bræc fif hlafas and twegen fixas, and hu fela wyligena ge namon
fulle? Hi cwædon tha, Twelfe.

Mark .... Verses ......

16. And ælc thæra the gehyrth thas mine word and tha ne wyrcth se bith gelic tham dysigan men the getimbrode his hus ofer sand-ceosel.

   Tha rinde hit and thær comun flod and bleowun windas . . . and thæt hus feoll.

   Matt. . . . . Verses . . . . . .

17. Moyses us wrat, gif hwæs brothor dead bith and læfth his wif and ne hæfth nan bearn, thæt his brothor nime his wif and his brothor sæd wecce.

   Eornostlice seofon gebrothru wæron, and se æresta nam wif and wearth dead na læfedum sæde.

   And tha nam se other hi and wearth dead, ne se sæd ne læfde. Gelice se thridda.

   And ealle seofon hi hæfdon and sæd ne læfdon.

   Ealra æftemest tha forthferde thæt wif.

   On tham æriste, hwilces thara seofona bith thæt wif?

   Hi ealle hi hæfdon.

   Tha andswarode him se Hælend . . . Sothlice thonne hi of deathe arisath, ne wifiath hi, ne ne giftiath, ac hi sind swilce Godes englas on heofonum.

   Mark . . . . Verses . . . . . .

18. Tha brohton hi him. Tha sæde he him, Hwæs is theos anlicnys and this gewrit? Hi cwædon, Thæs Caseres.

   Tha cwæth se Hælend to him, Agifath tham Casere tha thing the thæs Caseres sind, and Gode tha the Godes sind.

   Mark . . . . Verses . . . . . .

19. Tha andswarode se hundredes ealdor and thus cwæth. Drihten ne eom ic wyrthe thæt thu ingange under mine thecene; ac cweth thin an word and min cnapa bith gehæled. Sothlice ic eom man under anwealde geset and ic hæbbe thegnas under me, and ic cwethe to thisum, Gang, and he gæth; and ic cwethe to othrum, Cum, and he cymth; to minum theowe, Wyrc this, and he wyrcth.

   Matt. . . . . Verses . . . . . .

20. Thas thing he cwæth and siththan he cwæth to him, Lazarus ure freond slæpth, ac ic wille gan and awreccan hine of slæpe.

   His leorning-cnihtas cwædon. Drihten, gif he slæpth he bith hal . . .

   Tha cwæth se Hælend openlice to him, Lazarus is dead . . . Tha cwæth Martha to tham Hælende, Drihten gif thu wære her, ne wære min brothor dead . . . Tha cwæth se Hælend to hire, Thin brothor arist.

And Martha cwæth to him, Ic wat thæt he arist on tham ytemestan dæge.

And se Hælend cwæth to hire, Ic eom ærist and lif.

Se the gelifth on me, theah he dead sy, he leofath . . .

And tha heo thas thing sæde, heo eode and clypode digollice Marian hire swustor thus cwethende, Her is ure lareow and clypath the.

John . . . . Verses . . . . . .

21. And he com to his leorning-cnihtum, and he gemette hig slæpende. And he sæde Petre, Swa ne mihte ge nu wacian ane tid mid me?

Waciath and gebiddath eow thæt ge in ne gan on costnunge. Witodlice se gast is hræd and thæt flæsc is untrum. Eft othre sithe he ferde and hine gebæd and cwæth, Min fæder gif thes calic ne mæge gewitan, buton ic hine drince, gewurthe thin willa.

And he com eft, and gemette hig slæpende. Sothlice heora eagan wæron gehefegode.

Matt. . . . . Verses . . . . . .

22. Tha Maria com thar se Hælend wæs, and heo hine geseah, heo feoll to his fotum and cwæth to him, Drihten gif thu wære her, ne wære min brothor dead.

Tha se Hælend geseah thæt heo weop and thæt tha Judeas weopon the mid hire comon, he geomrode on his gaste . . . And cwæth, Hwar lede ge hine? Hig cwædon to him, Drihten, ga and geseoh.

And se Hælend weop.

And tha Judeas cwædon, Loca nu, hu he hine lufode . . .

And se Hælend cwæth, Doth aweg thone stan. Tha cwæth Martha to him, thæs swustor the thar dead wæs, Drihten nu he stincth, he wæs for feower dagum dead.

Se Hælend cwæth to hire, Hu ne sæde ic the thæt thu gesyhst Godes wuldor gif thu gelifst?

Tha dydon hig aweg thone stan . . . Se Hælend ahof his eagan up and cwæth, Fæder, ic do thancas the, fortham thu gehyrdest me . . . Tha he thas thing sæde, he clypode mycelre stefne, Lazarus, ga ut.

And sona stop forth se the dead wæs, gebunden handum and fotum . . . Tha cwæth se Hælend to him, Unbindath hine and lætath gan.

John . . . . Verses . . . . . .

23. And he cwæth, Godes rice is swilce man wurthe god sæd on his land and sawe. And arise dæges and nihtes, and thæt sæd growe and wexe, thonne he ne wat. Sothlice sylf-willes seo eorthe wæstm berath, ærest gærs, siththan ear, siththan fulne hwæte on tham eare.   Mark ....   Verses ......

24. Tha cwædon sume tha boceras him betwinan. Thes sprycth bysmor-spræce. Tha se Hælend geseah hira gethanc tha cwæth he. To hwi thence ge yfel on eowrum heortum?

    Hwæt is eathelicre to cwethenne, De beoth forgifene thine sinna oththe to cwethanne, Aris and ga?
    Thæt ge sothlice witon thæt mannes sunu hæfth anweald on eorthan sinna to forgifenne, tha cwæth he to tham laman, Aris, nim thin bedd and gang on thin hus.
    And he aras and ferde to his huse.   Matt. ....   Verses ......

25. Tha wæs him broht an deofol-seoc man se wæs blind and dumb, and he hine hælde swa thæt he spræc and geseah.   Matt. ....   Verses ......

26. Ut eode se sædere his sæd to sawenne. And tha he sew, sum feoll with thone weg and fugelas comon and hit fræton. Sum feoll ofer stan-scyligean thar hit ne hæfde mycele eorthan; and sona upeode fortham the hit ne hæfde eorthan thiccnesse.
    Tha hit up-eode, seo sunne hit forswælde; and hit forscranc, fortham hit wyrtruman ne hæfde.
    And sum feoll on thornas, tha stigon tha thornas and forthrysmodon thæt, and hit wæstm ne bær.
    And sum feoll on god land, and hit sealde uppstigende, and wexende, wæstm; and an brohte thritig-fealdne, sum sixtig-fealdne, sum hund-fealdne.
    And he cwæth, Gehire, se the earan hæbbe to gehiranne.   Mark ....   Verses ......

27. Tha cwæth he, Sylle ge him etan. Tha cwædon hi, Uton gan and mid twam hundred penegum hlafas bicgan and we him etan syllath.
    Tha cwæth he, Hu fela hlafa hæbbe ge? Gath and lociath. And tha hi wiston, hi cwædon, Fif hlafas and twegen fixas. And tha bebead se Hælend thæt thæt folc sæte ofer thæt grene hig.   Mark ....   Verses ......

28. Tha cwæth sum to him, Witodlice! thin modur and thine gebrothra standath her ute, the secende.

And he andswarode him secgendum and cwæth, Hwilc is min modur and hwilce sint mine gebrothra?

Witodlice, swa hwilc swa wyrcth mines fæder willan the on heofenan is, he is min brothur and min swustor and modor.

Matt. .... Verses ......

29. And thonne ge standath eow to gebiddenne, forgifath gif ge hwæt agen ænigne habbath thæt eow eower sinna forgife, eower heofonlica fæder se the on heofonum is.

Gif ge ne forgifath, ne eow eower sinna ne forgifth eower fæder.

Mark .... Verses ......

30. Tha cwædon tha bisceopas to Pilate, Ne writ thu Judea cyning, ac thæt he cwæde, Ic eom Judea cyning.

Tha cwæth Pilatus, Ic wrat thæt ic wrat.

John .... Verses ......

31. Johannes him sæde, Ne is the alyfed hi to wife to hæbbenne.

And tha he hine ofslean wolde, he adred him thæt folc, fortham the hig hæfdon hine for ænne witegan. Tha on Herodes gebyrd-dæge tumbude thære Herodiadiscean dohtur beforan him and hit licode Herode.

Matt. .... Verses ......

32. Tha cwæth he, Hwæt axast thu me be gode? An God is god. Sothlice gif thu wilt on lif becuman, heald tha beboda. Tha cwæth he, Hwilce? Tha cwæth se Hælend.

Ne do thu mann-sliht, ne do thu unriht-hæmed, ne stel thu, ne sege thu lease gewittnisse.

Wurtha thinne fæder and modor, and lufa thinne nehstan swa the silfne.

Tha cwæth se geonga, Eall this ic geheold. Hwæt is me git wana?

Matt. .... Verses ......

33. Tha he genealæhte Hierusalem and Bethania to Olivetes dune, he sende his twegen leorning-cnihtas.

And cwæth to him, Farath to tham castele the ongen inc is and git thar sona gemetath assan folan getigedne, ofer thæne nan man gyt ne sæt. Untigeath hine and to me gelædath.

And gif hwa to inc hwæt cwyth, secgath thæt Drihten hæfth his neode and he hine sona hider læt.

And tha hi ut-ferdon, hi gemetton thone folan ute on twycenan beforan dura getigedne. Tha untigdon hi hine.

And sume the thar stodon thus sædon him, Hwæt do git, thone folan untigende?

Tha cwædon hi, swa se Hælend unc bead.

Mark .... Verses ......

34. And tha sæton twegen blinde with thone weg, and gehyrdon thæt se Hælend ferde; and tha clypodon hig to him and cwædon, Drihten, gemiltsa unc, Dauides sunu ...

Tha stod se Hælend, and clypode hig to him, and cwæth, Hwæt wille git thæt ic inc do?

Tha cwædon hig Drihten, thæt uncre eagan sin ge-oponede.

Matt. .... Verses ......

35. Witodlice, æfter tham the ic of deathe arise, ic cume to eow on Galilea.

Tha andswyrde Petrus him and thus cwæth. Theah the hig ealle ge-untreowsion on the, ic næfre ne ge-untreowsige. Tha cwæth se Hælend, Soth ic secge the thæt on thissere nihte ærtham the cocc crawe thriwa thu withsæcst min.

Matt. .... Verses ......

36. Tha cwædon hig to him, Hu wæron thine eagan ge-openede.

He andswarode and cwæth, Se man the is genemned Hælend worhte fenn and smyrede mine eagan and cwæth to me, Ga to Syloes mere and thweah the, and ic eode and thwoh me and geseah.

Tha cwædon hig to him, Hwar is he? Tha cwæth he, Ic ne wat.

John .... Verses ......

37. Theof ne cymth buton thæt he stele and slea and fordo.

Ic com to tham thæt hig habbon lif and habbon genoh.

Ic eom god hirde. God hirde sylth his lif for his sceapum.

John .... Verses ......

38. Tha andswarodun hig we ne habbath her buton fif hlafas and twegen fixas.

Tha cwæth se Hælend, Bringath me hider tha.

Matt. .... Verses ......

39. And he cwæth to his leorning-cnihtum, Ne sy eower heorte gedrefed. Ge gelifath on God and gelifath on me . . .

And ge witon hwider ic fare and ge cunnon thone weg.

Thomas cwæth to him, Drihten, we ne witon hwider thu færst and hu mage we thone weg cunnan?

Se Hælend cwæth to him. Ic eom weg and sothfæstnis and lif, ne cymth nan to fæder buton thurh me.

Gif ge cuthon me, witodlice ge cuthon minne fæder and heononforth ge hine gecnawath and ge hine gesawon.

Phillipus cwæth to him, Drihten æt-yw us thone fæder and we habbath genoh.

Se Hælend cwæth to him, Phillipus, swa lange tid ic wæs mid eow and ge ne gecneowon me? Se the me gesyhth, gesyhth minne fæder.

John .... Verses ......

40. Witodlice, swa swa Jonas wæs on thæs hwæles innothe thri dagas and threo niht, swa bith mannes sunu on eorthan heortan thri dagas and threo niht.

Matt. .... Verses ......

41. Thær twegen oththe thri sint on minum naman gegaderode, thær ic eom on hira midlene.

Matt. .... Verses ......

42. Siththan he sæde, Thome, do thinne finger hider and geseoh mine handa, and nim thine hand and do on mine sidan and ne beo thu ungeleafful ac geleafful.

Thomas andswarode and cwæth to him, Thu eart min God and min Drihten.

Se Hælend cwæth to him, Thu gelifdest fortham thu me gesawe. Tha sind eadige, the ne gesawon and gelifdon.

Witodlice manege othre tacen se Hælend worhte on his leorning-cnihta gesyhthe, the ne sind on thisse bec awritene. Witodlice thas thing sind awritene thæt ge gelifon and thæt ge habbon ece lif thonne ge gelifath on his naman.

John .... Verses ......

6

Likenesses and Differences among the Sister Languages

People capable of learning anything easily, except how to think for oneself, if English-speaking with a smattering of French and of German, may not have noticed certain features common to both and some striking differences between the one and the other. It will be a fitting prelude to further familiarity with the New Look with which the English language confronts us in the pages of Chaucer or of the Wycliffe Bible in the latter years of the fourteenth century, if we now take stock of these likenesses and differences.

We may start by considering the so-called articles; in Modern English *a* or *an* (indefinite) and *the* (definite). All the sister languages, Teutonic and Latin descendants alike, have corresponding terms, though more variegated owing to the persistence of different gender and, in the case of the definite article, of different number forms. On the other hand many members of the Indo-Germanic family have no words which answer precisely to the uses of either.

Thus there is nothing that corresponds to the indefinite article in Latin, Welsh or O.E., except when it is necessary to convey explicitly that a speaker or writer is referring to *one* thing only; and to do so is essential only when neither its name nor any word (verb or adjective) associated with it has a distinctive singular form, e.g. when one says *he saw a sheep in the field*. In short, a so-called indefinite article is merely an overworked numeral, viz. unity. In the sister and half-sister languages, forms of the so-called indefinite article, French *un—une*, Italian *un(o)—una*, Scandinavian *en—et(t)*, Dutch *een* and German *ein* etc., are not indeed distinguishable from the equivalent of our word *one*, the latter being a corruption of the equivalent O.E. word AN. It has now lost its final N before another consonant, just as O.E. MIN (=*mine*) becomes *my* before a consonant in late Middle English, and eventually retains the *n* only when no noun follows it (e.g. *this is mine*). It should not therefore surprise us to learn that our Anglo-Saxon ancestors used AN only where we might now use *one* as an alternative. It is well to remember this, because few tricks tend to make English style more drastically congested than does indiscriminate use of the articles.

This is especially true of inserting *the* except where custom dictates its necessity. What we call the definite article in English or its sister languages is nothing more nor less than a demonstrative which has come down in the world; and where not used as a demonstrative, it is merely what the Chinese call an *empty* word. The origin of the definite articles in the descendants of Latin we can trace to their source during the period when the end of the Western Empire was in sight. In the parent language there were three demonstratives, each with more or less distinctive case and number forms for each of the three genders, of which the masculine has absorbed the neuter. The one which here concerns us is the one whose: (a) nominative singular forms are *ille* (masc.) and *illa* (fem.); (b) nominative plural forms are *illi* (masc.) and *illae* (fem.); (c) accusative plural forms are *illos* (masc.) and *illas* (fem.); (d) genitive plural forms are *illorum* (masc.) and *illarum* (fem.).

As our Museum Exhibit (p. 207) shows, we can derive all the definite articles of modern descendants of Latin by breaking up one or other of these, e.g. IL-LE, IL-LOS, etc. The only entry which might puzzle the reader is the Italian feminine plural LE, short for ILLAE (nom. fem. plur.). Each is translatable by the invariant Modern English *the*; but a Roman orator would use one of the ancestral forms only where we should use *that* (*one*) or *those* (*ones*).

It is indeed important to realise that our Roman orator, or for that matter any educated Roman citizen at the beginning of our era, did not usually pepper his sentences with *ille*, etc., as recklessly as the French, Italian or Spanish speakers to whom Latin bequeathed them use their definite articles. Nor is degradation of demonstratives in daily use peculiar to descendants of Latin. In the history of language, it happens again and again, each time to make way for a newcomer. Lucklessly, it is happening in contemporary English as one deplorable consequence of the military occupation of Britain by the United States of America (1943 onwards). Thus the following is a type specimen of General Intake Idiom now widely current especially in U.K. Midlands: "*I went into this* (hitherto unmentioned) *shop, and this* (not previously referred to) *man at the counter . . .*". That we can here (more acceptably) replace each *this* by the indefinite article suffices to show that neither has any demonstrative value, i.e. as *pointing* to anything in the preceding context.

Before we look at the downgrade process at work in O.E. and other Teutonic languages, it will be wise to take stock of another way in which demonstratives acquire new usage with no corrosion of meaning. Older Indo-European languages, including Caesar's Latin, had no unique personal pronouns which tally with *he—him, she—her* and *they—them*. To convey their meaning a Roman orator or writer used one of three demonstratives: (a) *ille—illa*, etc.; (b) *iste—ista*, etc.; (c) *is—ea*, etc., where we might write *this one* for *he, she, it*, etc. In provincial daily Roman speech we may assume that *ille*, etc., was the most popular with this end in view. Hence, with the exception of the Italian equivalent of *they*, words for *he, her, them*, etc., in modern descendants of Latin ring the changes on the same flexional forms as the definite article. The reader can see this by comparing Romance pronouns of the third person and Romance definite articles tabulated in the Museum Exhibit on the next page with their Latin ancestors.

MUSEUM EXHIBIT—THE ROMANCE PRONOUN OF THE THIRD PERSON

In the following two lines, we see nine of the fourteen flexional forms of the ancestral Latin demonstrative equivalent to *that—those*:

Masc. Sing. ILLE, ILLI, ILLO	*Fem. Sing.* ILLA, ILLI
Masc. Plur. ILLI, ILLOS, ILLORUM	*Fem. Plur.* ILLAE, ILLAS, ILLARUM

The next exhibit shows the flexional forms of the Romance equivalent of the definite article (English *the*):

	Masc. Sing.	Fem. Sing.	Masc. Plur.	Fem. Plur.
FRENCH	LE	LA	LES	
ITALIAN	IL	LA	I	LE
SPANISH	EL	LA	LOS	LAS

Compare with the above the forms of the Romance pronoun of the third person:*

	FRENCH	ITALIAN	SPANISH
he	IL	(ESSO)	EL
him	LE	LO	LO
to him	LUI	GLI	LE
she	ELLE	(ESSA)	ELLA
her	LA	LA	LA
to her	LA	LE	LE
they	ILS (m.), ELLES (f.)	ESSI (m.), ESSE (f.)	ELLOS (m.), ELLAS (f.)
them	LES	LI (m.), LE (f.)	LOS (m.), LAS (f.)
to them	LEUR	LORO	LES

However, the same family likeness does not emerge in the adjectival equivalents to the genitive case forms as below:

	FRENCH	ITALIAN	SPANISH
his, her, its	SON (m.s.)	SUO (m.s.)	SU
	SA (f.s.)	SUA (f.s.)	„
	SES (pl.)	SUOI (m. pl.)	„
		SUE (f. pl.)	„
their	LEUR-LEURS	LORO	„

---

* This does not include so-called disjunctive forms used when the pronoun is neither verb subject nor verb object.

While the first two entries of the last line recall the genitive plural forms ILLO-RUM, ILLARUM, the others clearly come from a different crib; and they exhibit a feature which is puzzling on first acquaintance, viz. *son—sa—ses*, etc., may each mean *his* or *her* or *its* in accordance with the gender of what follows. Thus in French:

> *son père*   = his *or* her father
> *sa mère*   = his *or* her mother
> *ses parents* = his *or* her parents

The explanation of this anomaly takes us back to another common ancestor. In the older Indo-Germanic languages, the only thing which answers to a personal pronoun in its own right is a reflexive S-form which admits of no distinction with respect to gender or number. Since there is nothing which uniquely answers to this in Anglo-American, and only a trace in early O.E., it is difficult to identify it without reference to usage in the sister languages. In Latin, as in French and Spanish, there is one and the same written form SE for *himself, herself, itself, themselves,* in such so-called *reflexive* constructions as *they washed themselves.* The Italian equivalent is SI. Latin had also a separate dative form SIBI, later supplanted by SE for such usage as: *she gave herself an ample helping.* However, Tudor English and Anglo-American *himself, herself, itself, themselves* are not intrinsically reflexive. They have also an *emphatic* and non-reflexive use, as when we say *he himself admitted it.*

In Latin we also find a genitive form SUI which we may translate as *his (her, its or their) own;* and since the essential characteristic of the reflexive illustrated above is that it refers back to the subject, the implication is here the same. SUI occurs only when it stands alone, as when we say *it was his* (etc.) *own;* but there are corresponding adjectival forms (as in *she remained in her own house*) distinguishable by gender, case and number—the nominative singular being *suus* (m.), *sua* (f.), *suum* (n.). The gender of these agrees with the noun they accompany, e.g. *house* in *his* (or *her*) *own house.* No ambiguity arose from this, since a Roman would use these forms only to refer back to the verb subject whose gender would be manifest. Otherwise, our Roman would use the genitive case form of a demonstrative. A trace of the latter (non-reflexive) use persists in LEUR(S) and LORO of p. 207. With this exception the entries are descendants of adjectival forms once, but no longer, with an exclusively reflexive meaning.

Let us now take a glance at what remains of the ancestral Indo-European reflexive pronoun in the Teutonic family. All Teutonic sisters of Anglo-American still have an S-form on all fours with Latin SE: *sig* in all Scandinavian dialects, *zich* in Dutch, *sich* in German. In Scandinavian dialects, there is a corresponding adjectival form, in Danish and Swedish *sin* (m. and f. sing.), *sit* or *sitt* (n. sing.) and *sine* or *sina* (plur.), all being *referable to the verb subject* in contradistinction to *hans* (his), *hendes* or *hennes* (her), *dets* or *dess* (its), *deres* or *deras* (their). Icelandic retains a dative form *sjer.* In Dutch *zijn(e)*, pronounced like its equivalent German *sein(e)*, corresponds to English *his*, but, like the relics of Latin SUI, etc., in its modern descendants, has lost its reflexive meaning. In O.E. no traces of the reflexive *sig*, *sich*, etc., remain, and only in its earliest phase do we meet the adjectival *sin*.

Having now had a look at the reflexive pronoun of the Teutonic clan, let us glance at the other Teutonic pronouns of the third person and at their relations to a demonstrative used where we might now use the definite article. From this point of view O.E. is very revealing because it preserves as pronouns of all three genders the several case, gender and number forms of a demonstrative which has left traces as such in Gothic, but has disappeared in German. In Dutch, the neuter singular article *het* pairs off with O.E. HIT (=*it*) but it is also the neuter singular form of the definite article for which *de* otherwise replaces Middle and later English *the*. The O.E. (HIT) form persisted into the beginning of the Tudor period, but we find it side by side with modern *it* in the Middle period. The Anglo-Saxon Bible has: *swa, hwylcne swa ic cysse, he hit ys* (Mark xiv. 44). The Wycliffe Bible here has: *whom euere I schal kisse, he it is*. In Tyndale's version this is: *whosoever I do kisse, he it is*. On the other hand, the disciples when charged *that won of you shall betraye me*, ask among themselves in Tyndale's version (Matt. xxvi. 22): *ys hit I, master?*

Our next Museum Exhibit shows the complete battery of this O.E. relic of what had been a demonstrative. The masculine forms have a peculiarly familiar aspect mentioned (p. 178) already. So have the neuter nominative and accusative case forms, if we drop the initial *h*. We may perhaps recognise at sight *hire* as the parent

MUSEUM EXHIBIT—THE TEUTONIC PERSONAL PRONOUN
OF THE THIRD PERSON

	OLD ENGLISH				MODERN ENGLISH			
	Masc.	Neut.	Fem.	Plur.	Masc.	Neut.	Fem.	Plur.
Nom.	HE	HIT	HEO	HIE	HE	IT	SHE	THEY
Acc.	HINE	HIT		HIE	HIM	IT		THEM
Gen.	HIS	HIRE	HIRA		HIS	ITS	HER	THEIR
Dat.	HIM	HIRE	HIM		HIM	IT	HER	THEM

FOSSIL REMAINS OF THE SIMPLE* DEMONSTRATIVE
(Parental Forms of THE, THAT, SHE, THEY, THEM, THEIR)

	GOTHIC			OLD ENGLISH			ICELANDIC		
	Masc.	Neut.	Fem.	Masc.	Neut.	Fem.	Masc.	Neut.	Fem.
Nom. Sing.	SA	THATA	SO	SE	THÆT	SEO	SA	†THAÐ	SU
Acc. Sing.	THANA	THATA	THO	THONE	THÆT	THA	THANN	†THAÐ	THA
Gen. Sing.	THIS	THIS	THIZOS	THÆS	THÆS	THÆRE	THESS	THESS	THEIRI
Dat. Sing.	THAMMA	THAMMA	THIZAI	THAM	THAM	THÆRE	THEIM	THVI	THEIRAR
Nom. Plur.	THAI	THO	THOS	THA	THA	THA	THEIR	THAU	THAER
Acc. Plur.	THANS	THO	THOS	THA	THA	THA	THA	THAU	THAER
Gen. Plur.	THIZE	THIZE	THIZO	THARA	THARA	THARA	THEIRRA	THEIRRA	THEIRRA
Dat. Plur.	THAIM	THAIM	THAIM	THAM	THAM	THAM	THEIM	THEIM	THEIM

---

* So-called because O.E. THES, etc. (and corresponding forms in Gothic and Old Norse) is a compound with the above and the suffix -SE.

† Ð = our *dh*-sound.

of *her*; but we look in vain for any clue to the ancestry of *its*, *she* and *they—them—their*. Just as the masculine dative HIM supplanted accusative HINE (p. 178), the accusative (H)IT supplanted dative HIM. We may dismiss *its* as a late sixteenth-century intruder seemingly due to an immigrant's mistake (*circa* A.D. 1598) accepted by his Elizabethan contemporaries as a welcome innovation. It is not in any issue of Shakespeare's plays printed before his death, and had not come into general use much before the time when Bunyan penned *The Pilgrim's Progress*. In its place *his* occurs in the first edition of the King James Bible (1611). Thus we meet: *put up again thy sword into his place* (Matt. xxvi. 52).

What is of more interest is the source of *she* for O.E. HEO, and of TH forms of the modern plural (*they*, etc.). To complete this part of our story, we need to take a look at the second part of the same Museum Exhibit. This shows the Gothic, O.E. and Icelandic forms of a demonstrative whose neuter singular form is the ancestor of Modern English *that*. In O.E., we often find the several forms of this demonstrative used as pronouns in much the same way that a Roman might use *ille*, etc., or *iste*, etc. Thus we read in the Anglo-Saxon Gospels: *he ge-hierth min word and tha wyrcth* (=he heareth my words and *those* worketh, i.e. does *them*). It was therefore entirely consistent with usage to use SEO, the feminine singular equivalent of *that one*, to replace the highly ambiguous HEO which had become indistinguishable from HIE for *they* in the period transitional to Middle English.

The example cited from the O.E. Gospels shows how a TH-form could supplant HIE for *them*; and here the process of replacement would gain impetus from contact with Scandinavian conquerors and settlers, especially in the North, where the change began. Our exhibit (p. 210) shows the Icelandic equivalents of the demonstrative battery from which *that* survives as such; but it does not show, as is true, that the *plural case forms in Icelandic are identical with those of the third person plural pronoun*. Clearly, HIE would make no contact with Old Norse *their*; but by dropping its final *r*, it would be recognisably equivalent to O.E. *tha*, whence *they*. Substitution of *they* for HIE occurred early in the transitional period from Old to Middle English, but replacement of *them* for the ambiguous *him* or *hem* and *their* for *hiera* or (by the beginning of the transitional period) *hiere* took place much later (between A.D. 1400 and 1500). Thus we read in the Wycliffe Bible (A.D. 1389) the following (Matt. vii. 27-29):

> And rayn came doun and floodis camen and wyndis blewen, and *thei* hurliden in to that hous . . . he was techynge *hem* as a man hauynge power, and nat as the scribis . . .

On the other hand, Tyndale's Bible of 1526 renders the last few words as:

> he taught *them* as one havynge power, and not as the scribes.

As a further illustration, we may refer to Luke xxiv. 31 in the English Bible of 1389:

> And the yȝen of *hem* weren opened and thei knewen him, and he vanyschide fro *her* yȝen."

The Tyndale version has: "and *their* eyes were openned and he vanisshed out of *their* syght." Note here that Wycliffe retains the -EN plural of *eye* (cf. *een* for *eyes* in the folk song *Annie Laurie*) and the -EN terminal of the verb after a plural subject.

To return to an earlier theme, we have now to account for the origin of the modern plural form *those* corresponding to *that*, and of the modern unchangeable definite article *the*. O.E. had a compound demonstrative form comparable with Latin *idem*, *eadem*, etc., made up by tacking on a particle *dem* to *is*, *ea*, etc. By uniting the simple demonstrative last mentioned with a particle *se* (*behold!*, *see!*) we obtain in O.E. (cf. German *diese*, etc.) a new demonstrative THES. The singular neuter nominative and accusative survives as *this*, just as THÆT survives in *that*, and the plural THAS is the parent of both *those* and *these*. The origin of *the*, which established itself during the transitional period as the invariant definite article, is not so clearly traceable. In O.E. THE was an invariant relative pronoun (see p. 187), replaced as such by *that* during the transitional period of two centuries after the Norman Conquest. One commonly meets it as a personal pronoun when preceded by the simple demonstrative, e.g. SE THE = *he who*. It is perhaps simplest to infer that SE (masc. nom. sing.) assimilated the initial consonant of THÆT (neut. nom. sing.) to become the article of today. In this context we should recall a change which did not appreciably* begin before the Middle period. Originally HWA (*who*), HWÆS (*whose*), HWÆM (*whom*), HWILC (*which*) were interrogatives only, and at the beginning of the Middle period *that* had become the only relative. In Chaucer's time *whose* was already current, and by the end of the Middle period the (now so spelt) WH-forms were in common use as relatives. A similar spread of function occurred at a very much earlier date in the corresponding QU (=*kw*) interrogatives of the Latin family.

What has gone before sufficiently discloses why pronouns of the third person need show no manifest family likeness even in closely related languages. The recognition that this is so prompts the question: why do some pronouns conform to a pattern recognisably common to widely different families of the Indo-European group, and why do not others (excluding those of the third person) do so? We have already (p. 151) drawn attention to the pattern of interrogative pronouns and adverbs (e.g. *who*, *when*) common to the Latin, Celtic and Teutonic clans. The common ancestry

---

* In the O.E. gospels we meet more than once the construction *swa hwylc . . . swa* as in Matt. x 11 *On swa hwylce othe cæstre swa ge ingath.* The Wycliffe Bible renders this: *In to whatever citee or castel ȝe shulen entre.*

of the singular pronouns of the first and second persons is also conspicuous; but this is far from true of the corresponding plural forms. To be sure, English *I* (Du. and Goth. *ik*, Germ. *ich*) is not at first sight recognisably like Latin and Greek *ego*, but *ego* itself is as clearly like Old Icelandic *ek* as is the latter like O.E. IC. The Modern and O.E. ME is identical on the written page with *me* in Latin and in its modern descendants (French, Italian, Spanish). It is recognisably like the equivalent Dutch *mij*. The equivalent in Greek is *me*, in Irish *me* and in Welsh *mi*. The equivalent of *ti* (=*thou*) in Welsh, *tu* in Irish, *tu* in Latin and its descendants, is *su* or *tu* in Greek, THU in O.E., Gothic and Icelandic, *du* in Modern Scandinavian and German, the differences (*t—th—d*) being consistent with sound shifts already mentioned.

If the resemblance of singular pronouns of the first and second person is crystal clear throughout the Indo-Germanic group, our next Museum Exhibit (p. 214) shows that no such widespread similarity confronts us when we turn our attention to the corresponding plural ones. Within the Latin clan there is a family likeness of both—at least of the literary forms. Within the Teutonic clan there is also a recognisable similarity of pronouns of the so-called first person plural. None the less, with all due allowance for regular sound-shifts dealt with in Chapter 4, these have no resemblance whatever to those of the Latin clan; and Teutonic pronouns of the so-called second person plural conform to no uniform pattern at all. The expression *so-called* directs attention to several reasons why such differences have come about. One is that the meanings of the words referred to are far less clear-cut than those of *I* and the now somewhat archaic *thou*.

Consider first the meaning of *we*, for which some Oriental languages distinguish inclusive and exclusive forms: viz.: (a) I and thou with or without another or others (as when one says to another person, *we can both agree*); (b) I and another or others not including the person or persons addressed (as when one says, *we disagree with you*). As regards *you*, the situation is even more confused. In Modern English, one commonly uses it as an impersonal singular or plural pronoun of the third person, where *one* (French *on*) would be more appropriate (e.g. *you turn it this way* = *one turns it this way*). This usage draws attention to a secondary use of the numeral in English and Scandinavian other than as the indefinite article. What is more important, however, is that the so-called second person plural may be the formal and usual, in contradistinction to the familiar and intimate, mode of address to either a single person or more than one of them. As it happens, some languages enlist the third person to that end, as when a shop assistant says, *Would Madam like this?* In Italian, Danish and German, the most commonly used so-called pronoun of the second person (see the Museum Exhibits on page 214) is indeed the pronoun of the third.

Aside from the diversities of meaning last mentioned, another intelligible circumstance may give rise to diversity of form. In the older Indo-European languages, in

MUSEUM EXHIBIT
THE TEUTONIC PERSONAL PRONOUN OF THE FIRST AND SECOND PERSON

The following correspond to Middle English *we—us—our* and *ye—you—your*. (Dual forms on the left, plural on the right.)

GOTHIC		OLD ENGLISH		ICELANDIC*	
WIT	WEIS	WIT	WE	VIÐ	VJER
UGKIS	UNS	UNC	US	OKKUR	OSS
UGKARA	UNSARA	UNCER	URE	OKKAR	VOR
JUT	JUS	GIT	GE	THIÐ	THJER
IGGIS	IZWIS	INC	EOW	YKKUR	YÐUR
IGGARA	IZWARA	INCER	EOWER	YKKAR	YÐAR

Next are their descendants in contemporary Teutonic languages:

SWEDISH	DANISH	DUTCH	GERMAN
VI	VI	WIJ	WIR
OSS	OS	ONS	UNS
VÅR(T)	VOR(T)	ONZE, ONS	UNSER(E)
NI	DE (*or* I)	U	SIE (*or* IHR)
EDER	DEM (*or* JER)	U	SIE (*or* IHNEN)
ER(T)	DERES (*or* JERES)	UW	IHR(E)

Below are the equivalents of *we—us—our, ye—you—your* in the Latin sister languages. The forms cited in parentheses are for polite usage.

FRENCH	ITALIAN	SPANISH
NOUS	NOI	NOSOTROS, NOSOTRAS
NOUS	CI	NOS
NOTRE	NOSTRO (etc.)	NUESTRO, NUESTRA
VOUS	VOI (*or* LEI)	VOSOTROS, VOSOTRAS (*or* USTEDES)
VOUS	VI (LI *or* LE)	OS (LOS, LAS, LES)
VOTRE	VOSTRO (etc.)	VUESTRO (etc.)

---

* In Icelandic script, Ð (ð) stands for the *dh*-sound of *this* and *then*. For the corresponding voiceless sound in *thick* and *thin*, Icelandic script employs the runic þ (Þ), written here as TH.

particular Sanskrit and the Greek of Homeric times, we meet, side by side with singular and plural (*we* and *you*), dual forms which we may render as: *we two, our two, the two of us* and *you—your two, the two of you*. As our Museum Exhibit shows, Gothic and O.E. had dual forms. Icelandic still has them. Otherwise, the dual has disappeared in modern Teutonic languages. Except in very formal discourse, it happens that the Icelandic dual is now the one most commonly used, regardless of whether one is addressing two or more persons. Accordingly, one may surmise that the dual forms will eventually supplant the plural, as the latter has supplanted the former in other members of the Teutonic clan. Separate dual and plural forms must have ceased to exist side by side in the Latin (and indeed throughout the Celto-Italic) stem at a remote date. Which supplanted which is therefore a matter of speculation. However, it is highly suggestive to compare Latin *nos* (= *we*) with early Greek *νω*=NO (*we two*) in contradistinction to the corresponding plural *ἡμεῖς*=HEMAIS. In short, comparison of so-called plural forms of personal pronouns of the first and second person may be misleading in the sense that what we now call plural form is the descendant of a dual.

Only one other feature of our last-mentioned Museum Exhibit calls for comment. The reader should now be able to recognise the parentage of *ye* (nom.) and *you* (accus. and dat.). The distinction between the uses of these forms persisted into the modern period. The King James Bible consistently employs *ye* as the verb subject, *you* otherwise, e.g. *ye have not chosen me, but I have chosen you* (John xv, 16). The disappearance of *thou* (except in places of worship) took place later, and is a story with some relevance to what has gone before. By the time *you* had everywhere replaced *ye* it had also become customary to use the former when addressing a person—other than one of the three persons of the Trinity—of higher social standing than the speaker. Gradually, it came into use to address a person regarded as a social equal, though *thou—thee* long remained the usual forms of address for a single person, if either inferior or non-existent. In the latter half of the seventeenth century, the Quakers sought a remedy for such an unfriendly distinction by trying to restore the O.E. (singular *versus* plural) usage. What eventually happened was the reverse. *Thou* is totally dead in daily speech. In Anglo-American, one uses *you* to address a single or more than one person, regardless of social status.

Let us now turn to another topic relevant to the theme of this chapter. In a remarkable way, an O.E. manuscript would have a less unfamiliar aspect than its Tudor English or Anglo-American equivalent to a Norman invader (if literate) or to a half-literate absentee landlord of the Plantagenet period. The O.E. negative particle corresponding to *not* was NE. That of Latin was *non* in simple assertions, *ne* in commands and wishes, *nonne* in questions. The corresponding negative particles in Italian and Spanish are respectively *non* and *no*. Like O.E. NE and Gothic *ni* all the last-named customarily come before the verb, and a family likeness is apparent. In

French, the negative particle (before the verb) is also *ne*, customarily reinforced (after the verb) by *pas*, or more emphatically by *point*. Such reinforcement of a negative particle, as when we now say *not . . . a bit* or *not . . . at all*, is a very common linguistic trick. Thus colloquial Welsh employs the corresponding construction *nid . . . ddim*, and Italian employs *non . . . punto* (=*not . . . a point*) for emphasis. Like Italian *punto*, French *pas* (=*pace* or *trace*) and *point* (for *punto*) and Welsh *ddim* (=*anything*) may all acquire a negative value by association, though their original meanings were not negative. On the other hand, Spanish resorts to reinforcement by use of double negatives, viz. *no . . . ninguno* and *no . . . nadie* (=*not . . . none*).

Although use of a double negative (e.g. *he didn't see nobody*) is a hallmark of illiteracy in Anglo-American usage, it was highly fashionable in O.E. There we meet the negative particle both before the verb and glued on to certain reinforcing words which came after it. Two of the latter are of especial importance, OWUHT and AWIHT. We may interpret the precise difference between their respective meanings as *anything* and *anybody*. Seemingly, the latter lingered on as *wight* (*person*) in Tudor English and later for poetic usage. What is more certain is that both lingered into Tudor English (and later) as respectively *ought* and *aught*. Now, NE could glue itself on to some O.E. words, e.g. NÆS for NE WÆS, where *not* now glues itself on to *was* as in *wasn't*. Whence we get NOWUHT (*nought*) and NAWIHT (*naught*) for *none* (i.e. *nothing* or *nobody*). During the Middle period these contracted to *not* and *nat*; and they had gained importance during the previous transitional period as particles to reinforce NE, but, unlike the latter, placed after the verb. Hence it happens that we find side by side throughout the Middle period the following ways of expressing negation:

(a) *ne* with nothing to reinforce it;
(b) *ne . . . nat* or *not*;
(c) *nat* or *not* after the verb without the preliminary O.E. negative particle *ne*.

The last (and modern) usage is the one we find in the Wycliffe Bible with the modern spelling *not*, e.g. Rev. xiv: *these it ben that ben not befoulid with wymmen* (these it be that be not corrupted with women). However, a metrical version of Psalm li. composed (1450) nearly a century later reads: *Lat thi pite sprynge and sprede. Off thi mercy that I ne mys.* We meet all three of the constructions mentioned above in Chaucer, who may well have cherished usages already archaic in conversation, to make his verses scan. Here is a nosegay of examples:

(i) From the *Prologue* to the *Canterbury Tales*:

     (a) O.E. simple form:
       That he ne knew his sleighte (line 604) (cf. sleight of hand)
       I noot (=ne wot) *how men him calle* (line 284)

(b) Double O.E. negative:
Hir frendschipe nas (=ne was) *nat newe to biginne* (line 428)
Ne studieth noght (line 841)

(c) Simple modern form (spelt *nat* or *noght*):
It is nat honest (line 246)
A bettre felawe sholde men noght finde (line 648)

(ii) From the *Monk's Tale:*

Ther nas (=ne was) *no remedie* (line 3183)

Had thou nat told to wommen thy secree
In al this worlde ne hadde been thy pere (lines 3243-44)

God that sit in magestee
Ne mighte him nat bireve of his estaat (lines 3358-59)

No tere out of his yĕn for that sighte
Ne cam (lines 3677-78)

Pitously he preyde
For socour, but it mighte nat bityde (lines 3729-30)

No man ne truste upon hir favour longe (line 3914)

The genesis of *niet* in Dutch and *nicht* (cf. *gh* in *naught* and *nought*) in German followed a course parallel to that of *not* in English, and English usage throughout the sixteenth century was on all fours with that of Dutch and German today—that is to say, *not* followed the verb in a negative statement as in the King James Bible, e.g. *he came unto his own and his own received him not.* During the seventeenth century a form of negation peculiar to Anglo-American gained ground. While the older usage persisted with helper verbs (e.g. *have not, shall not, ought not*, etc.) and has remained to this day, we otherwise enlist the helper verb *do* (e.g. *do not believe, did not suspect*) followed by the so-called infinitive, i.e. dictionary form, of the verb. The use of *do* for emphasis in a simple assertion, as when we say *I do insist*, is of great antiquity in the English story, and it is odd that it did not enlarge its territory still further during the seventeenth century when it also appropriated the older Teutonic form of interrogation (e.g. *do you say?* for *sayest thou?*).

Like the protean uses of the -ING derivative, whose terminal now attaches itself to every Anglo-American verb other than some of the more defective auxiliaries (*shall, can, may, must*), this use of *do* as an auxiliary in negative and interrogative constructions places the language in its present stage of development in a class apart both from other members of the Teutonic and from all of the Latin clan. In the latter and in other Teutonic languages, as indeed in Tudor English, the usual written device for conversion of a statement into a question is to place the subject after the verb; but in speech one commonly has recourse to an interrogative phrase or particle without change of word order, as when we say: *he is leaving, eh?* This is a trick of widespread occurrence. Welsh preserves *a* in writing, an equivalent to *eh*, and Finnish has *ko*. In speech a comparable usage involving a phrase occurs commonly, e.g. *est-ce-que?* (=*is it so?*) in French before what would otherwise be an assertion and *eller hur?* (=*or how?*) or *inte sant?* (=*not true?*) in Swedish tacked on to the end of it.

The last remarks lead us to what may be one of the most formidable difficulties of learning a foreign language if its word order is different from one's own. Although Dutch is ancestrally more akin to English than is Swedish, most English-speaking adults or adolescents are likely to find Swedish easier to learn. This is so for a reason lightly touched on in Chapter 2, i.e. the word order of Anglo-American and indeed of Middle English is far more like that of a Scandinavian than like that of a West Germanic language, including early O.E. Indeed, Anglo-American word order is nearer to that of French or Italian than to that of German or of Dutch. It will therefore furnish a fitting conclusion to our survey of likenesses and differences among the sister languages, if we now look more closely at word-order patterns.

First, however, we may pause to dispose of a superstition which would merit no consideration if we no longer met it in textbooks and quasi-popular expositions. It has been customary to say that a more highly flexional language (e.g. O.E.) can have a more highly flexible word order than one that is more *isolating* (e.g. Anglo-American). This oft-repeated statement rests on several misconceptions. As applied to English prose, it is not literally true. O.E.—especially early O.E.—prose had its own pattern of word order which has much in common with that of contemporary Dutch and German. Anglo-American has a different pattern which we shall discuss later; but the difference has very little to do with flexibility. To get to grips with the last word in the last sentence we have to take stock of several circumstances.

One of these is that the gap between written and spoken word in ancient times was, and still is in many speech communities, enormous. Another is that the itinerant bard had a unique social function as custodian of an *oral* tradition when writing was in its infancy, and likely enough long before alphabetic writing. As such, he cultivated a word-for-word preservation of the story by recourse to tricks of alliteration, scansion, etc., enlisted to aid the memory in performance of a repetitive task. To preserve such a prescribed bardic pattern, poets play havoc with the word order of everyday speech, and preserve words, prefixes or terminals which have long been extinct in daily intercourse. Much of our earliest written record (e.g. our first notable sample of O.E., the heroic poem *Beowulf*), like the Homeric saga of prehistoric Greek culture, records bardic incantations centuries after the events described had actually or supposedly occurred. The written record of a highly flexional language is therefore very misleading as a picture of contemporary speech.

However, the plea that flexions make flexibility of word order more feasible is intrinsically foolish because it presumes that flexional terminals (or vowel changes as in *man—men, give—gave*) are necessarily unequivocal. Ludicrous at any level, this is also pernicious because the underlying assumption adds to the difficulty of learning a flexional language. For instance, it perpetuates unintelligible instructions. One such is that we must use the nominative case for the *subject* of a verb, an injunction which could be meaningful only if the so-called subject of the verb had a singular meaning in its own right. This is not true. That *he* (subject) *strikes the table* conveys something he does to the table; but that *he* (subject) *sees the flash* conveys something the flash does to his retina. We recognise the subject by no intrinsic peculiarities. We do so because it has the nominative case form of the noun or pronoun in a language which preserves case flexion, or otherwise if it occupies a certain place in the customary and stable word-order pattern of unaffected vocal communication in contradistinction to the vagaries of poetic usage.

When we contrast the word order of classical Latin with that of modern descendants of provincial Roman speech, we must recall that it was a highly artificial medium not uncommonly committed to writing by slaves for leisurely decipherment by an aristocracy with time to burn. How much so in Caesar's time, when the writing surface was still commonly wax, will be self-evident if we stop to compute the size of a building to house a single Sunday issue of the *New York Herald Tribune* or the *Kansas City Star* produced on wax tablets. The Latin translation of the Bible, St. Jerome's Vulgate, was the first substantial example of writing addressed to plebeians who could read, and appeared after the Romans had adopted, as had the Greeks at a much earlier date, papyrus from the Egyptians. From this we may infer that the pattern of word order common to everyday communication in French, Spanish and Italian was far nearer to the normal speech of Caesar's soldiers than the written Latin of Tacitus, more than a century later.

For the purpose of intelligible human communication between people of different speech communities, the only common denominator of language has two components: (a) what individual words mean; (b) what additional restriction their place in a sequence imposes on them. If we know the meanings of *against, crimson, goat, hairy* and *sky*, we still need to distinguish *hairy goat against a crimson sky* from *crimson goat against a hairy sky*. Any such rule, like the rule of the road (right- or left-hand drive), is arbitrary in one sense. What matters is not what rule we adopt (e.g. *goat hairy sky crimson against* or *against sky crimson goat hairy*). It is important only that we consistently conform to rules prescribed by local custom. This simple reflection seems to have escaped the attention of the egregious Dr. Zamenhof who concocted Esperanto. To be sure, he at least showed that even a badly constructed language purged of irregularities can be more teachable than the best natural one; but the Esperanto noun retains in the ostensible interests of suppositious "flexibility" an accusative case terminal which Swedish, Danish, Norwegian, Dutch, French, Spanish, Portuguese, Italian and English even among western Indo-European languages get on very well without. Who conceivably wants to attach to the tail of the *goat* an accusative terminal to make sure that *the man shot the goat*, when word order makes clear (as does the sense) that the goat did not shoot the man?

The only outstanding difference between the word order of the Latin family and that of the Teutonic as a whole is that the French, Italian or Spanish adjective, with few exceptions, comes after the noun, as in *the home beautiful* or *the light divine*. This is characteristic of all the Italo-Celtic (e.g. Welsh and Gaelic) branch of the Indo-European family. Aside from the usage of poets, and salesmen of *the home beautiful*, it is the obverse of the rule that the Teutonic adjective precedes the noun, as the adjective *Teutonic* here precedes the noun *adjective*. Normally, in all the sister (or half-sister) languages, the pronoun or noun designated as subject: (a) precedes the verb with its so-called object thereafter in an *assertion*; (b) follows it in a *question* unless fortified by an interrogative particle (e.g. *eh*) or expression (e.g. French *n'est ce pas*, Swedish*eller hur* or *inte sant*).

To this rule, two qualifications are important to the student of a Teutonic sister language: (a) when a qualifying word or expression precedes the subject, the latter follows the verb as in Tudor English (e.g. *then came the word of the Lord unto . . ., therefore say I to you*, etc., of the 1611 Bible); (b) one can eliminate the equivalent of *if* by using a so-called subjunctive (p. 182) form of the verb as in *were I to do so = if I did so*.

To proceed further, we take cognisance of two classes of auxiliary verbs in all sister languages of either clan: (a) in all of them the equivalent of *have* can precede the past participle (or in Scandinavian the so-called *supine*, see p. 183) to make constructions such as *have* or *had gone*; (b) in all of them the equivalents of *can, must, should* can precede the dictionary form (so-called *infinitive*) of another verb (e.g. *can do, should go, must come*). Having made this distinction we may classify the following patterns of word order in simple assertions.

A. MODERN DESCENDANTS OF LATIN

1. Subject precedes both pronoun object and verb.
2. Pronoun object precedes, and noun object follows, simple tense form of the verb.
3. Direct precedes indirect object.
4. Pronoun object precedes the equivalent of *have*, but noun object follows the past participle in a *have* construction (e.g. *have* or *had eaten*).
5. Both pronoun and noun object follow the verb infinitive of Italian and Spanish constructions involving *can, must, might*, etc.; but the French pronoun object precedes the infinitive.

B. WEST GERMANIC (DUTCH AND GERMAN)

1. Subject precedes verb unless itself preceded by an adverb or qualifying expression (cf. Tudor English, *thus saith the Lord*).
2. Both verb and subject precede an object, direct or indirect.
3. A simple tense form or an auxiliary verb immediately follows the subject, but the infinitive or past participle of an auxiliary couplet trails at the end of the sentence.
4. The indirect pronoun object follows the direct pronoun object, but both precede a noun object.
5. Negative particles *niet* (Du.) and *nicht* (Ger.) follow the direct object.

C. SCANDINAVIAN

1. As for B1 and B2 above.
2. The supine (p. 183) or infinitive of an auxiliary construction precedes an object, whether direct or indirect.
3. Whether pronoun or noun, an indirect object, if not itself preceded by a preposition, comes before the direct object of the verb.
4. Whether direct or indirect, an object follows a simple tense form and both come after the supine or infinitive in an auxiliary verb construction.
5. The negative particle follows a simple tense form of the verb and its pronoun object preceding a noun object, and in an auxiliary construction, it precedes the supine or infinitive.

From the above emerge several conclusions which emphasise previous remarks (p. 57) about the influence of the Norse settlers on English grammar. One is that the word order of Middle and Tudor English, in every particular mentioned above, agrees with that of the modern Scandinavian languages; but that of neither Old nor of later English tallies with French *vis-à-vis* the position of the pronoun object. Contrariwise, O.E. tallies more closely with Dutch and German than with Scandinavian or with Tudor English in so far as the participle or infinitive is apt to come at the end of a sentence involving an auxiliary verb construction. Anglo-American word order is out of step with Scandinavian, and with Tudor (and earlier) English, order in so far as the subject, when preceded by a qualifying word or phrase, retains its precedence over the verb.

The foregoing remarks consistently apply only to simple sentences and to the so-called *principal clause* of a complex one. As regards Anglo-American, we need to take stock of several amendments customarily subsumed by saying that they concern only the type of so-called subordinate clause labelled *relative*. However, a precise delimitation of what we care to label as such is impossible; and it will suffice if we distinguish three categories of clauses in which one of the following pronouns precedes the subject of the verb in the subordinate clause.

(a) The direct object of the verb may be one of the set THAT, WHOM, WHICH, WHAT, e.g.
     This is the house *that* Jack built (subject, *Jack*);
     Jack is the man *whom* you saw building it (subject, *you*);
     You now know *which* (house) I mean (subject, *I*);
     What he built you now see (subject, *he*);
(b) WHOSE followed by a noun, e.g.
     This is the man *whose* house Jack built (subject, *Jack*);
(c) WHOM or WHICH follow a preposition, e.g.
     Jack is the man *from whom* we bought it (subject, *we*);
     Such was the price *at which* he sold it (subject, *he*).

The reader will note that Anglo-American increasingly preserves normal word order in a subordinate clause either by: (a) dropping *that, which* or *whom* as direct object (e.g. *the house Jack built, the man you saw*); (b) taking the preposition to the end of the sentence and dropping out *whom* or *which* (e.g. *the man we bought it from, the price he sold it at*). Otherwise, the foregoing categories cover what is relevant to French word order in contradistinction to that of any of the Teutonic languages.

All of the Teutonic languages exhibit some departure from the dominant pattern in subordinate clauses of any category one sees fit to distinguish. The departure in Scandinavian is trifling. The only important feature to note is a shifting forward of the negative particle (*inte* or *ikke*) when present from its usual position to precede the verb, as if one were to say *when I not do so*. On the other hand, the pattern of the German or Dutch subordinate clause challenges Anglo-American—or Middle English—habits of speech much more formidably. The tense form of the simple verb, and of the auxiliary if the verb is compound, goes to the *end* of the clause. In an auxiliary construction therefore the past participle or infinitive *precedes* the auxiliary, as if one were to say: (a) *I knew that he it her gave*; (b) *she came after I away gone had*. Before Norse settlements and Norman influence began to change O.E., its word order conspicuously betrayed its Low German ancestry in such constructions as:

THÆT HIE THONE GODES MANN A-BITAN SCOLDEN
that they this man of God bite-up should
(=that they should devour this man of God)

Anglicised examples of word order used for explanatory purposes in the foregoing paragraphs illustrate a mnemotechnic (memory-saving) device which can be of great use, if we are alert to the diverse difficulties which learning a foreign language entails. These are of four kinds: (a) memorising new words; (b) learning how to pronounce them correctly; (c) memorising the many terminals or internal vowel changes which the same dictionary entry may undergo if the language is flexional; (d) getting at home in a new word-order pattern. Of (b) it suffices to say that one cannot get guidance in writing unless already familiar with the international phonetic script. Otherwise, one depends on a teacher, on radio or on gramophone records such as those of the *Linguaphone* series. Of (a) enough has been said in our first four chapters, and of (d) in this and in its predecessor. The relative importance of the four categories of obstacles depends on the language. If our own battery includes all the sounds of a foreign language, (b) is of minor importance. If our language is very closely related thereto a little premedication, with information about spelling conventions (Chapter 3) and with changes of pronunciation (Chapter 4), greatly reduces the mnemotechnic load of (a); and (c) will be of no significance if we set out to learn an isolating language or a so-called *agglutinative* language such as Finnish or Hungarian, i.e. one of which all attachable terminals follow a regular pattern. If one or more of the other three obstacles to learning is trivial, the last one, i.e. pattern of word order, may be the most, albeit more than necessarily, formidable.

Since it is always more difficult to learn at the same time two (or more) unrelated skills than to learn one, we may best accustom ourselves to a word-order pattern totally different from our own by divorcing the task of doing so from the use of an unfamiliar vocabulary, an unfamiliar flexional apparatus and an unfamiliar phonetic apparatus. The last statement is equally true if a person reared in Anglo-American speech should wish to know *Breton* (weakly flexional), *Basque* (agglutinative) or *Burmese* (isolating). Consider Welsh, which employs subordinate clauses very sparsely. Here the most common pattern for a so-called adverbial clause is like the following:

Before I see him = *Before to me his seeing.*

The second formula illustrates how we may reproduce Welsh word order without the additional burden of Welsh vocabulary and flexions. Such an exercise is much more rewarding in terms of effort expenditure than memorisation of rules set forth formally above.

The Anglo-American learner can take advantage of this device for getting familiar with an unfamiliar pattern of word order by interpreting such rules by recourse to such models as:

I had told him the story:

ANGLO-AMERICAN	I	HAD	TOLD	HIM	IT
FRENCH	I	IT	HIM	HAD	TOLD
SWEDISH	I	HAD	TOLD	HIM	IT
GERMAN	I	HAD	IT	HIM	TOLD

QUIZ CORNER 6

Code for Quizzes 1-6

In each Quiz numbered from 1–7 you have before you a specimen of English of the Middle period (A.D. 1200-1400). The puzzle is to identify relics of O.E. grammar which have since disappeared, or Modern English forms which had not as yet become universal. Since the change from Old to New went on unequally in different parts of Britain, the home county of the authors of pieces chosen is instructive in the light of the foregoing text. To answer the Quizzes it suffices to use the same code as below. Printing had not yet standardised spelling. Each *scrivener* (scribe) who copied a manuscript by penmanship for circulation relied on his own taste influenced by local sound values. He did not always spell the same word on the same page in the same way. So we are here at liberty to spell words in what looks the most familiar way, when more than one way would be true to the time. In particular, Y more usually appears where we use I, and Y itself most usually where there had once been the prefix GE- or the Old Germanic J. Similarly, we often find -IS for -ES at the end of a plural noun.

- (a) O.E. NE for *not* or *nor*.
- (b) O.E. HER or HIR for *their*.
- (c) YE for *you*.
- (d) Y- for O.E. GE- of past participle.
- (e) -N terminal of O.E. verb after *to*.
- (f) -N terminal of O.E. verb after a helper verb.
- (g) -N terminal of some O.E. plural nouns.
- (h) -N terminal with plural subject in past tense of O.E. verb.
- (i) -N terminal of the subjunctive tenses of the O.E. verb when the subject is plural.
- (j) -EN terminal for the -AN of certain O.E. prepositions.
- (k) -TH terminal with plural subject in present tense of O.E. verb.
- (l) In the English of the Middle period, the case form *me* sometimes replaces *I* and in the present tense the verb then takes the -TH terminal following *he, she, it.*
- (m) O.E. MID for *with*.
- (n) O.E. HIE for *they*.
- (o) Our modern *the* for O.E. SE, THÆT or SEO, etc.

(p) O.E. THINE, MINE, where we now use *thy, my.*

(q) The modern terminal -S in the present tense where the King James Bible would use -TH.

(r) Verb with plural subject but without -N terminal of O.E.

(s) The new hybrid preposition BY-CAUSE, now written *because.*

(t) The new -ING form of the verb as adjective.

(u) O.E. HIM or HEM for *them.*

(v) The -E terminal of an adjective before a plural noun.

(w) The use of the -ING form of the verb with the helper verb *be,* as in *I am (was, will be) writing.*

(x) Loss of the -N terminal of the O.E. verb after *to.*

(y) Survival of the O.E. case ending -E of the adjective after a preposition.

(z) Middle period THO equivalent to O.E. THA for Modern English *those.*

(aa) O.E. MIN or THIN for *my* or *thy.*

(bb) O.E. BEN for *were.*

(cc) Late O.E. CHILDER or CHILDRE for *children.*

(dd) In Northumbrian dialect of the Middle period, QU for O.E. HW.

(ee) Late O.E. ICH for *I.*

(ff) O.E. AC for *but.*

(gg) O.E. ILKA for *every.*

(hh) O.E. BETH for *is.*

(ii) O.E. WITAN for *know.*

(jj) Late O.E. WONETH for *dwells.*

(kk) -N terminal of past participle retained.

(ll) -N terminal of past participle dropped.

(mm) Loss of the -N terminal of the O.E. verb after a helper verb.

Quiz 1

Chaucer

From the *Prologue* (*circa* 1387) to the *Canterbury Tales*
 Bifel that, in that seson on a day,
In Southwerk at the Tabard as I lay
Redy to *wenden*[1] on my pilgrimage
To Caunterbury with ful devout corage,

At night was come into that hostelrye
Wel nyne and twenty in a companye,
Of sondry folk, by aventure *y-falle*[2]
In felaweshipe, and pilgrims were they alle,
That toward Caunterbury *wolden*[3] ryde.
The chambres and the stables *weren*[4] wyde,
And wel we *weren*[5] esed atte beste.
And shortly, whan the sonne was to reste,
So hadde I spoken with *hem*[6] everichon,
That I was of *hir*[7] felaweshipe anon,
And made foreward erly for to ryse,
To take oure wey, ther as I yow devyse.
    But nathelees, whil I have tyme and space,
Er that I ferther in this tale pace,
Me thinketh[8] it acordaunt to resoun
To telle yow al the condicioun
Of ech of *hem*,[9] so as it semed me,
And whiche they *weren*,[10] and of what degree.

            .   .   .   .

    A KNIGHT ther was, and that a worthy man,
That fro the tyme that he first bigan
To *riden*[11] out, he loved chivalrie,
Trouthe and honour, fredom and curteisie

        .   .   .   .

For he was late *y-come*[12] from his viage,
And went for to *doon*[13] his pilgrimage.

        .   .   .   .

    Ther was also a Nonne, a PRIORESSE,
That of hir smyling was ful simple and coy;
Hire gretteste ooth was but by Seynte Loy;
And she was cleped madame Eglentyne.

        .   .   .   .

And Frenssh she spak ful faire and fetisly,
After the scole of Stratford atte Bowe,
For Frenssh of Paris was to hire unknowe.
At mete wel *y-taught*[14] was she with-alle;

        .   .   .   .

A MONK ther was, a fair for the maistrie,
An out-ridere, that lovede venerie;
A manly man, to *been*[15] an abbot able.

.   .   .   .   .

He hadde of gold *y-wroght*[16] a ful curious pin:
A love-knotte in the gretter ende ther was.
His heed was balled, that shoon as any glas,
And eek his face, as he hadde been enoynt.
He was a lord ful fat and in good point;
His *eyen*[17] stepe, and rollinge in his head.

.   .   .   .   .

An HABERDASSHER and a CARPENTER,
A WEBBE, a DYERE, and a TAPICER,

.   .   .   .

Hir[18] knyves were *chaped* noght with bras,
But al with silver; wroght ful clene and weel,
Hire girdles and hir pouches every-deel.
Wel semed ech of *hem*[19] a fair burgeys,
To *sitten*[20] in a yeldhalle on a deys.
Everich, for the wisdom that he can,

.   .   .   .   .

I saugh nat this yeer so mery a companye
At ones in this herberwe as is now.
Fayn wolde I *doon*[21] yow mirthe, *wiste*[22] I how.
And of a mirthe I am right now bithoght,
To *doon*[23] yow ese, and it shal coste noght.

Ye[24] *goon*[25] to Caunterbury; God yow speede,
The blisful martir quite yow your meede.
And wel I woot, as *ye*[26] *goon*[27] by the weye,
Ye shapen yow to *talen*[28] and to pleye;
For trewely, confort ne mirthe is noon
To ride by the weye doumb as a stoon;
And therfore wol I *maken*[29] yow disport,
As I seyde erst, and doon yow som confort.
And if yow *liketh*[30] alle, by oon assent,
For to *stonden*[31] at my juggement,

And for to *werken*[32] as I shal yow seye,
To-morwe, whan ye *riden*[33] by the weye,
Now, by my fader soule, that is deed,
But ye be merye, I wol *yeve*[34] yow myn heed.
Hold up youre hondes, *withouten*[35] more speche.

From the *Pardoners Tale*

In Flaundres whilom was a companye
Of yonge folk, that *haunteden*[36] folye,
As riot, hasard, stewes, and tavernes,

.   .   .   .   .

Hir[37] othes been so grete and so dampnable
That it is grisly for to heere *hem*[38] swere;

.   .   .   .

'Now,' quod oure host, 'I wol no lenger pleye
With thee, *ne*[39] with noon other angry man.'
But right anon the worthy knight bigan,

.   .   .   .

'And ye, sir host, that been to me so deere,
I prey yow that ye kisse the pardoner.
And pardoner, I prey thee, drawe thee neer,
And, as we *diden*,[40] lat us laughe and pleye.'
Anon they kiste, and *riden*[41] forth *hir*[42] weye.

1.	2.	3.	4.	5.	6. ......
7.	8.	9.	10.	11.	12. ......
13.	14.	15.	16.	17.	18. ......
19.	20.	21.	22.	23.	24. ......
25.	26.	27.	28.	29.	30. ......
31.	32.	33.	34.	35.	36. ......
37.	38.	39.	40.	41.	42. ......

Quiz 2

Wycliffe's Bible (circa 1379)

Forsothe there *weren*[1] summe of the scribis *sittynge*[2] and *thenkynge*[3] in *her*[4] hertis, What *spekith*[5] he thus? He *blasfemeth*[6]; who may *forgeve*[7] synnes no but God alone? . . . What *thenken*[8] yee these thingis in youre hertis? What is lightere for to *seie*[9] to the *sike*[10] man in palasie, Synnes *ben*[11] *forgoven*[12] to thee or for to *seie*,[13] Rise, take thy bed and walke?

Mark ii. 6-9

And alle men of Jerusalem *wenten*[14] out to him and **al** the cuntre of Judee; and *weren*[15] baptisid of him in the flood of Jordan *knowlechinge*[16] *her*[17] synnes.

Mark i. 5

I *knelinge*[18] am not worthy for to *undo*[19] the thwong of his *schoon*.[20]

Mark i. 7

And in the morewynge ful erly he . . . wente in to desert place and preiede there. And Symont suede him and *they*[21] that *weren*[22] with him. And whanne *they*[23] *hadden*[24] *founden*[25] him they *seiden*[26] to him, For alle men *seeken*[27] thee. And he *seith*[28] to hem,[29] Go we in to the *nexte*[30] townes and citees that and there I preche, for to this thing I came. And he was *prechynge*[31] in the synagogis of *hem*[32], and in *alle*[33] Galilee, and *castynge*[34] out fendis.

Mark i. 35-39

Go shewe thee to the princis of prestis and offre for thy clensynge *tho*[35] thingis that Moyses badde.

Mark i. 44

For *thei*[36] thoughten so with inne *hem self*.[37]

Mark ii. 8

I seie to thee, Rise up, take *thy*[38] bed, and go in to *thin*[39] hous.

Mark ii. 11

And Jhesu passynge thennes, twey *blinde*[40] men *sueden*[41] him, crynge and saynge, Thou sone of Davith have mercy of us. . . . Than he touchide *her*[42] *eeyen*,[43] saynge Up your feith be it don to you. And the *eeyen*[44] of bothe *ben*[45] opnyde.

Matt. ix. 27, 30

And these it *ben*[46] that ben *sowun*[47] on good lond, the whiche *heren*[48] the word and *taken*[49] and *maken*[50] fruit.

Mark iv. 20

1.	2.	3.	4.	5. . . . . . .
6.	7.	8.	9.	10. . . . . . .
11.	12.	13.	14.	15. . . . . . .
16.	17.	18.	19.	20. . . . . . .
21.	22.	23.	24.	25. . . . . . .
26.	27.	28.	29.	30. . . . . . .
31.	32.	33.	34.	35. . . . . . .
36.	37.	38.	39.	40. . . . . . .
41.	42.	43.	44.	45. . . . . . .
46.	47.	48.	49.	50. . . . . . .

Quiz 3

Mandeville

Sir John Mandeville, born A.D. 1300, went travelling in the East at twenty-two years of age and wrote in 1356 an account of his journeys, in the Midland dialect. In his book called *Contrees beyond Cathay*, he refers to the Goose Barnacle legend:

I tolde *hem*[1] of als gret a merveylle to *hem*[2] that is amonges us . . . For I tolde hem that in oure contree weren trees that baren a fruit that *becomen*[3] briddes fleeynge; and tho that *fellen*[4] in the water *lyven*[5], and they that fallen on the erthe *dyen*[6] anon; and they *ben*[7] right gode to mannes mete.

. . . . .

There ben vines that *beren*[8] so grete grapes that a strong man scholde *have*[9] ynow to *done*[10] for to *bere*[11] a clustre with alle the grapes.

. . . . .

And therefore alle the Jewes that *dwellen*[12] in alle londes *lernen*[13] alle weys to *speken*[14] Ebrew in hope that whanne the other Jewes schulle *gon*[15] out that thei may *understonden*[16] *hire*[17] speche . . . And yif that yee wil *wyte*[18] how that thei schulle *fynden*[19] *hire*[20] weye . . . I schalle *telle*[21] you.

1.	2.	3.	4.	5. . . . . . .
6.	7.	8.	9.	10. . . . . . .
11.	12.	13.	14.	15. . . . . . .
16.	17.	18.	19.	20. . . . . . .
21.				

Quiz 4

Robert of Gloucester

Almost exactly a century before Chaucer finished the *Canterbury Tales*, Robert of Gloucester, a monk in the abbey of that city, completed about the year A.D. 1298 a chronicle of England in rhymed verse. Being a Southerner he uses some O.E. forms which had made way in the North for more modern ones at an earlier date. Among other things the Chronicle emphasises how the Normans failed to impose the French language on the conquered people.

Tho Willam bastard hurde telle of Haraldes suikelhede,
Hou he (h)adde *ymad*[1] him king & *mid*[2] such falshede.

. . . . .

Harald him sende worde 'that folie it was to *truste*[3]
To such oth as was *ido*'[4] . . .

So that bi-side Hastinge to Engelond *hii*[5] come
Hom[6] thoghte tho *hii*[7] come alond that al was in *hor*[8] hond.

As sone as the duc Willam is fot sette alond
One of his knightes gradde, "hold vaste Willam nou" . . .

Tho duc Willam wuste that he was *icome*[9] so nei
A monek he sende him in message & . . .
That lond that him was *igive*[10] that he sholde him up-yelde.

The Englisse al *the*[11] night bivore vaste bigonne to *singe*[12]
& *spende*[13] al the night in glotonie & in *drinkinge.*[14]
The[15] Normans ne dude noght so, ac criede on God vaste
& shrive *hom*[16] ech after other the wule *the*[17] night ylaste.

Thus com lo! Engelond in to Normandies hond
& the Normans ne couthe *speke*[18] tho bote *hor*[19] owe speche,
& *speke*[20] French as *hii*[21] dude at om & *hor*[22] children dude also teche.

Ac[23] lowe men *holdeth*[24] to English & to *hor*[25] owe speche . . .
Ich[26] wene ther ne beth in al *the*[27] world, contreyes none
That ne *holdeth*[28] to *hor*[29] owe speche, bote Engelond one.

1.	2.	3.	4.	5.	6. . . . . . .
7.	8.	9.	10.	11.	12. . . . . . .
13.	14.	15.	16.	17.	18. . . . . . .
19.	20.	21.	22.	23.	24. . . . . . .
25.	26.	27.	28.	29.	

Quiz 5

Some Northumbrian Manuscripts

Two religious books, a Psalter and a Homily, written in the Northumbrian dialect are contemporary with, or possibly earlier than, the Chronicle of Robert of Gloucester. Their special interest for us here is the early appearance of some modern forms of speech, one of which did not come into use in the South till long after Chaucer's time. *The Ayenbite of Inwit,* a religious poem in the Northern dialect, is of a later date. Its author, Richard Rolle de Hampol, was a monk of Doncaster in Yorkshire. The author of a fourth specimen of the Northern dialect was a John Barbour of Aberdeen. It is a chronicle about the life and adventures of Robert Bruce, King of the Scots.

I.
  Sain Matheu *the*[1] wangeliste
  Telles[2] us todai hou Crist
  Schipped[3] into *the*[4] se a time
  And his decipelis al wit him.
  And *quen*[5] *thair*[6] schip com on dep
  Jesu selven fel on slep,
  And gret tempest bigan to rise . . .
  Thai[7] wakned Crist and said yare
  Help us Lauerd for we forfare.
  And Crist, als mihti Godd, ansuerd
  And said, Foles *qui*[8] er ye fered . . .
  And Crist comanded wind and se
  To lethe and fair weder be.
  This is *the*[9] strenthe of our godspelle
  Als man on Ingelis tong mai *telle*[10].
  Al hali kirc als thinc me
  Mai bi this schippe takened be . . .
  For schip *fletes*[11] on the flode
  And hali kirc wit costes gode
  Fletes[12] aboven this werldes se
  Flouand wit sin and caitifte . . .

  Bot for our godspel *spekes*[13] of se
  Quarbi this werld mai bisend be
  Forthi wil I schaw other thinges . . .

II. From the *Northumbrian Psalter* (before A.D. 1300)
  Lauerd, oure Lauerd, hou selkouth is
  Name *thine*[14] in alle land this . . .

Of mouth of *childer*[15] and soukand
Made thou lof in *ilka*[16] land

Psalm viii

That winsom es to alle *thine*[17] wickenesses
That *heles*[18] alle thine sekenesses

Psalm cii

In *mi*[19] drouing Lauerd called I,
And to *mi*[20] God cried I witerli

Psalm xvii

III. From *The Ayenbite of Inwit* (*The Pricke of Conscience*) (about A.D. 1340)

Alle mans lyfe *casten*[21] may be
Principaly in this partes thre
That er thir to our undirstandyng
Begynnyng, midward and endyng...

And by that cry men *knaw*[22] than
Whether it be man or weman,
For when it es born it *cryes*[23] swa;
If it be man, it says "a, a",
That the first letter es of the nam
Of our forme-fader Adam.

IV. From *John Barbour's Chronicle* (about A.D. 1375)

Thus eschapit the nobill kyng;
But sum *sais*[24] this eschaping
Apon ane othir maner fell.

The king *has*[25] furth his wayes is tane.

For the thre tratouris *took*[26] gud hede
That he on slep wes and his man.

God and my hound *has*[27] *slane*[28] the twa
... For richt wicht men all thre *war*[29] thai.

1.	2.	3.	4.	5. ......
6.	7.	8.	9.	10. ......
11.	12.	13.	14.	15. ......
16.	17.	18.	19.	20. ......
21.	22.	23.	24.	25. ......
26.	27.	28.	29.	

Quiz 6

John of Trevisa

Midway between the deaths of Wycliffe and of Chaucer, John of Trevisa, like Robert of Gloucester, completed a chronicle of England. Born a Cornishman, he became a village priest in Gloucestershire, and translated several works, including, it is said, an English version of the Bible, no remains of which survive. Being a Southerner his language is in some ways more conservative than that of either Wycliffe or Chaucer.

As hit is *yknowe*[1] hough meny people *buth*[2] in this ilonde, ther *buth*[3] also of so meny people longages and tonges. Notheles Walschemen and Scottes that buth noght *ymelled*[4] with othere nacions, *holdeth*[5] wel nigh *here*[6] furste longage and speche.... Bote the Flemynges that *woneth*[7] in the west side of Wales *habbeth*[8] *yleft*[9] *here*[10] straunge speche and *speketh*[11] Saxonlych inow. Also Englischemen ... hadde fram the beginninge thre maner speche, Southeron, Northeron and Middel speche (in the middel of the lond), as *hy*[12] *come*[13] of thre maner people of Germania; notheles by commyxstion and mellinge furst with Danes and afterward with Normans, in menye the contray longage is apeyred.... This apeyryng of the burthe-tonge is *by-cause*[14] of twey thinges. On ys for childern in scoles agenes the usage and manere of al othere nacions *buth*[15] compelled for to leve *here*[16] oune longage and for to construe here lessons and here thingis a Freinsch.... Also gentilmen *children*[17] buth ytaught for to speke Freinsch fram time that a buth yrokked in here cradel ... and uplondysche men wol likne *ham-sylf*[18] to gentilemen and fondeth with gret busines for to *speke*[19] Freinsch for to *be*[20] more *ytold*[21] of.

Whanne the victory was *ydo*,[22] William buriede his men that were y-slawe, and grauntede his enemies to do the same who that wolde, and sent Harold his body to

Harold his moder withoute eny myde, as *hie*[23] hadde y-prayed; and *hie*[24] buriede him at Waltham in the Abbay of Chanons that Harold hadde *yfounded.*[25]

1.	2.	3.	4.	5. ......
6.	7.	8.	9.	10. ......
11.	12.	13.	14.	15. ......
16.	17.	18.	19.	20. ......
21.	22.	23.	24.	25. ......

7
The Greek Legacy

No one who has written about the Mother Tongue has failed to pay tribute to the Greek legacy; but one may doubt whether any have as yet composed an unwritten chapter on the theme of this one. Most of us think of the Greek contribution to the stock-in-trade of Anglo-American as a bequest of a now out-dated classical scholarship. This is a misconception shared by many pundits. What classical scholarship contributed during the preceding three centuries was a trickle contributory to another source which had let loose a torrent in the nineteenth century. To trace the origin of the new wellspring we have to familiarise ourselves with the genesis of what is now the world-wide vocabulary of Western science. It is a bilingual vocabulary in which Latin, the other contributor, blends with the now dominant Greek. It is one which the Mother Tongue, having enriched its resources from Latin, can assimilate all the more readily because Latin had itself borrowed extensively from Greek.

If we are to discuss without misunderstanding the Greek legacy to the Mother Tongue, it may not be amiss to dispose of a misunderstanding very prevalent among otherwise well-educated people who have never taken much interest in ancient history. When one speaks of the Glory that was Greece, one is not speaking of a nation, still less of a nation mainly located on the European mainland west of the Dardanelles. What one calls Ancient Greece was an assortment of city states, monarchies and colonies extending from the coastal region of Asia Minor to Marseilles, embracing not only mainland Greece, but an equally large part of the toe of Italy, with Sicily, Crete, Cyprus, and a multitude of smaller islands and coastal settlements. These communities, intermittently at war among themselves for many centuries and with no lasting framework of alliances, had an overall government only during the brief period of a generation under Philip of Macedon and his son Alexander. Generals of the latter established dynasties in Egypt, Mesopotamia and Syria, where the one common possession of what we call the Greeks (or as they called themselves, the Hellenes) achieved its expression of most enduring benefit. They shared at all times nothing consistently other than a language which became a unique vehicle for the written word.

In Chapter 2 we have seen that the Tudor period was one during which Greek scholarship, for the first time since the Norman Conquest, established itself in England at English seats of learning. The enthusiasm it evoked is partly explicable because the temper of religious controversy in the latter three-quarters of the century favoured interest in probing Greek sources of the New Testament and of the early Fathers of the Church. However, Greek literature had compelling attractions to those who had little use for the reformed teaching. To understand fully how power-ful was the impact of Greek on scholars of Western Europe during the century which followed Caxton's work, we must first recognise that writing of any sort, and especi-ally priestly sign-writing of the more ancient civilisations, had a very limited use as a means of communication between human beings before printing encouraged a new standard of literacy. Ancient scripts, at first a jealously guarded secret of the priest-hoods, were cumbersome to use and laborious to learn. No writing conveyed the rich content of the spoken word before Greek-speaking people with a reformed alphabet at the disposal of free citizens not subject to a priestly hierarchy began to exploit its possibilities. For centuries thereafter, a wide gap between the written and the spoken word remained where there was no Greek literature—even where the art of alpha-betic writing was in use. There was a vast chasm between written and spoken Latin of the Roman Empire. A wide gap still persisted in nineteenth-century Germany.

In the West at least, it is certain that the Hellenes were first among peoples speak-ing a language of the Indo-Germanic family to adopt and to adapt to their own needs the art of alphabetic writing already used by their Semitic trade rivals. Whether the Romans learned it from them when South Italy and Sicily were Greek-speaking, and Latin the tongue of the tiny province of Latium round the city itself, is a matter of conjecture. What is certain is that their Etruscan neighbours who spoke a language unrelated to languages of the Indo-European group had already adopted and adapted the Phoenician alphabet. In 400 B.C. there was already a considerable Greek literature of hitherto unprecedented variety, when the same small province circumscribed the boundaries of Roman rule. Threatened with Celtic neighbours who occupied North Italy and with the navy of Phoenician Carthage on its sea-board, there must then have seemed little prospect that Rome would master the Western world.

That Greek civilisation produced so rich a literature we may partly explain by saying that Greek script was a finer tool of communication than the consonant alphabet of the Semitic-speaking peoples who took the first and decisive step to alphabet writing; but this is not enough to explain why Latin-speaking pupils of the Greeks fell so far short of Greek achievement. When Rome was in its infancy, Greek literature already had a quality alien to the writings of other civilisations which preceded our own. A decisive circumstance contributory to its growth was that Greek civilisation had already institutionalised as drama of a sort the tribal chorus of its forefathers when the age of alphabet writing began. To an extent which was true of no other civilisation before the age of printing, its dramatists wrote as people actually talk; and Greek drama had a material ally unknown to authors of the Roman Republic. At an early date, when clay or wax tablets were still widely in use elsewhere, Greek-speaking merchant mariners had learned from Egypt the art of using papyrus. Thus, Greek literature had at its disposal a writing surface neither

CAROLI LINNÆI

Equitis De Stella Polari,

SYSTEMA NATURÆ

Per
REGNA TRIA NATURÆ,

Secundum
CLASSES, ORDINES, GENERA, SPECIES,

Cum
CHARACTERIBUS, DIFFERENTIIS, SYNONYMIS, LOCIS.

TOMUS II.

Editio Decima, Reformata.

Cum Privilegio S:æ R:æ M:tis Sveciæ.

HOLMIÆ,
Impensis Direct. LAURENTII SALVII,
1759.

Fig. 20a. Specimen Page from Linnaeus.

DELINEATIO PLANTÆ.

I. THEORIA.

GENUS. Nomen *selectissimum*.
  Character naturalis, essentialis, artificialis.
  Classis Ordoque *Systematis præstantissimi*.
  Ordo naturalis *demonstrandus*.

SPECIES. Nómen triviale.
  Differentia specifica *demonstranda* : *certissima*, *brevissima*.
  Synonyma *ex* descriptione *s.* figura *selecta*; vernacula

CRITICA. Etymologia nominis *generici*, *specifici*.
  Inventor *cum* tempore.
  Eruditio Historica, Critica, antiqua.

II. DESCRIPTIO.

RADIX *duratione* annua, biennis, perennis.
  figura a. fibrosa, ramosa, fusiformis, præmorsa,
    b. repens, articulata, dentata.
    c. globosa, tuberosa, fascicularis, palmata.
    d. bulbosa, granulata,

TRUNCUS *specie* Caulis, Culmus, Scapus, Stipes.
  duratione herbaceus, suffruticosus, fruticosus, arbreus.
    solidus, inanis, fistulosus,
  mensura a. linearis, ungvicularis, pollicaris,
    palmaris, spithameus, dodrantalis,
    pedalis, orgyjalis.
    (proportio *ad folia reliquasque partes.*)
    b. crassities *ex simili notissimo.*
  directione a. erectus, strictus, rigidus,
    laxus, obliqvus, adscendens,
    declinatus, incurvatus, nutans,
    diffusus, procumbens, stoloniferus.
    b. sarmentosus, radicans, repens.
    c. geniculatus, flexuosus, scandens,
    volubilis: *sinistrorsum*, *dextrorsum.*

Fig. 20b. Specimen page from Linnaeus.

unwieldy to hold nor bulky to store; and cultivation of the dramatic form was to influence profoundly a literature of instruction rooted in the medium of debate.

More than three centuries before the fall of Carthage, Greek merchant pilots garnered the secret lore of priestly civilisations, and argumentative listeners were avid for proof when they returned from their travels. Teachers skilled in argument gathered pupils to learn about their discoveries and about strange beliefs held by people of other lands. At first transmitted under oath of secrecy, such as bound the disciples of Pythagoras to their master, instruction soon came into the open. Both teachers and pupils committed it to writing, often in dialogue which recalls the manner of a dramatist. Though we may dismiss much of the reasoning as primitive, such dialogues as those between Socrates and his associates, set down by Plato, contain something more than a record of information about auspicious events and ritual, accounts of revenues, or rules of measurement. They convey the atmosphere of human beings conversing together in a language which addresses itself to the reader directly. To those who had hitherto known Aristotle only through Latin translations, the lucidity of Greek texts dispersed from the printing press was thus a new impetus to writing clearly about controversial matters.

This is perhaps the most remarkable and novel thing about Greek writing; but it is equally true that secular curiosity flourished in the ancient world only where Greek was the speech of daily use. Indeed, Greek-speaking mathematicians and astronomers were responsible for all major advances in scientific knowledge from 500 B.C. to A.D. 300. During that period, the Roman contribution to natural science was negligible; and Latin literature, unless admittedly inspired by Greek authors, conspicuously lacks the speculative temper which we find in the writings of Greeks who discussed politics and human duty. It is therefore worthy of comment that a lively dramatic tradition did little or nothing to shape the Latin of the classical authors as a written language. For the most part, literary Latin was as remote from informal Roman speech as the language of T. S. Eliot from the language of a radio newscaster. No Roman read his classical authors as one reads a bedside book. Even to the educated Roman of the age of Augustus, reading had something of the flavour of a crossword puzzle, and writing, often left to a slave, something of the art of composing a telegram.

The Latin of the Roman Empire had absorbed almost its entire technical vocabulary of medicine, mathematics and astronomy from its Greek teachers. As it is true to say that many words ultimately traceable to Latin came into English through Norman French, many words of Greek parentage have therefore come into English as rendered by Latin writers. This accounts for an inconsistency with respect to English and continental spelling of words of Greek origin. A circumstance undoubtedly propitious to such assimilation is that the flexional systems of Greek and Latin have many similarities. Thus it was that Latin writers rendered the Greek terminals *-os*, *-e* (η) and *-on* by their own corresponding endings *-us*, *-a* and *-um*. At an earlier period, before they appropriated the Greek K for use in loan words, they used C in its place. Earlier writers used PH for φ, which had ceased before the end of the Empire to have the value suggested thereby. Accordingly later writers, as do the Scandinavians and French, represented it by F. Having themselves no sound corresponding to θ (as in *thin* or *thick*) they rendered this sign by TH; likewise, having no sound answering to χ (as in Scots *loch*) they represented it by CH (cf. *christian* and *chalice*); and having no single sign for ψ they represented it correctly as PS. As regards vowels, Latin writers replaced αι by AE (cf. παιδος and *paediatrics*), ει by I (cf. *dinosaur* from δεινος = *terrible* and σαυρος = *lizard*), and ου by U (cf. πους and *Platypus*).

Through Church Latin a handful of Greek words invaded later O.E., in particular *Christmas, psalter, Pharaoh, Pharisee, alms* and *crism* (oil mixed with balm for anointing). Of the last two the former is referable to a corruption of the same root as in *eleemosynary* (1620) for *alms-giving = charity*. A corruption of *crism* from Old French *crème* came back in Middle English as *cream*. To the Middle period belong other Greek loan words introduced by *ecclesiastics* (itself of this vintage), including some referable to treatment of the sick in monasteries, and to the curricula of mediaeval universities. *Inter alia*, we may record the following, mostly late arrivals:

angel, arithmetic, astrology, astronomy, catholic, choir, charity, chronicle (same root as *chronic*, 1601*), *chrysoprase* (cf. the Apocalypse, spelt *crisoprase*), *eclipse, ecliptic, harmony, lyre, monarchy, phantom, pharmacy, pheasant* (through French), *philosophy, phlegm, phylactery, physician, rhetoric* (through Old French with R for RH), *rheumatic, rhinoceros, theatre, theme, theology, thesis, thorax, thyme*.

In view of the interest in Greek studies on the threshold of the Tudor period, intruders assignable thereto are not notably numerous. Such as they are, they do, however, display the *imprimatur* of Holy Church far less than the foregoing. Noteworthy examples are the following, of which only two gainsay the foregoing remark:

amnesty (1580), *christian* (1526), *chrysanthemum* (1578), *democracy* (1574), *ephemeral* (1576), *epic* (1589), *epigram* (1538), *episcopal* (1483), *genus* (1551), *geodesy* (1570), *hexagon* (1571), *hydrophobia* (1547), *monogamy* (1612), *monogram* (1610), *nephritis* (1580), *parabola* (1579), *phenomenon* (1576), *phrase* (1530), *phthiriasis*[1] (1598), *physics* (1589), *physiology* (1564), *Rhamnus*[2] (1562), *rhapsody* (1542), *rhododendron* (1601), *rhomboid* (1570), *rhythm* (1557), *temperature* (1531), *tetrahedron* (1570), *theodolite* (1571), *theorem* (1551), *theory* (1597), *therapeutic* (1541).

---

* All dates given in the next paragraphs are taken from the 1959 reprint of the *Shorter Oxford Dictionary*.

[1] = *lice-infestation*, [2] = *buckthorn*.

During the century and a half after the Tudor period, the secular aspect of the picture becomes more striking, and the influence of the nascent physical sciences becomes more noticeable. A few examples will illustrate this, including, as they do, six names for instruments destined to have a sturdy progeny during the nineteenth century:

barometer (1665), *hydrometer* (1675), *hyperbola* (1668), *microphone* (1683), *microscope* (1656), *philology* (1614), *phraseology* (1664), *psoriasis* (1684), *psychical* (1642), *psychology* (1693), *Ptolemaic* (1674), *telescope* (1648), *thermometer* (1633).

The tempo of Greek invasion did not greatly increase till towards the end of the eighteenth century, and classical scholarship had little directly to do with a process of assimilation which continues with undiminished vigour to this day. Undoubtedly, the pacemaker was the progress of natural sciences handicapped by poverty of the vernacular to supply suitable names for the vast number of new objects discovered or invented during the past two centuries. From 1750 onwards, manufacture of Greek words follows a recognisable pattern. That its increasing momentum thereafter has had little recognition from historians of the Mother Tongue may have something to do with the circumstance that dictionary makers formulate no easily intelligible criterion of what words are current in common speech and what are now *jargon*, i.e. technical terms used only by specialists. For instance, the *Concise Oxford* abounds with agricultural relics such as *gelding, steer, wether*, with architectural labels such as *minaret, casement, plinth*, with heraldic terms such as *puissant* and *rampant*, with legal terms such as *barratry* and *simony* and with nautical terms such as *hatch, poop, schooner*. The truth is that few comparatively well-educated people living in what is now a highly urban civilisation have occasion to use any of these words. Nor will they be familiar with precise distinctions recognised only in Canon Law, as between *adultery* and *fornication*. Contrariwise, many words we commonly meet in an article on baby feeding or on child health in a women's magazine, and on radio or space travel in a magazine of hobbies for boys, are not yet in the dictionary list. A scrutiny of these discloses a number of bricks such as *photo, graph, logy, tele, psycho, geo, hydro, zoo, bio, gen, gram, path, phobia, scope*. By putting these together in different ways we can make an enormous variety of new words whose component parts give a direct clue to meaning. One example is enough to make this clear. Starting with *telephotography* we may form *telepathy, psychopath* and *psychiatry, pathology, zoology, zooscope, telescope, telegram, gramophone, phonetic, phonograph, telegraph*; or *photophobia, hydrophobia, hydrant, hydrogen, photogenic, geography, geology, biology, biography* and so on.

To get into focus the origins of this new word-making pattern, and to understand how what had been but a trickle before 1750 had become a cataract in 1850, we must take stock of several historical circumstances. The little knowledge of Greek astronomy, medicine, mechanics and mathematics available in Northern Europe during the period immediately before printing began came from Arabic translations current in the Moslem universities of Spain; but substantial progress in the study of medicine, of mining and of navigation did not begin till after the introduction of printing and the discovery of the New World. Throughout Western Europe, Latin was the language of nearly all learned treatises, scientific or otherwise, till after the Puritan Revolution, and the study of Greek did not start in Britain till the movement for Reformation in the English Church encouraged theologians to search the earliest available sources of Christian scriptures. Above all, England and Scotland did not begin to become manufacturing countries in the modern sense till the time of the French Revolution, that is to say the end of the eighteenth century. In Chaucer's time, the stock-in-trade of the apothecary and of the manufacturer called for few terms other than those widely current. Chaucer himself uses:

quicksilver, litharge, brimstone, boras, sal armoniak, verdegrees, arsenik, alkali, sal tartare, vitriole, sal peter, alum, magnesia, unslekked lym.

By A.D. 1450 we also find in general use among men of learning:

algebra, antimony, azimuth, amber, distil, duodenum, iris, magnet, nitre, rheumatic, sciatica, semen, thorax, ventricle.

Several terms in the last two lists are from Arabic. Of about 100 words of Arabic origin now part of current speech, a high proportion bear testimony to our debt to Moslem science. To Moorish pharmacy we owe: *alchemy, alcohol, alkali, amber, ambergris, attar, camphor, carat, chemistry, damson, elixir, hashish, jar, lime, mummy, naphtha, nard, opium, saffron, sugar, syrup, talisman.* To Moorish astronomy, mathematics and meteorology we owe: *algebra, almanac, cipher, monsoon, nadir, sirocco, zenith* and *zero.* Expanding trade between Europe and the more prosperous Moslem communities during and after the Crusades brought in many other words: *artichoke, bazaar, caravan, coffee, cotton, crimson, damask, divan, lute, mattress, ottoman, tambourine, tariff* from Arabic; and from Persian: *azure, barbican, chess, check* and *checkmate, emerald, lilac, musk, orange, pawn* and *rook, sash, shawl, taffeta.* Aside from many words which describe life in the Near East, such as *Koran, Sultan* and *Vizier* (Arabic) or *sepoy, Pasha* and *turban* (Persian), a few others are familiar to all of us, but less easy to classify. Such are (Arabic) *admiral, assassin, arsenal, dragoman, hazard, magazine, gazelle, giraffe, scullion,* and (Persian) *jackal, kaffir, paradise, scimitar.*

A landmark of language change in the period 1500-1550 was the publication of the first illustrated work of anatomy, the *de Humani Corporis Fabrica* of Vesalius, printed in Latin. It signalises a new species of scientific writing, easily intelligible because beautifully illustrated; and it made available to the secular physician, now a man of substance, a rich fund of word-material for the names of organs and bones. In the century of Vesalius several scientific terms other than those already cited above came into use, viz. *alga, alloy, dissection, evaporate, leprosy, mosquito, mumps, smallpox, scurvy, vacuum*. Aside from the stimulus printing imparted to the study of human anatomy, it also made possible for the first time in history the production of illustrated treatises on supposedly medicinal plants. This novel amenity for spreading scientific knowledge came about when the discovery of the New World familiarised Europe with many hitherto unknown species such as cinchona bark from which we get quinine. The subsequent invention of the microscope in the first half of the seventeenth century and the rise of commercial horticulture also enlarged man's knowledge of the diversity of animals and plants. Between 1680 and 1730 new data and a new interest in living things bore fruit in a succession of treatises on individual assemblages both of plants and of animals.

How vast was the number of newly-named species will be evident from a few figures. The Greek pharmacopoeias of Theophrastus (*circa* 300 B.C.) and of Dioscorides (first century A.D.) respectively listed about 500 and 600 species of plants, the Moorish pharmacopoeias (*circa* A.D. 800) scarcely twice as many. Indeed, the famous Elizabethan *Herbal* of Gerard (*circa* A.D. 1590) names no more than 1,033. A century later, the number of names for plant species had increased more than fourfold. In the setting of Gerard's *Herbal*, names for familiar creatures and for substances in daily use were by no means equivalent in different countries. Indeed, folk-names for plants are not necessarily the same in different parts of the same country. Thus the *mountain ash* of southern England is the *rowan* of Scotland. Scottish *blaeberries* are *wimberries* in Wales, *whortleberries* in one part of England and *bilberries* in another. Thus intelligible and useful communication about either living creatures or inert materials could be possible only if naturalists of all sorts systematically undertook the task of citing individual names of international currency: (a) for each species of plant or animal and each variety of mineral used as a raw material for industry of one sort or another; (b) for the characteristics by which we identify as such the objects so named.

To understand fully the accomplishment of this undertaking, we need to recall that Latin was the medium of instruction in all disciplines of the mediaeval universities of Christendom at a time when scholars came to them from all parts of Europe, that the efflorescence of natural science in Europe, other than Moorish Spain, began in the Italy of Leonardo da Vinci (1452-1519), and that the whim of the Italian renaissance favoured the crossword puzzle model of Ciceronian rhetoric in contradistinction to a more flexible, so-called *vulgar*, Latin lately current in the lecture room. When Galileo set a new fashion in Padua by lecturing in the vernacular, i.e. his native Italian, students from abroad may well have found his lectures more easy to follow than discourses in the grand manner of classical rhetoric. At the death of Galileo (1642), the Thirty Years' War (1618-1648) had eclipsed the culture of what we now call Germany. Within two decades thereafter, France and Britain shared equal distinction as the successors of their Italian teachers in the forefront of scientific discovery, and savants of both countries in their respective associations, the French Academy of Sciences and the British Royal Society, followed the Galilean tradition by conducting public discussion in their own vernaculars.

It goes without saying that Galileo's practice entailed no inconvenience through paucity of descriptive terms used by predecessors who taught and wrote in Latin. In his native Italian, novel Latin adjectives and nouns fall into line with the contemporary pattern by a simple process of discarding terminals, as had happened in the past. The same is true of French and, through French, of English. Indeed, English had assimilated at an early date formative French suffixes not necessarily restricted to use with roots of French origin (cf. *righteous, bumptious, Muscovite*). Some of these have proved to be instruments for welding Anglo-American into a medium

MUSEUM EXHIBIT—SUFFIXES OF THE CLASSICAL LEGACY

-IC   Latin -*ica*, Greek -*ike*, French -*ique* as in *historic, public, endemic, politic;*

-ITE   Latin -*ita*, Greek -*ite*, French -*ite* as in *erudite, composite, tripartite, Muscovite, apposite, polite, opposite, Carmelite;*

-ATE   Latin -*ata*, French -*ate* as in *alternate, articulate, sedate, ornate, desolate, prostrate, innate, ovate;*

-OUS and -OSE   Latin -*osa*, French -*euse* and -*ose* as in:
(a) *righteous, luscious, anxious, gracious, ligneous;*
(b) *grandiose, otiose, bellicose, globose, varicose;*

-IFEROUS   Latin -*fer* (=*bearing*), French -*fère* as in *carboniferous, coniferous;*

-ACEOUS   Latin -*aceosa* as in *foliaceous, herbaceous, carbonaceous;*

-AR and -ARY   From Latin -*aria*, French -*aire* or -*ière* as in *lunar, solar, regular* and in *plenary, arbitrary, rotary;*

-ANT and -ENT   From Latin (nomin. sing. -*ans* and -*ens*, abl. sing. -*ante* and -*ente*) as in *appellant, sentient, rampant;*

-AL   From Latin (abl. sing.) -*ale* as in *lateral, partial, radical, general;*

-ILE   From Latin (abl. sing.) -*ile* as in *sessile, fissile, labile, prehensile, agile, servile;*

-INE   From Latin -*ina* as in *canine, feline, pristine;*

-FIC   Latin -*fica*, French -*fique* (same root as *faciens*=*making*) as in *soporific, pacific, beatific, colorific, terrific, prolific, horrific;*

-FID   From perfect tense stem (-*fid*) of Latin *findere* (=*to split*) as in *bifid, trifid, pinnatifid;*

-FORM   Latin *forma*, French *forme* (=*shape*) as in *cruciform, vermiform* and (metaphorically) *uniform.*

for world-wide communication about what is of common interest to all on the threshold of an Age of Potential Plenty. As such, they deserve detailed comment. For a good enough reason, which we shall later see, they are all adjectival endings. Our Museum Exhibit (p. 246) cites the feminine nominative singular Latin or French form, as nearest to the English. The sixth term (-ACEOUS) calls for additional comment, because it is *technically* formative as both adjective and noun. It has the force of the native suffix -LIKE in *life-like*, *god-like*, *bird-like*. As such, it has generated a list of names, for plant groups, e.g. *Liliaceae* (=*lily-like*), *Rosaceae* (*rose-like*), and for a few classes of animals, e.g. *Crustacea*. As will transpire more clearly in what follows, the circumstance that English had already acquired this equipment of suffixes by the beginning of the Tudor period and that it had then shed the flexional handicaps of its Teutonic ancestry makes it easy to understand two things. One is why Latin remained the language of science among Europeans of Teutonic stock throughout the eighteenth—and in Germany well into the nineteenth—century. The other is why German forfeited any claims to be a *lingua franca* of science in the world of today by relapsing into *Volksprach* when it abandoned Latin. The consequence was unavoidable. So highly flexional a language as High German cannot assimilate, to any simple pattern, affixes foreign to its own heritage.

The reader may here feel that we have anticipated too much of what follows, and will therefore ask: why do we attach so much importance to the Anglo-American outfit of Latin-Greek terminals which are adjectival and as such descriptive? To answer this, let us retrace our steps to Galileo. In his time, the mechanical sciences were on the march and medicine had inherited, through Latin, a Greek vocabulary adequate to the needs of what little medical science there was. This was still almost entirely descriptive in the service of human anatomy and identification of plants with alleged curative properties. A century after Galileo's death, the prospect for scientific discovery was different in two ways. One of these has already provoked comment, i.e. that discovery of the New World and navigations along the coasts of Africa and the Far East had brought into the picture a vast treasury of previously unfamiliar plant and animal species, whence an impetus to a technique of identification alien to earlier herbals and pharmacopoeias. Meanwhile, Galileo's own demonstration that air has weight had opened the door to a hitherto unrecognised third state of matter, the gaseous. Thereby, chemical science was eventually able to explore a new territory for inventive ingenuity. Such was the setting in which Linnaeus published (1735) the first edition of his *Systema Naturae*, in three volumes devoted respectively to what he called the '*animal, vegetable* and *mineral* kingdoms.'

The piety of the author provides more than enough comic relief for adverse comment in the manner of Lytton Strachey's *Great Victorians*. In many ways, the *Systema* is well behind piecemeal work of naturalists regarded by later botanists and zoologists as more *en rapport* with a so-called *natural* approach to classification; and its mineralogy discloses no hint of an already nascent understanding of the rôle of gaseous elements in chemical combination. None the less, the *Systema Naturae*, in one sense at least, is stupendously unique. In what categories Linnaeus classified animals, plants and minerals is now of trivial importance; but his recognition of the need for a new vocabulary of descriptive terms remains a landmark in the history of science. None of the herbalists, nor even their more sophisticated successors who had written about particular groups, as did Morrison and Ray in the preceding half century, had recognised that a prerequisite for clear directives relevant to the task of identification is unequivocal definition of the adjectives we use when we describe creatures.

It is here pertinent to our theme to recall that the total number of named plants and animals known to European civilisation before exploration of the New World began was less than 1,000. By the time when Linnaeus wrote, the total was about 10,000. This signifies that the task of codifying their characteristics with a view to subsequent identification called for precisely defined descriptive terms vastly more numerous than those hitherto in use. For two reasons, demand was greatest to meet the needs of botanical classification. One is that medicine had already equipped comparative anatomy with a sizeable vocabulary. The other is that practical objectives, supposedly medical or authentically horticultural, fostered the description of new plant species while zoological classification was still in its infancy. A few figures will spotlight the rôle of Linnaeus as a language-maker with this end in view. At the beginning of the second volume of the *Systema* dealing with the vegetable kingdom, we encounter a complete glossary of all adjectives used for labelling the variety of forms the several parts of plants display: 16 to specify the longevity and shape of the RADIX (*root*); 122 in nine categories for different characteristics of the TRUNCUS (*trunk*); 203 in eighteen categories to describe the site, shape, etc., of the FOLIA (*leaves*); 175 in seven categories for the FULCRA (*petioles, bracts, spines*); 57 also in seven categories to describe the *inflorescence*; 181 in six categories for the FRUCTIFICATES (*floral organs*) and nearly 200 others for uses, texture, habit, climate, site, etc.

In all, the list cites a few more than 950 terms, Latin like the rest of the text, and almost all with one or other of the adjectival suffixes which French and English had already assimilated as thoroughly as Galileo's Italian. For instance, the root may be *bulbosa*; the trunk *procumbens, herbaceus*; the leaves *alternata, axillaria, tripartita, 5-fida, sessilia, radicalia* and so on. Every item of the 950-word list is transparently adaptable to English usage. With the aid of very little elementary natural history, anyone familiar with French or Anglo-American can translate most of the text without recourse to a dictionary or Latin grammar. Accordingly, the reader might even suspect that the main outcome of the *Systema* was to reinstate Latin by a back-door. However, the *Systema*, and especially the second volume, is notable for a reason other than the wealth of descriptive Latin words which it enlisted in the service of science. Perhaps because the author felt that he had usefully exhausted his resources of Latin with the end in view, he systematically recruited only Greek roots for naming the major groups of plants in his so-called *sexual system*. As we have seen, this innovation was consistent with medical tradition, since the jargon of medicine, if spelt in conformity with Latin conventions, had come almost exclusively from Greek sources; but we can view it in retrospect as a watershed in the story of what was to be the world-wide vocabulary of Western science. Henceforth science, at first chemistry in particular, was to turn more and more to Greek for its word-building bricks.

Chemistry therefore claims our attention as we approach the end of the century; and the third volume (*Mineral Kingdom*) makes no contact with classificatory procedure subsumed by what we ordinarily call chemistry today. It is therefore mentionable that the first edition antedated the beginnings of chemical industry when Dr. Roebuck (1749) set up a factory to produce sulphuric acid in Birmingham. During the eighteenth century, expanding manufacture in Britain had outgrown resources of crude natural substances upon which it had hitherto relied, such as *sand, chalk, sea-salt, vinegar, lard, potashes, saltpetre* and so forth. Before the turn of the century, chemical industry, which started with large-scale manufacture of sulphuric acid, embraced synthetic *alkali, bleaching powder, ammonia* and *coal gas*. Discovery of a large number of new elements and of their compounds accompanied the change, and multiplication of *ersatz* substitutes called for *ersatz* names. Within the half century after Roebuck obtained his patent, all the above-named commercial processes for manufacturing pure substances had begun in Britain. Thus the social setting in which successive later editions of the *Systema* appeared was favourable to an entirely new approach to classification of inert materials. The new need was for names which could convey a recipe for making them. Creation of such a system was the work of French theoretical chemists, in close correspondence with the British pioneers of chemical industry.

Foremost among the French circle was Lavoisier, who had been commissioned at one time by his government to carry out a mineralogical survey of France. Undoubtedly he was well acquainted with the work of Linnaeus, whose undertaking may well have quickened his interest in classification and nomenclature; and Bergman, like Linnaeus a Swede, was foremost in making a plea for a new approach to chemical nomenclature. With him, Guyton de Morveau, at first independently, later jointly, explored (1780-82) the possibility of breaking through the miasma of meaningless names of current chemistry with a view to naming substances in terms relevant to, and indicative of, their ingredients. In a memoir communicated to the French Academy of Sciences in 1782, Lavoisier cites such examples of the fatuity of contemporary nomenclature as: *powder of algaroth, salt of alembroth, pompholise, phagedauic water, turbith material, aethiops, colcothar, oil of tartar per deliquium, oil of vitriol, butter of arsenic, butter of antimony, flowers of zinc.* To these one may add *blue vitriol* (copper sulphate), *litharge* (lead monoxide), *Rochelle salt* (potassium sodium tartarate), *tartar emetic* (potassium antimony tartarate), *Glauber's salt* (sodium sulphate), *Epsom salt* (magnesium sulphate), *calomel* (mercurous chloride), *corrosive sublimate* (mercuric chloride).

Bergman and de Morveau formulated a programme which laid down principles which posterity has endorsed; but they left its implementation to Lavoisier and his colleagues, notably Berthollet, at the invitation of de Morveau (1787) after Bergman's death (1784). To Lavoisier the challenge had a wider significance than the intention. "If languages really are instruments fashioned by men to make thinking easier, they should be of the best possible kind, and to strive to perfect them is indeed to work for the advancement of science." The immediate outcome was a joint publication, translated into English and published in London in 1788. The following excerpt from the translator's (Pearson's) introduction to the second edition (1799) illustrates the immensely important rôle in the reformed nomenclature of affixes which English had so copiously assimilated from Latin only because it had earlier done so as part of its hybrid heritage. The reader will see that a prominent feature of the system was regularisation of the significance attachable to terminals of the pairs -*ous*, -*ic* and -*ite*, -*ate* which had already (e.g. *ferrous*, *cupric*) invaded the terrain of chemistry, but hitherto with no reason for preferring one or other member of a pair. A single example, taken from the *New System of Chemistry*, should explain clearly how much brevity and simplicity in terms, provided the terms have a proper import, facilitate the acquisition, retention and communication of chemical knowledge. What follows reproduces typographical conventions of the 1799 translation.

SULPHUR may be a component of a great number . . . of substances . . . SULPHUR may unite with OXYGEN by which combination it is rendered into the ACID STATE; but this ACID is of three different species, according to three quantities of Oxygen which may combine with a given quantity of Sulphur; and these three species are named the *Sulphu*REOUS, the *Sulphu*RIC and the OXY-GENATED *Sulphu*RIC acids. . . . Each of these acids may unite with at least twenty-six different kinds of substances, which are metallic Oxides, Earths and Alkalis, and consequently produce seventy-eight different compound bodies. . . . Accordingly, the word *Sul*PHITE denotes compounds consisting of the *Sulphu*-REOUS Acid and each of the above twenty-six different kinds of substances; *Sul*PHATE implies compounds consisting of *Sulphu*RIC Acid and each of the above twenty-six . . . and . . . *Oxysul*PHATE signifies compounds consisting of the OXYGENATED SULPHURIC Acid and the above twenty-six. . . . The particular species of compound substances belonging to each of these three genera, named *Sul*PHITE, *Sul*PHATE and *Oxysul*PHATE are signified by subjoining the name of the basis as an adjective to these generic names. Accordingly, the meaning of the names *Sul*PHITE of Soda, *Sul*PHATE of Soda, *Oxysul*PHATE of Soda will, without difficulty, suggest the composition of these substances. . . . SULPHUR may unite with Metals, Earths, Alkalis, Hydrogen Gas and other bases which are not acidified or are not acidifiable. The compound bodies produced by these combinations are denominated SULPHURETS.* . . . By the names SUL-PHURET OF POTASH . . . OF SODA . . . OF IRON . . . OF LIME . . . OF HYDROGEN GAS, etc., a just notion may be acquired of the composition of the compound just mentioned to consist of SULPHUR AND CERTAIN BASES NOT ACIDIFIED or NOT ACIDIFIABLE (pp. 4-7) . . . It appears therefore, that by four different terminations of the word Sulphur and two different abbre-viations of it, and by adding the word which is the name of the species of substance united to Sulphur, or by prefixing a word which signifies the substance combined with a compound of Sulphur, Oxygen, and a basis, above 300 different kinds of substances (which consist of Sulphur united to other bodies) may be denominated so as to import the most essential properties of the things which these terms are intended to signify . . . (p. 8).

Against the background of this testimony, it is scarcely too much to say that two dates are of cardinal importance in connexion with the genesis of the international vocabulary of modern science. One is A.D. 1066. The Norman Conquest was instrumental in preparing a way for linguistic innovations which facilitated English assimilation of a battery of Latin affixes, mainly through French at first, later more often directly from classical authors. The other is 1749, the year which signalises the beginning of chemical industry in Britain, and anticipates close links between British discoverers and inventors with utilitarian preoccupations and French pioneers of linguistic reform. From the memoir last cited, we get a clear picture of the contemporary unreadiness of the Teutonic bloc for a reform which British men of science cordially welcomed from the start:†

"In Germany, Gulanner appears to have been the first who introduced the new chemical Nomenclature of the French; but in rendering it into the German language, he has made *several changes in the words of the names suitably to the nature of the language*. . . . As instances may be mentioned, Salpetergesaure Pottasche, Salpeter-gesaurte Pottasche, ueber saure Salpetergesaurte Pottasche, for nitrite, nitrate and oxynitrate of Potash." (Italics inserted.)

Without compunction, Lavoisier's successors exploited Greek roots, in particular the numerals, as in *monoxide, dioxide, trioxide, tetroxide, pentoxide*, though sometimes

* Now *sulphides* in agreement with *oxide* which the new nomenclature adopted from the start. The affix *-ide* is a classical assimilation from Greek εἶδος (=*species*, in contradistinction to *genus*).
† From 1803 onwards, Dalton followed the new usage in his own teaching, and his *New System of Chemistry* (1808) established it firmly throughout Britain.

associated with Latin in the same word (e.g. *sesquioxide*). However, chemistry did not circumscribe Lavoisier's creative genius as a language maker. Indeed, the reader may have noticed in a previous citation that he wrote for posterity of the language of science as a whole. He actively participated in a notable contribution to the nomenclature of the physical sciences as secretary of a commission set up in 1790 by the Revolutionary government to reform the French system of weights and measures. The outcome, published after his death, was our now international (C.G.S.) system. Here again, Greek roots annexed new territory; and chemical manufacture was now competing with commercial horticulture as the pacemaker of word-building. A need was soon to arise in another domain.

A mechanical revolution was now under way. More extensive use of steam power and electrical inventions followed in rapid succession. By 1840 Europe, and especially Britain, was beginning to exploit resources of power hitherto unknown and hence with no native stock of suggestive roots to describe such inventions as *electrolysis, telegraphy, galvanometers, dynamos, photography* and *telephones*. Between 1800 and 1850 these followed in rapid succession. By the latter date, the same pattern of ringing the changes on a few Greek roots (as in *lithograph, neolithic, monolith*) was beginning to permeate the whole of industry and newer branches of scientific enquiry such as *archaeology*.

The nomenclature of the *Centigrade—Gram—Seconds* (C.G.S.) system was, like many chemical terms (e.g. *sesquioxide* and *pentavalent*) of a later vintage, a blend of Latin and Greek roots in the same word, with results which are open to criticism. Unhappily, it transmitted to posterity a new source of confusion with reference to the meaning of a Greek root by adopting the French convention K indiscriminately for the *k*-sound so represented in Greek and the *kh*-sound represented in Greek by χ and in Anglo-American more commonly by CH (as in Scots *loch*). As regards blending Greek and Latin roots in the same word, men of science at one time adhered to the rule that a new term should consist of only Greek or of only Latin roots.

To be sure, we cannot apply a comparable rule consistently unless we exclude native and French terminals such as -LY in *confidently* and -OUS in *righteous*. Nor is it possible to lay down a hard and fast distinction between Latin and the many Greek roots which Latin authors borrowed. None the less, the objection to mixing roots is not mere pedantry. The spelling of a Latin root may be like that of a Greek one with a totally different meaning or *vice versa*, and it may suggest the latter if in company with a second root which is truly Greek. For instance *homo-* attached to a Latin root, as in *homosexual*, may wrongly recall the root in *homicide*, suggestive of common *man-love = love of male for male*. It is in fact the Greek root signifying *likeness*, as in *homogeneous*. The alternative *homoerotic*, based wholly on Greek, conveys more precisely the correct meaning, which includes *Lesbian*, and does not distract us on first acquaintance with a false clue.

After Linnaeus and after Lavoisier, new circumstances conspired to call for new names both for living creatures and for substances. Between A.D. 1780 and 1850 trade with and colonisation of Australasia greatly enlarged our knowledge of the vast variety of animals and plants. Meanwhile, steam navigation gave new opportunities for travel to explorer-naturalists such as Alfred Russell Wallace and Charles Darwin. Whereas the total number of named living creatures was only about 10,000 in 1750, the number of named species of plants was about 225,000 in 1950 at which date the number of named animals was over a million. There are today about a quarter of a million named species of beetles alone. Between 1850 and 1870, the discovery of how to make dyes from coal-tar constituents led to the manufacture of compounds which almost wholly displaced the traditional use of vegetable dyes. The first synthesis of an organic compound (urea) occurred in 1828. By 1954 the number of organic compounds synthesised was over 750,000; the number of dyes already synthesised exceeded 10,000 and of these 1,200 were on the market. In the same year, the rate at which chemists were making new organic compounds was about 400 a week in Britain alone; but the task of naming so many things and of naming many more in future is no longer formidable. From only ten roots, we can make ten different words containing one only (e.g. *electron*), ninety different words containing two only (e.g. *telegraph*), and 720 different words with three only (e.g. *gynandromorph, telephotography*), giving a total of 820 derivative words containing only three roots or less. From twenty roots we can make 7,240.

An account of the impact of natural science on language, and of the rôle it has played in fostering adoption of Greek roots as bricks for word-building, would be incomplete without any reference to modern medicine. The *Systema* of Linnaeus set a pattern for the production of pretentious medical textbooks such as that of Cullen (1784) in which many new, but few useful, names for diseases crop up. Some of these have entered common speech, but only because of knowledge gained later and only because of a new need. The urbanisation which accompanied the rising tempo of industrialisation in Britain from 1800 to 1850 made the need for improved sanitation greater than ever before, encouraged the study of epidemics on the threshold of new knowledge, associated especially with the names of Pasteur and Koch, and promoted two social innovations. One was the legal obligation to register the so-called cause of death. The other, and later, was the inauguration of public health authorities. Well before the end of the nineteenth century, death registration led to international conferences to get agreement about naming diseases in a useful and suggestive way. Thenceforward, the work of public health authorities has promoted an ideology of health and a growing interest of the ordinary citizen, especially the parent, in advancing medical science. Consequently, words such as *tuberculosis, immunity, calorie, vitamin, serum* and *anti-biotic* are now more truly part of the vocabulary of everyday usage than are such dictionary exhibits as *gelding, minaret, galleon, bell-wether* or *barratry*.

To use this emotionally neutral language of science intelligently, and to add to its stock-in-trade, we do not need to be proficient in Greek or in Latin; but we do need to know a few hundred current roots derived from Greek words and a few hundred from Latin words with the meaning they now have by general consent in current speech. Unless we have such knowledge we shall miss useful clues to meaning and we shall adopt or coin meaningless new words. An example of the latter is the title *Auto-electric* of three garages in one English city. The root common to *automatic*, *autonomous* and *autarchy* might suggest that the proprietors have at last discovered a form of perpetual motion for generating electricity. Truth to tell, they merely sell electric devices for *automobiles*, the latter so-called because equipped with an inanimate source of power in contradistinction to the horse-drawn vehicles they displaced.

Today the international vocabulary of scientific terms numbers more than three million items, mainly based on less than a thousand Greek and a thousand Latin roots. Other speech communities have been less receptive than English and French to their assimilation into the daily speech of the citizen. None the less, the common stock of international word-material in daily use is daily growing. Indeed, commerce and a common interest in technological advances sooner or later impose the same pattern on all alike. The gain is enormous for a reason not sufficiently recognised by those who wistfully plead for native compounds such as *sand-waste* for *desert* or *sky-line* for *horizon*. While such are sometimes attractive and often harmless, any attempt to build a vocabulary of exact science from native roots alone would have one great disadvantage. Advancing knowledge of fact has brought about a deeper insight into nature and new ways of thinking about it. If we agree to give native words such as *force* or *soul* a new meaning in a new context, we find ourselves carrying into the new context old ideas which make it difficult to think clearly. Those who talk, as in Hitler's Germany, about *race* (*Ras*) and *blood* (*Blut*) are inviting passion, misunderstanding and muddle. In the emotionally neutral language of science, *localised communities* and *genes* are a challenge to curiosity, calm reflection and clear thinking.

QUIZ CORNER 7

Quiz 1

Latin and Greek Prepositions, Adverbs and Pronouns used as Prefixes

	LATIN	MEANING	AS IN	GREEK	AS IN
1.	SUPER *or* SUPRA	above	......	ὑπερ	......
2.	SUB	below	......	ὑπο	......
3.	ANTE *or* PRE	before	......	προ	......
4.	POST	after	......	μετα	......
5.	RETRO	backwards	......	ὀπισθεν	......
6.	PRO	on behalf of, in favour of	......		
7.	CONTRA	against	......	ἀντι	......
8.	CUM	together with	......	συν *or* συμ	......
9.	SINE	without, not	......	ἀν *or* ἀ	......
10.	AD *or* A	up	......	ἀνα	......
11.	DE	down	......	κατα	......
12.	EX *or* E	out of	......	ἐξ *or* ἐκ	......
13.	EXTRA	outside	......	ἐκτος	......
14.	IN *or* IM	in	......	ἐν *or* ἐμ	......
15.	INTRA	inside	......	ἐνδον	......
16.	INTER	between	......		
17.	PER	through	......	δια	......
18.	AB *or* A	away from	......	ἀπο	......
19.	CIRCUM	around	......	περι	......
20.	PROXIME	beside, near	......	παρα	......
21.	TRANS	across, through	......	δια	......
22.	ULTRA	beyond	......	ὑπερ	......
23.	EGO	I	......	ἐγω	......
24.	IPSE	self	......	αὐτος	......

Notes:

3, 4 and 15 have comparative forms ANTERIOR, POSTERIOR, INTERIOR from which we get prefixes ANTERO-, POSTERO-.

8. Greek N becomes M in compounds before P, B or PH, and drops out before S or L (with doubling of L).

9. Greek AN is shortened to A before a consonant.

10-11. Latin AD may be shortened to A before a consonant. AD means more generally *towards*, DE more generally *from*.

12. Latin EX may be shortened to E, and Greek to EC.

14. For Greek, see note on 8; but note that IN- as a Latin prefix which changes to IM- before B, M and P is more often equivalent to NON- and to the Teutonic affix UN- as in *unwary*. So also before L and R, IN- becomes IL- and IR-, as in *illegal* and *irresponsible*.

1, 13 and 22 have comparative and superlative SUPERIOR-SUPREMUS, EXTERIOR-EXTREMUS and ULTERIOR-ULTIMUM.

Quiz 2

Prefixes based on the Latin and Greek numerals, the Colours and the Elements

Fill in the blanks.

LATIN	MEANING	AS IN	GREEK	AS IN
1. UNI-	......	......	ἐν	......
2. DI- *or* DU-	......	......	δι-	......
3. TRI-	......	......	τρια	......
4. QUADR-	......	......	τετρα-	......
5. QUINQUE	......	......	πεντε	......
6. SEX	......	......	ἐξ	......
7. SEPT-	......	......	ἑπτα	......
8. OCTO	......	......	ὀκτω	......
9. NOVEM	......	......	ἐννεα	......
10. DECEM	......	......	δεκα	......
11. DUODECIM	......	......	δωδεκα	......
12. CENT-	......	......	ἑκατον	......
13. MILLE	......	......	χιλιοι	......
14. (VIGINTI)	......	—	εἰκοσι	......
15. PRIM-	......	......	πρωτω	......
16. SECUND-	......	......	δευτερω	......
17. TERTI-	......	......	τριτω	......
18. SINGULI	......	......	μονω	......

LATIN	MEANING	AS IN	GREEK	AS IN
19. BI-	......	......	διπλω	......
20. TRI-	......	......	τριπλ-	......
21. SEMI-	......	......	ἡμι	......
22. AMBI-	......	......	ἀμφι	......
23. SIMPL-	......	......	ἁπλω-	......
24. ALBO	......	......	λευκω	......
25. NIGRO	......	......	μελανι	......
26. RUBRO	......	......	ἐρυθρω	......
27. CAERULO	......	......	κυανεω	......
28. VIRIDI or GLAUCO	......	......	χλωρω	......
29. LUTEO	......	......	ξανθω	......
30. CINERACEO	......	......	πολιω or φαιω	......
31. PURPUREO	......	......	πορφυρω	......
32. —	......	—	ῥοδο-	......
33. VIOLA	......	......	ἰοειδει	......
34. TERRA	......	......	γη	......
35. INCENDIO	......	......	πυρι	......
36. AQUA	......	......	ὑδατι	......
37. AERE	......	......	ἀερι	......

Quiz 3

Word Bricks based on Latin and Greek Adjectives and Adverbs

LATIN	MEANING	AS IN	GREEK	AS IN
1. SANCTO	holy	......	ἁγιω	......
2. ALTO	high	......	ἀκρω	......
3. ACRI	bitter, sharp	......	ὀξει	......
4. ALTERO	other	......	ἀλλω	......
5. LIBERO	free	......	ἐλευθερω	......
6. OPTIMO	best	......	ἀριστω	......
7. PROFUNDO	deep	......	βαθει	......

LATIN	MEANING	AS IN	GREEK	AS IN
8. BREVI	short	......	βραχει	......
9. LONGO	long	......	δολιχω	......
10. DULCI	sweet	......	γλυκει	......
11. SIMILI	alike	......	ὁμω	......
12. BENE	well	......	ἐυ	......
13. MALE	ill	......	δυς or κακω	......
14. MEDICO	medical	......	ἰατρικω	......
15. PROPRIO	individual, proper	......	ἰδιω	......
16. AEQUO	equal	......	ἰσω	......
17. BELLO	beautiful	......	καλω	......
18. FRIGIDO	cold	......	κρυο-εντι	......
19. MOLLI	soft	......	μαλακω	......
20. GRANDI	big	......	μεγα-λω	......
21. (PARVO)	small	—	μικρω	......
22. SALUBRI	healthy	......	ὑγιει	......
23. MORTUO	dead	......	νεκρω	......
24. MEDIO	middle	......	μεσω	......
25. ALIENO	foreign	......	ξενω	......
26. SICCO	dry	......	ξηρω	......
27. PAUCO	few	......	ὀλιγω	......
28. NOVO	new	......	νεω	......
29. OMNI	whole	......	ὁλω	......
30. RECTO	straight	......	ὀρθω	......
31. VENERABILI	old	......	παλαιω	......
32. OMNI	all	......	παν-τι	......
33. GROSSO	thick	......	παχει	......
34. PLANO	flat	......	πλατει	......
35. MULTO	many	......	πολλω	......
36. AURO	gold	......	χρυσω	......
37. SATURO	full	......	πλεω	......
38. DURO	hard	......	σκληρω	......
39. TENUI	thin	......	στενω	......
40. SOLIDO	solid	......	στερεω	......
41. UMIDO	moist	......	ὑγρω	......
42. CALORI	heat, hot	......	θερμω	......
43. LONGO	distant, afar	......	τηλε	......

LATIN	MEANING	AS IN	GREEK	AS IN
44. ITERUM	again	......	παλιν	......
45. NUDO	naked	......	γυμνω	......
46. VARIO	unlike	......	ἑτερω	......
47. GRAVI	heavy	......	βαρει	......
48. PAUPERI	poor	......	πενητι	......
49. SENI	old	......	πρεσβει or γεροντι	......
50. INSANO	foolish	......	μωρω	......

Notes:

(i) The Latin and Greek adjectives have masculine, feminine and neuter case forms in both numbers. The one given here is the masculine singular dative corresponding to O.E. HIM. Greek adjectives with the dative ending ει may have the nominative ending υς in which case they commonly appear with the ending -U in compounds, e.g. βραχυς—βραχει in *brachydactyly*.

(ii) For 42, the adjectival form of the Latin is *calido*, which has few derivatives; *calori* is the corresponding noun.

Quiz 4

Latin Phrases

PHRASE	MEANING
1. Ave atque vale	....
2. ad hoc	....
3. ad nauseam	....
4. per os	....
5. post mortem	....
6. brev	....
7. exempli gratia (e.g.)	....
8. ceteris paribus	....
9. semper eadem	....
10. ibidem (ibid.)	....
11. idem	....
12. id est (i.e.)	....

PHRASE	MEANING
13. ipsissima verba	. . . .
14. in vino veritas	. . . .
15. ipso facto	. . . .
16. nil desperandum	. . . .
17. per cent(um)	. . . .
18. ad valorem	. . . .
19. per annum	. . . .
20. ad vitam aut culpam	. . . .
21. post script(um)	. . . .
22. pro bono publico	. . . .
23. quod vide (q.v.)	. . . .
24. sine die	. . . .
25. solvitur ambulando	. . . .
26. vice versa	. . . .
27. vide infra	. . . .
28. et alia	. . . .
29. pro forma	. . . .
30. et sequentes	. . . .
31. non sequitur	. . . .
32. et cetera	. . . .
33. nihil obstat et imprimatur	. . . .
34. quod erat demonstrandum	. . . .
35. mutatis mutandis	. . . .
36. pro rata	. . . .
37. Ora pro nobis	. . . .
38. ex libris	. . . .
39. Adeste Fideles	. . . .
40. Te Deum	. . . .
41. De Profundis	. . . .
42. De Re Metallica	. . . .
43. De Humani Corporis Fabrica	. . . .
44. De Revolutionibus Orbium Coelestium	. . . .
45. De Motibus Stellae Martis	. . . .
46. Pseudodoxia Epidemica	. . . .
47. Novum Organum	. . . .
48. inter se	. . . .

PHRASE	MEANING
49. Lux Mundi	. . . .
50. Nunc dimittis	. . . .
51. Magnificat	. . . .
52. Gloria in excelsis Deo	. . . .
53. De Magnete	. . . .
54. mens sana in corpore sano	. . . .
55. viva voce	. . . .
56. Agnus Dei	. . . .
57. non compos mentis	. . . .
58. post hoc, ergo propter hoc	. . . .
59. locum tenens	. . . .
60. ad infinitum	. . . .
61. ex cathedra	. . . .
62. quid pro quo	. . . .
63. cui bono	. . . .
64. ecce homo	. . . .
65. dulce domum	. . . .
66. dulce et decorum est pro patria mori	. . . .
67. per procurationem (p.p.)	. . . .
68. ante meridiem	. . . .
69. deo volente (D.V.)	. . . .
70. ars longa, vita brevis	. . . .
71. tempus fugit	. . . .
72. bona fide	. . . .
73. sic transit gloria mundi	. . . .
74. Stabat Mater	. . . .
75. vox populi, vox Dei	. . . .
76. anno domini	. . . .
77. ad libitum	. . . .
78. fons et origo	. . . .
79. sine qua non	. . . .
80. persona grata	. . . .
81. De Rerum Natura	. . . .
82. Pax vobiscum	. . . .
83. Virginibus Puerisque	. . . .
84. dies irae	. . . .

PHRASE	MEANING
85. habeas corpus	. . . .
86. deus ex machina	. . . .
87. corona lucis	. . . .
88. in camera	. . . .
89. quot homines tot sententiae	. . . .
90. veni, vidi, vici	. . . .
91. timeo Danaos et dona ferentes	. . . .
92. nota bene (N.B.)	. . . .
93. pax romana	. . . .
94. cogito, ergo sum	. . . .
95. casus belli	. . . .
96. aetatis (aet.)	. . . .
97. de minimis non curat lex	. . . .
98. inter alia	. . . .
99. annus mirabilis	. . . .
100. mirabile dictu	. . . .

Quiz 5

Latin Comparison

ADJECTIVE	MEANING	COMPARATIVE	SUPERLATIVE
1. BONO	. . . . . .	MELIORE	OPTIMO
2. MALO	. . . . . .	PEIORE	PESSIMO
3. PARVO	. . . . . .	MINORE	MINIMO
4. MULTO	. . . . . .	PLURI	PLURIMO
5. MAGNO	. . . . . .	MAIORE	MAXIMO
6. SENI	. . . . . .	SENIORE	—
7. IUVENI	. . . . . .	IUNIORE	—

ADVERB OR PREPOSITION	MEANING	COMPARATIVE	SUPERLATIVE
8. EXTRA	. . . . . .	EXTERIORE	EXTREMO
9. INTRA	. . . . . .	INTERIORE	INTIMO

LATIN	MEANING	AS IN	GREEK	AS IN
74. FLORE	......	......	ἀνθιε	......
75. URSO	......	......	ἀρκτω	......
76. DOMO	......	......	οἰκω	......
77. PECTORE	......	......	στηθει	......
78. IDEM (Nom.)	......	......	ταυτο	......
79. FERA	......	......	θηρι	......
80. SANGUINE	......	......	αἱματι (Nom. αἱμα)	......
81. POMO	......	......	μηλω	......
82. PLUMBO	......	......	μολυβδω	......
83. CORDE	......	......	καρδια	......
84. VOCE	......	......	φθογγω	......
85. POTENTIA	......	......	δυναμει	......
86. CAPRO	......	......	τραγω	......
87. ARCU	......	......	τοξω	......
88. DUCE	......	......	ἀγωγει	......
89. FEMINA	......	......	γυναικι (Nom. γυνη)	......
90. CRURE	......	......	σκελει	......

Note:
Ablative singular case form of Latin, Dative singular case form of Greek; diction-(nom. singular) form added in brackets where grossly irregular.

Quiz 7

... important Greek Verbs

GREEK	MEANING	EXAMPLE
ἀγγελλειν	......	evangelist
ἀκουσεσθαι	hear	......
ἀρχειν	......	tetrarch
βαλλειν	......	ballistics
βαπτειν	dip	......
βιων	......	amphibious

ADVERB OR PREPOSITION	MEANING	COMPARATIVE	SUPERLATIVE
10. SUPRA	......	SUPERIORE	SUPREMO
11. INFRA	......	INFERIORE	(INFIMO)
12. ULTRA	......	ULTERIORE	ULTIMO
13. PRAE	......	PRIORE	PRIMO
14. POST	......	POSTERIORE	(POSTREMO)
15. PROPE	......	(PROPIORE)	PROXIMO

Give Derivatives of:

ADJECTIVE OR ADVERB	COMPARATIVE	SUPERLATIVE
2.	1.	1. ......
4.	2.	2. ......
5.	3.	3. ......
6.	4.	5. ......
7.	5.	8. ......
8.	6.	9. ......
9.	7.	10. ......
10.	12.	12. ......
11.	13.	13. ......
12.		15. ......
13.		
14.		
15.		

Quiz 6

Word bricks based on some Greek and Latin Nouns

LATIN	MEANING	AS IN	GREEK	AS IN
1. AGRO	......	......	ἀγρω	......
2. CAELO	......	......	οὐρανω or αἰθερι	......

LATIN	MEANING	AS IN	GREEK	AS IN
3. VENTO	......	......	ἀνεμω	......
4. STELLA	......	......	ἀστερι	......
5. VAPORE	......	......	ἀτμω	......
6. SOLE	......	......	ἡλιω	......
7. LUNA	......	......	σεληνη	......
8. MARI	......	......	θαλασση	......
9. OCEANO	......	......	ὠκεανω	......
10. UNIVERSO	......	......	κοσμω	......
11. GLACIE	......	......	κρυσταλλω	......
12. INSULA	......	......	νησω	......
13. FLUVIO	......	......	ποταμω	......
14. LUCE	......	......	φωτι	......
15. VITA	......	......	βιω	......
16. MORTE	......	......	θανατω	......
17. AMORE	......	......	ἐρωτι	......
18. TIMORE	......	......	φοβω	......
19. SONORE	......	......	φωνη	......
20. TEMPORE	......	......	χρονω	......
21. MENTE	......	......	ψυχη	......
22. ODIO	......	......	μισει	......
23. MEMORIA	......	......	μνησει	......
24. INSANITATE	......	......	παθει	......
25. SENSU	......	......	αἰσθησει	......
26. LABORE	......	......	ἐργω	......
27. FORMA	......	......	μορφη	......
28. IMITATIONE	......	......	μιμησει	......
29. VERBO	......	......	λογω	......
30. LITTERA	......	......	γραμματι	......
31. LIBRO	......	......	βιβλιω	......
32. CIVITATE	......	......	πολει	......
33. CIVE	......	......	πολιτη	......
34. LIBERATIONE	......	......	λυσει	......
35. PETRA	......	......	λιθω	......
36. LACTE	......	......	γαλακτι	......
37. ITINERE	......	......	ὁδω	......
38. CARNE	......	......	κρεα	......

LATIN	MEANING	AS IN	GREEK
39. AURE	......	......	ὠτι (Nom. οὐς)
40. ORE	......	......	στοματι
41. DENTE	......	......	ὀδοντι
42. MANU	......	......	χειρι
43. PEDE	......	......	ποδι (Nom. πους)
44. INFANTE	......	......	παιδι
45. OCULO	......	......	ὀφθαλμω
46. OVO	......	......	ὠω
47. DOLORE	......	......	ἀλγει
48. UNDA	......	......	κυματι
49. SPECTRO or IMAGINE	......	......	πλασματι (Nom. πλασμα)
50. VESPERE	......	......	ἑσπερω
51. DIE	......	......	ἡμερα
52. NOCTE	......	......	νυκτι
53. ANNO	......	......	—
54. HORA	......	......	ὡρα
55. DEO	......	......	θεω
56. CANE	......	......	κυνι
57. EQUO	......	......	ἱππω
58. AVE	......	......	ὀρνιθι
59. PISCE	......	......	ἰχθυι
60. PATRE	......	......	πατρι
61. MATRE	......	......	μητρι
62. FRATRE	......	......	ἀδελφω
63. HOMINE	......	......	ἀνθρωπω
64. REGE	......	......	βασιλει
65. FOLIO	......	......	φυλλω
66. FRUCTU	......	......	καρπω
67. LOCO	......	......	τοπω
68. RADICE	......	......	ῥιζη
69. GLOBO	......	......	σφαιρα
70. SCRIPTO	......	......	γραφη
71. ARBORE	......	......	δενδρω
72. SOPORE	......	......	ὑπνω
73. NASO	......	......	ῥινι

GREEK	MEANING	EXAMPLE
7. γαμειν	marry	......
8. γεινεσθαι	......	eugenics
9. γραφειν	......	graphite
10. διακονειν	......	diaconal
11. διψαν	thirst	......
12. δυνασθαι	be able	......
13. ἐργαζεσθαι	......	erg
14. καλυπτειν	......	eucalyptus
15. κινειν	......	cinema
16. κλινειν	......	klinostat
17. κρατειν	rule	......
18. κρυπτειν	conceal	......
19. μετρειν	measure	......
20. μιξειν	......	amphimixis
21. ὁρμαν	......	hormone
22. ῥειν	......	rheostat
23. σημανειν	......	semantics
24. σηψειν	rot	......
25. σκοπειν	look at	......
26. σχιζειν	split	......
27. τοχεων	shoot (with arrow)	......
28. τριβειν	......	diatribe
29. φαγειν	......	entomophagous
30. φανειν	......	phenotype
31. φιλειν	......	Philadelphia
32. φοβειν	fear	......
33. φορειν	......	melanophore

The form of the verb given is that known as the present active infinitive if with the terminal ειν (cf. O.E. -AM) or passive if with ἐσθαι. Number 2 has the future form.

Quiz 8

Greek Roots in Common Terms of Medicine and Natural History

Give two examples of words containing each root.

	GREEK	MEANING	AS IN	SECOND EXAMPLE
1.	αἱματι			
2.	ἀλγει			
3.	ἀρθρω			
4.	βρογχω			
5.	γαστρι			
6.	γλωσση			
7.	γναθω			
8.	δερματι			
9.	ἐνκεφαλη			
10.	ἐκτομη			
11.	ἐντερω			
12.	ζωω			
13.	ἰχθυι			
14.	καρδια			
15.	καρπω			
16.	κερατι			
17.	λεπιδι			
18.	λινω			
19.	νευρω			
20.	νεφρω			
21.	ξυλω			
22.	ὀδοντι			
23.	ὀρνιθι			
24.	ὀστω (ὀστεον)			
25.	οὐρα			
26.	ὀφθαλμω			
27.	ὀψει			
28.	πεψει			
29.	πλευρα			
30.	πνευματι			
31.	ποδι (πους)			

GREEK	MEANING	AS IN	SECOND EXAMPLE
32. πτερω	. . . .	. . . .	. . . .
33. πυρετω	. . . .	. . . .	. . . .
34. πυω (πυον)	. . . .	. . . .	. . . .
35. ῥινι	. . . .	. . . .	. . . .
36. σαυρα	. . . .	. . . .	. . . .
37. φαρμακω	. . . .	. . . .	. . . .
38. φλεβι	. . . .	. . . .	. . . .
39. χειρι	. . . .	. . . .	. . . .
40. ὠτι (οὖς)	. . . .	. . . .	. . . .

Quiz 9

Each word here shown in the third column comes from two Greek roots, one given with meaning in the first two columns. To answer, look through Quizzes 1-8. Then fill in the number of the Quiz and the code number of the second root in the fourth column, and give the meaning of the whole word in the fifth.

GREEK	MEANING	DERIVATIVE	OTHER ROOT	MEANING OF WHOLE WORD
1. ἀγωνι	contest	protagonist	. . . . . .	. . . . . .
2. ἀγωγη	training	pedagogue	. . . . . .	. . . . . .
3. αἰτια	cause	aetiology	. . . . . .	. . . . . .
4. ἀρχη	beginning	archetype	. . . . . .	. . . . . .
5. βιω	life	symbiosis	. . . . . .	. . . . . .
6. βολη	toss	hyperbole	. . . . . .	. . . . . .
7. γενει	race	photogenic	. . . . . .	. . . . . .
8. γνωσει	knowledge	diagnostic	. . . . . .	. . . . . .
9. δοξη	opinion	orthodoxy	. . . . . .	. . . . . .
10. δρομω	race	hippodrome	. . . . . .	. . . . . .
11. δωρω	gift	Dorothea	. . . . . .	. . . . . .
12. ἐργω	work	energy	. . . . . .	. . . . . .
13. ἐπιστημη	knowledge	epistemology	. . . . . .	. . . . . .
14. ἐρωτι	love	autoerotic	. . . . . .	. . . . . .
15. θανατω	death	euthanasia	. . . . . .	. . . . . .

	GREEK	MEANING	DERIVATIVE	OTHER ROOT	MEANING OF WHOLE WORD
16.	θεσις (Nom.)	arrangement	antithesis	......	......
17.	κεντρω	centre	egocentric	......	......
18.	λογω	word, reasoning	apology	......	......
19.	λυσις (Nom.)	release	analysis	......	......
20.	μνησει	memory	amnesia	......	......
21.	μορφη	form	metamorphosis	......	......
22.	ὀνοματι	name	onomatopoeia	......	......
23.	παθει	suffering	pathology	......	......
24.	σθενει	strength	neurasthenia	......	......
25.	ῥυθμω	rhythm	eurhythmic	......	......
26.	στασει	standing	apostasy	......	......
27.	στροφη	twist	apostrophe	......	......
28.	σοφια	wisdom	philosophy	......	......
29.	τελει	end	teleology	......	......
30.	τεχνη	art	pyrotechnic	......	......
31.	νω (νους)	mind	paranoia	......	......
32.	τονω	stretching	hypertonic	......	......
33.	τοπω	place	topography	......	......
34.	τυπω	impression, model	typography	......	......
35.	φοβω	fear	hydrophobia	......	......
36.	φρενι	understanding	schizophrenia	......	......
37.	φυσει	nature	physiology	......	......
38.	φωνη	sound	gramophone	......	......
39.	χρωματι	colour	panchromatic	......	......
40.	χρονω	time	chronometer	......	......
41.	βροντη	thunder	Brontosaurus	......	......
42.	ἱππω	horse	hippopotamus	......	......
43.	ζυγω	yoke	monozygous	......	......
44.	κυτει	cell	phagocyte	......	......
45.	ταφω	grave	epitaph	......	......
46.	τροφη	food	atrophy	......	......
47.	ἁλι	salt	halogen	......	......
48.	λιθω	stone	palaeolithic	......	......
49.	πολλω	much, many	polygyny	......	......
50.	ἀνθρωπω	human being	misanthrope	......	......

ADVERB OR PREPOSITION	MEANING	COMPARATIVE	SUPERLATIVE
10. SUPRA	......	SUPERIORE	SUPREMO
11. INFRA	......	INFERIORE	(INFIMO)
12. ULTRA	......	ULTERIORE	ULTIMO
13. PRAE	......	PRIORE	PRIMO
14. POST	......	POSTERIORE	(POSTREMO)
15. PROPE	......	(PROPIORE)	PROXIMO

Give Derivatives of:

ADJECTIVE OR ADVERB	COMPARATIVE	SUPERLATIVE
2.	1.	1. ......
4.	2.	2. ......
5.	3.	3. ......
6.	4.	5. ......
7.	5.	8. ......
8.	6.	9. ......
9.	7.	10. ......
10.	12.	12. ......
11.	13.	13. ......
12.		15. ......
13.		
14.		
15.		

Quiz 6

Word bricks based on some Greek and Latin Nouns

LATIN	MEANING	AS IN	GREEK	AS IN
1. AGRO	......	......	ἀγρω	......
2. CAELO	......	......	οὐρανω or	......
			αἰθερι	......

LATIN	MEANING	AS IN	GREEK	AS IN
3. VENTO	......	......	ἀνεμω	......
4. STELLA	......	......	ἀστερι	......
5. VAPORE	......	......	ἀτμω	......
6. SOLE	......	......	ἡλιω	......
7. LUNA	......	......	σεληνη	......
8. MARI	......	......	θαλασση	......
9. OCEANO	......	......	ὠκεανω	......
10. UNIVERSO	......	......	κοσμω	......
11. GLACIE	......	......	κρυσταλλω	......
12. INSULA	......	......	νησω	......
13. FLUVIO	......	......	ποταμω	......
14. LUCE	......	......	φωτι	......
15. VITA	......	......	βιω	......
16. MORTE	......	......	θανατω	......
17. AMORE	......	......	ἐρωτι	......
18. TIMORE	......	......	φοβω	......
19. SONORE	......	......	φωνη	......
20. TEMPORE	......	......	χρονω	......
21. MENTE	......	......	ψυχη	......
22. ODIO	......	......	μισει	......
23. MEMORIA	......	......	μνησει	......
24. INSANITATE	......	......	παθει	......
25. SENSU	......	......	αἰσθησει	......
26. LABORE	......	......	ἐργω	......
27. FORMA	......	......	μορφη	......
28. IMITATIONE	......	......	μιμησει	......
29. VERBO	......	......	λογω	......
30. LITTERA	......	......	γραμματι	......
31. LIBRO	......	......	βιβλιω	......
32. CIVITATE	......	......	πολει	......
33. CIVE	......	......	πολιτη	......
34. LIBERATIONE	......	......	λυσει	......
35. PETRA	......	......	λιθω	......
36. LACTE	......	......	γαλακτι	......
37. ITINERE	......	......	ὁδω	......
38. CARNE	......	......	κρεα	......

LATIN	MEANING	AS IN	GREEK	AS IN
39. AURE	......	......	ὠτι (Nom. οὐς)	......
40. ORE	......	......	στοματι	......
41. DENTE	......	......	ὀδοντι	......
42. MANU	......	......	χειρι	......
43. PEDE	......	......	ποδι (Nom. πους)	......
44. INFANTE	......	......	παιδι	
45. OCULO	......	......	ὀφθαλμω	
46. OVO	......	......	ὠω	......
47. DOLORE	......	......	ἀλγει	......
48. UNDA	......	......	κυματι	......
49. SPECTRO or	......	......	πλασματι	......
IMAGINE		......	(Nom. πλασμα)	
50. VESPERE	......	......	ἑσπερω	
51. DIE	......	......	ἡμερα	
52. NOCTE	......	......	νυκτι	......
53. ANNO	......	......	—	—
54. HORA	......	......	ὠρα	
55. DEO	......	......	θεω	
56. CANE	......	......	κυνι	......
57. EQUO	......	......	ἱππω	
58. AVE	......	......	ὀρνιθι	......
59. PISCE	......	......	ἰχθυι	......
60. PATRE	......	......	πατρι	
61. MATRE	......	......	μητρι	......
62. FRATRE	......	......	ἀδελφω	......
63. HOMINE	......	......	ἀνθρωπω	
64. REGE	......	......	βασιλει	......
65. FOLIO	......	......	φυλλω	......
66. FRUCTU	......	......	καρπω	
67. LOCO	......	......	τοπω	......
68. RADICE	......	......	ῥιζη	
69. GLOBO	......	......	σφαιρα	......
70. SCRIPTO	......	......	γραφη	......
71. ARBORE	......	......	δενδρω	......
72. SOPORE	......	......	ὑπνω	......
73. NASO	......	......	ῥινι	......

LATIN	MEANING	AS IN	GREEK	AS IN
74. FLORE	......	......	ἀνθιε	......
75. URSO	......	......	ἀρκτω	......
76. DOMO	......	......	οἰκω	......
77. PECTORE	......	......	στηθει	......
78. IDEM (Nom.)	......	......	ταὐτο	......
79. FERA	......	......	θηρι	......
80. SANGUINE	......	......	αἱματι	......
			(Nom. αἱμα)	
81. POMO	......	......	μηλω	......
82. PLUMBO	......	......	μολυβδω	......
83. CORDE	......	......	καρδια	......
84. VOCE	......	......	φθογγω	......
85. POTENTIA	......	......	δυναμει	......
86. CAPRO	......	......	τραγω	......
87. ARCU	......	......	τοξω	......
88. DUCE	......	......	ἀγωγει	......
89. FEMINA	......	......	γυναικι (Nom. γυνη)	......
90. CRURE	......	......	σκελει	......

Note:

Ablative singular case form of Latin, Dative singular case form of Greek; dictionary (nom. singular) form added in brackets where grossly irregular.

Quiz 7

Some important Greek Verbs

GREEK	MEANING	EXAMPLE
1. ἀγγελλειν	......	evangelist
2. ἀκουσεσθαι	hear	......
3. ἀρχειν	......	tetrarch
4. βαλλειν	......	ballistics
5. βαπτειν	dip	......
6. βιων	......	amphibious

	GREEK	MEANING	DERIVATIVE	OTHER ROOT	MEANING OF WHOLE WORD
51.	ἀρχω	ruler	heptarchy	......	......
52.	γενεα	birth	eugenics	......	......
53.	ἀνδρι	male	polyandry	......	......
54.	δημω	people	democratic	......	......
55.	διακονω	deacon	archdeacon	......	......
56.	κλεπτη	thief	kleptomania	......	......
57.	κριτη	judge	hypercritical	......	......
58.	ναυτη	sailor	aeronautics	......	......
59.	νομω	law	antinomian	......	......
60.	νυμφη	bride	nymphomania	......	......
61.	παιδι	child	paediatrics	......	......
62.	παρθενω	virgin	parthenogenesis	......	......
63.	πλουτω	wealth	plutocracy	......	......
64.	πολει	city, state	cosmopolitan	......	......
65.	πρεσβει	old man	presbyopia	......	......
66.	τεκτονι	builder	architect	......	......
67.	φυλη	tribe	phylogeny	......	......
68.	κολεω	sheath	coleoptera	......	......
69.	βιβλιω	book	bibliophile	......	......
70.	γραμματι	letter	cryptogram	......	......
71.	λατρεια	worship	idolatry	......	......
72.	μονω	single	monotheism	......	......
73.	ἱερει	priest	hierarchy	......	......
74.	μυθω	fable	mythology	......	......
75.	ἑλικι	spiral	helicopter	......	......
76.	κυνι	dog	cynosure	......	......
77.	πτερω	wing	Archeopteryx	......	......
78.	γωνια	angle	diagonal	......	......
79.	περι	round	perianth	......	......
80.	φυλλω	leaf	phylloxera	......	......

Quiz 10

Similar Roots

COUPLET	MEANING OF SIMILAR ROOT IN		LATIN(L), GREEK(G), TEUTONIC(T)	
	1ST	2ND	1ST	2ND
1. sinecure—cynosure	......	......	......	......
2. homicide—homosexual	......	......	......	......
3. epicene—eocene	......	......	......	......
4. valedictory—valuation	......	......	......	......
5. equitation—equitable	......	......	......	......
6. aviary—Ave Maria	......	......	......	......
7. prognosis—pro-British	......	......	......	......
8. antenatal—antibiotic	......	......	......	......
9. ingrained—innocuous	......	......	......	......
10. sincere—syncope	......	......	......	......
11. diary—diarrhoea	......	......	......	......
12. dislocation—dyspepsia	......	......	......	......
13. international—intravenous	......	......	......	......
14. introduce—intervene	......	......	......	......
15. ambidextrous—amphibious	......	......	......	......
16. archaic—archangel	......	......	......	......
17. hypertrophe—hypothesis	......	......	......	......
18. immersion—immature	......	......	......	......
19. perforate—peripheral	......	......	......	......
20. anodyne—anabolism	......	......	......	......
21. avert—aphasia	......	......	......	......
22. parachute—paraffin	......	......	......	......
23. penultimate—pentathlon	......	......	......	......
24. aliform—alimentary	......	......	......	......
25. chromograph—chronometer	......	......	......	......
26. antiseptic—septuagenarian	......	......	......	......
27. archetype—heptarchy	......	......	......	......
28. morphine—morphology	......	......	......	......
29. misanthrope—mistake	......	......	......	......
30. Chilognatha—Chilopoda (zool.)	......	......	......	......

COUPLET	MEANING OF SIMILAR ROOT IN		LATIN(L), GREEK(G), TEUTONIC(T)	
	1ST	2ND	1ST	2ND
31. sexagenarian—sexuality	......	......	......	......
32. acrimony—acromegaly	......	......	......	......
33. inelastic—infiltrate	......	......	......	......
34. oboe—obese	......	......	......	......
35. plantar—plantation	......	......	......	......
36. ironwork—ironical	......	......	......	......
37. fortitude—fortuitous	......	......	......	......
38. pedagogue—quadruped	......	......	......	......
39. audacious—audience	......	......	......	......
40. volatile—volition	......	......	......	......
41. edible—editable	......	......	......	......
42. plane—planet	......	......	......	......
43. transept—septicaemia	......	......	......	......
44. voluntary—voluble	......	......	......	......
45. germinate—gerundive	......	......	......	......
46. maritime—marital	......	......	......	......
47. tactics—tactile	......	......	......	......
48. pastime—pastoral	......	......	......	......
49. quinsy—quintet	......	......	......	......
50. ballast—ballistics	......	......	......	......

8

Semantics in Overalls

The keyword of the title of this chapter comes from a Greek one which signifies a *sign*, whence *signal* as in *semaphore*. Today, it most usually refers to the recognition of pitfalls of verbal communication due to inadequacy of many words we use to fulfil their ostensible function as signals, i.e. as meaningful symbols. To speak here of symbols, uttered or written, as meaningful, signifies that the recipient (listener or reader) can decode the message of the transmitter (speaker or writer) in terms consistent with the intention of the latter, a proceeding which would entail no hazards if each of the words we use had only one meaning in a particular context. This is probably true of no natural language. Relatively few words in common use have an authentically unique meaning regardless of context. Many have no meaning if divorced from a context of other words.

Within one and the same speech community, meanings of words may be more or less unique only in so far as we date the period to which they are referable; and, even during the same period, members of the same speech community do not necessarily decode those of the same message in the same way. For instance, members of the Anglo-American speech community with different theological, philosophical, political, ethical and aesthetic preoccupations attach different code values, or as we more customarily say, definitions, to a host of terms such as: *real, natural, good, integrity, sincerity, justice, freedom, democracy, morality, virtue, courage.* Moreover, some words have no meaning in their own right. For instance, Anglo-American *of* in *X of Y* is at best a vague indication that there is some connexion between X and Y. The signaller (speaker or writer) leaves to the recipient (listener or reader) the obligation to decode what connexion there is; and the connexion is very different if we substitute *dentures, debts* and *death* for D in the formula: *D of your father.*

The term *semantics* first came into use to label enquiries about how words change their meaning in the course of time. This was the theme of our first chapter, which cited many examples of such changes, e.g. the relation of *knight* and *knave* to their ancestral forms CNIHT and CNAFA. As we have seen, semantics in this sense of the term has a direct bearing on the uppermost intention of our story of the Mother Tongue inasmuch as it shows how an understanding of our hybrid heritage may help the Anglo-American to learn any one of more than a dozen languages most closely related to his or her native tongue by disclosing lively associations to lighten the tedium of memorising a vocabulary.

If the meaning of the term were now precisely as when first used, semantics would therefore have no relevance to our final theme. Actually, one now uses it in a more general sense, indicated in the opening sentence of this chapter, i.e. the scrutiny of how different contemporary meanings of one and the same word in different contexts may prevent *rapport* between transmitter and recipient of a message. So defined, and more especially during the past three or four decades, semantics has exerted a very salutary influence on philosophical discussion by forcing proponents of traditional metaphysics tailored to theological dictates to ask themselves awkward questions, in particular whether enigmas portentously but fruitlessly discussed since the beginning of Greek philosophy mean anything more intelligible than: What is the colour of Wednesday? Such issues lie outside the scope of our story; but study of the diverse meanings a single word may have is highly relevant to one aspect of language learning. Such is the topic of what follows.

In speaking of different aspects of learning a language, we may cross-classify four several skills involved in terms of (a) correct transmission and correct reception; (b) whether the receptor organ is the eye or the ear. This leads us to a 4-cell grid as shown below:

	Mode of Transmission *or* Reception	
	(voice *or* ear)	(pen *or* print)
Transmitter (speaker *or* writer)	1. speaking correctly	2. writing correctly
Recipient (listener *or* reader)	3. understanding conversation	4. being able to read with ease

The distinction between these aspects of learning is of much more importance to a learner than most of us realise. This is because learning a foreign language confronts adults and intelligent adolescents with a seemingly limitless load on the memory before there is any noticeable pay-off for expenditure of effort. We can, indeed, set no limit to the size of an indispensable vocabulary of recognition for wide reading; and it would be an exaggeration to state that we can set an absolute limit to what we require for self-expression. None the less, it is at least possible to programme the requirements of a minimum vocabulary of *recall* with the prospect of reaching a high level of proficient self-expression, if one sets about the task in the right way; and if we can indeed attain self-expression speedily we can expeditiously offload some of a burden of otherwise unrewarded effort. To set about the task of constructing for individual use a minimal *recall*-vocabulary for transmission, in contradistinction to a nodding acquaintance with a much wider *recognition*-vocabulary for reception, we need to take stock of an important difference between the two activities. To a recipient there is always an explicit context to prompt memory; but the transmitter must be able, with no external aid, to select the correct alien equivalent of a native word. We can accomplish the task of making an abridged code-book which suffices for the needs of the signaller only if we realise where comparison between a bilingual dictionary and the official code-book of the signaller of the Armed Services ceases to hold good.

Signalling messages by movement or display of flags, by light flashes or by electro-magnetic impulses has this in common: the symbol sequence which the signaller transmits for a word is unique; and if it has more than one meaning, the recipient, a member of the same speech community as the transmitter, interprets it appropriately. Thus a dictionary exhibiting Morse code equivalents for every Anglo-American word in common use would cite only one entry against each word transcribed in the usual way. A bilingual dictionary is not like this. For a word W in language L we are likely to find several entries w_1, w_2, etc., of language l; and for a word w in language l we are likely to find several entries W_1, W_2, etc., in language L. This is necessarily so, because meaning changes in course of time for different reasons, mainly classifiable under three headings. Since few teachers and fewer textbooks teach us how to use a dictionary with a view to constructing our abridged code, i.e. minimum recall vocabulary, we may usefully pause at a later stage to consider how one does so. First, however, a few hints at a more elementary level may not be amiss.

Bilingual dictionaries are of two sorts, bulky or conveniently small for carriage in constant use. The former commonly illustrate the uses of the several equivalents they cite by short sentences or phrases. Otherwise, the reader has to make a decision without explicit guidance. If the L-l dictionary cites w_1, w_2, etc., against W, one can sidestep the sometimes embarrassing consequences of lazily choosing the first by turning to the other half (l-L) to find which W_1, W_2, etc., corresponds to the W for which one needs an equivalent. This is often more laborious and less instructive than to look up a few lines below or above some of the near relations of W on the same page of the same half of the dictionary. To do so one has to be clear about different meanings which the same word, i.e. dictionary entry, may have in one's own language; and with that end in view we may usefully speak of couplets as *paranyms* if they share a common meaning but have widely different alternative meanings. A clear-cut example is the couplet BUT—YET.

BUT   1. YET, 2. *except*.
YET   1. TILL NOW *or* TILL THEN, 2. *but*.

When we can pair native words in this way, the recipe for choosing an appropriate alien word is clear. The indispensable meaning of BUT is the one it shares with YET. So we select from the alternatives which our dictionary cites for BUT, one which corresponds to an entry against YET. When using a compact bilingual dictionary which cites no examples of the use of more than one entry as the alien equivalent of a native word, one can proceed advantageously in more than one way, if first clear about the several meanings the native word may have. For illustrative purposes we may consider how to find equivalents of two Anglo-American verbs, the principal meanings of which are as cited below:

ABUSE   1. *revile*, 2. *misuse*.
SUCCEED   1. *prosper*, 2. *follow*.

A pocket Danish dictionary will cite for ABUSE: 1. *misbruge*, 2. *skælde ud*; and for SUCCEED: 1. *følge*, 2. *lykkes*. In the same context a little further on, we find that the equivalent of SUCCESS is *lykke* (*cf.* LUCK), and we should expect that *følge* comes from the same Teutonic root as FOLLOW, whence we scarcely need to look up the Danish equivalent for the latter. The Danish equivalent cited for ABUSIVE does not help us to distinguish the meanings of *misbruge* and *skælde ud*. However, we know that *mis-* (=BADLY) is a Teutonic affix, and we find that *bruge* means USE. By consulting the other end of the dictionary we expect to find, as we do, that *skælde ud* means REVILE, ABUSE. Before consulting our English-Danish dictionary it is a wise precaution to look up ABUSE, REVILE, FOLLOW and SUCCEED, etc., in the *Concise Oxford Dictionary* to locate their origins in the sister languages. As an exercise, the reader should now be able to identify the Welsh equivalents for each member of the same pair, after consulting the entries shown in parenthesis below:

ABUSE (v)   *camddefnyddio, difrio* (USE = *defnyddio;*   MISTAKE = *camgymeriad;*
            ABUSIVE = *difriol*).
SUCCEED   *llwyddio; canlyn* (SUCCESSFUL = *llwyddianus;*   SUCCESSOR = *can-
            lynydd*).

The foregoing examples are by no means atypical. Indeed, Anglo-American verbs with a clear-cut core of meaning are a small minority of the total in common use. This is a tiresome defect of the language from the viewpoint of a learner reared in another speech community, but perhaps even more so from that of the user, if habit has made him insensitive to its shortcomings. When the dictionary confronts one with a choice of several words of a foreign language for a single word of one's own, the dilemma should be a challenge to examine more closely what one really means. Unhappily, we are too prone to take refuge in abuse of the plaintiff's counsel, blaming the language of the foreigner for the shortcomings of our own. Only the effort of studying a foreign language can make most of us aware of such shortcomings. A semantic defect which Anglo-American shares with Teutonic, in contradistinction to Romance, languages will illustrate this forcibly. The word *only* and its equivalent in German (*nur*), in Swedish (*bara*), etc., has no single acceptable substitute in French, Italian, nor in Welsh; and a learner who stumbles over the correct French (etc.) translation, need not do so if alert to the various meanings it embraces in

English. The reader who has never done so will find it instructive to make up sentences in which *only* can replace the following: 1. ONE; 2. SOLE; 3. NO MORE THAN; 4. NOTHING EXCEPT; 5. WITHOUT A BROTHER OR A SISTER. After completion of the foregoing exercise, the reader will also find it instructive to distinguish between what the following sentence rightly conveys when one replaces each of the dots (one at a time) by *only*: .THE.BISHOP.GAVE.THE.BABOON. THE.BUN.

When learning a foreign language, we should thus be ready at all times to recognise defects in our own; and such shortcomings may not occur to us unless the study of another language brings them into focus. Thus one word, *with* in Anglo-American, *met* in Dutch, *mit* in German, *med* in Scandinavian, *avec* in French, *con* in Spanish and in Italian, covers two different notions distinguished in Welsh as follows:

> GYDA = *in the company of*, e.g. *came with her boy*
> AG = *by means of*, e.g. *cut with a knife*

Similarly, Welsh makes what is, from a mathematical viewpoint, a highly significant distinction between two meanings of Anglo-American *always*, Dutch *altijd*, German *immer*, Scandinavian *alltid* (or *altid*), French *toujours*, Italian *sempre*, Spanish *siempre*. No one Welsh word covers the foregoing. Instead, we have:

> YN WASTAD = *ceaselessly*, e.g. *always love you, honey friend*
> BOB AMSER = *on each occasion*, e.g. *always brought his flute*.

The examples cited to show how we can get the best out of a pocket-size dictionary do not suffice to programme the preparation of an abridged code-book for self-expression with the minimum number of indispensable words. Before proceeding in search of a recipe, it will clear the air if we now ask the question: why do words have so many different meanings? In seeking an answer, let us recall that few words in languages used by people who have attained a high level of literacy have so unique a meaning as *nineteen*, *whereby* and *elsewhere* in Anglo-American. However, it is also true to say that all languages accommodate many *good* words in the sense that we recognise the primary meaningful core in *father*, *mother* and *brotherhood* when we speak of the *Holy Father*, a *Mother Superior* or the *Brotherhood of Man*. These examples, which we sometimes speak of as *figures of speech*, illustrate one of several ways in which otherwise indistinguishable words, i.e. speech symbols spelt and pronounced in the same way, come to convey different meanings.

Figuratively, one may speak of the outcome as *semantic erosion*. In course of time the connexion between figurative substitute and primary intention may become less evident than it is in the foregoing triplet. Eventually, we may be able to expose a now missing link only with effort or by special pleading, if at all. For instance, there is no very obvious connexion between a cricket *match* and a love *match*, except when the cricketers are playing for charity or the lovers are quarrelling. As it happens, we can trace back both to O.E. GEMÆCCA = *mate*. Contrariwise, we may be able to trace the two meanings of a pair of words spelt and pronounced in the same way to different sources, as is true of *match* as above and *match* for lighting one's pipe (cf. French *mèche* for *wick*). We then speak of them as *homonyms*. *Date* (fruit) and *date* (calendar reckoning) are *homonyms*.

CNAFA and CNIHT illustrate another way in which the meaning of words may change, viz. by acquiring a denigratory or exalted connotation. Denigratory usage accounts for the modern meaning of the terms *crafty* and *artful*, whose earlier meanings are respectfully close to *skilful* (= *craftsmanlike*) and *artistic*. Doubtless, this arose (cf. the contemporary English lower-middle-class sneer: *just like the British workman*) from a suspicion that the craftsman or the artist was trying to cheat his customer. Lately in Britain, *smashing* has undergone an upgrading to signify *worthy of esteem*. The reader will doubtless be able to recall other examples of such elevation or downgrading.

Far more important than the process last mentioned is a slovenly habit of reluctance to take sufficient trouble to use what the French call the *mot juste*. The *mot juste* is the word which most explicitly conveys the intention of a speaker or writer. By the same token, it is also the word least subject to semantic erosion. The temptation to sidestep the obligation to use it is greatest if the native language is very rich in near-synonyms. When this is so, one has a nodding acquaintance with the common core of meaning in many couplets, triplets, etc., which one does not in practice distinguish in conformity with dictates of a dictionary. For instance, most educated people recognise that *encomium*, *panegyric* and *eulogy* imply (as does *flattery*) a notion of high praise; but few could cite any clear-cut difference between them. If one actually uses them in speech or writing, one is apt to choose the one which sounds best in a particular context.

It follows, and is highly relevant to our theme, that there is least check on semantic erosion when one's native language is a hybrid and, being a hybrid, has shed grammatical terminals which obstruct the assimilation of loan words from sources other than its ancestral partners. Needless to say, this is pre-eminently true of Anglo-American which has added to its ancestral stock an enormous battery of loan words, part Teutonic, part Romance, and not merely from Greek, but from all parts of the world through maritime trade, conquest and colonisation. Accordingly, the words one most often uses in the Anglo-American speech community of today are those whose meanings are most diverse. By the same token, they are words which are pitfalls for a hopeful Anglo-American beginner in quest of an abridged code-book for self-expression in a foreign language.

The cream of a bad joke is that such *bad* words are the ones beloved by schoolmasters and lady teachers who counsel their pupils to use *simple* words. They also take first place on the word-frequency lists compiled by pupils of Professor Thorndike, whose otherwise most stupendous exploit of profitless arithmetic has only one useful outcome. What its promoters presumably intended was to help those of other speech communities to get a reading knowledge of Anglo-American by disclosing what words we most often use. What they unwittingly disclosed for others to discover is that words which top the list are words to avoid at all costs. Let us look at a few Thorndike top-priorities (our next Museum Exhibit) as a preliminary to clarifying what to exclude as native entries, or in what of several senses we need to retain them if indispensable, if we hope to assemble a battery of the fewest alien words essential for unambiguous self-expression in a foreign language. We do not need JUST, QUITE, RATHER; and because we cannot dispense with AS for entries 1 and 2, it is indefensible to use it instead of 3 and 4.

The *bad* words of our next Museum Exhibit do not include two which are as multivalent as any of them; but have one saving grace. The right use of words cannot be wholly divorced, as can the best use of mathematical symbols, from a living context. Thus, many living languages have a niche for two terms with a considerable common territory of intelligibility in a living context as respectively intensifiers or the opposite. Such are STRONG and WEAK, against which we may cite in different contexts a *mot juste* as below.

STRONG: 1. (PHYSICALLY) POWERFUL. 2. NOT PRONE TO BAD HEALTH. 3. RESOLUTE. 4. INTENSE. 5. CONCENTRATED. 6. NOT EASILY BREAKABLE, CONQUERED *or* DISPOSED OF. 7. EMPHATIC. 8. INTOXICATING. 9. SAFE. 10. WITH MANY ALLIES.

WEAK: 1. (PHYSICALLY) FEEBLE. 2. SICKLY. 3. IRRESOLUTE. 4. EASILY BREAKABLE, CONQUERED, DESTROYED *or* DISPOSED OF. 5. DILUTE. 6. UNSAFE. 7. WITH FEW ALLIES.

Even the reader who is no crossword-puzzle addict should be able to construct sentences to illustrate all usages cited above. It is a rewarding exercise, because the dictionary entry of a non-native equivalent, though sharing a considerable common domain with one or other word, may not be invariably appropriate.

Two features of the following list merit mention. One is that a multivalent word (i.e. one with many meanings) may have one use covered by no other more specific word in common speech. For instance, LEFT, with at least four meanings, has one (the first cited on p. 281) which is indispensable without recourse to a pedantic alternative. Similarly, RIGHT, in contradistinction to *left* in the foregoing sense, as when we speak of turning *left* or *right*, is even more indispensable as such, but in

MUSEUM EXHIBIT OF BAD WORDS

ANY: 1. even a little. 2. even one. 3. even a few. 4. every.

APPARENT: 1. seeming. 2. manifest.

AS: 1. in the way that. 2. in like measure to (as *or* so . . . as). 3. while. 4. because.

BAR: 1. rod. 2. drinking place. 3. prisoner's place in court. 4. advocate's profession. 5. obstacle. 6. except.

BRIGHT: 1. shining. 2. conspicuous. 3. intense. 4. intelligent.

CLEAR: 1. manifest. 2. understandable. 3. translucent. 4. cloudless.

DULL: 1. not shining. 2. blunt. 3. unintelligent. 4. wearying *or* unstimulating. 5. with cloud-covered sky.

EVER: 1. even once. 2. at all times.

FACTOR: 1. divisor. 2. land agent. 3. merchant. 4. gene. 5. component. 6. aspect. 7. circumstance. 8. consideration. 9. thing. 10. what-not.

FAIR: 1. pale. 2. equitable. 3. beautiful. 4. neither good nor bad.

FINE: 1. very small and/or thin. 2. dry, cloudless, sunny. 3. good, fitting, worthy of esteem.

FUNNY: 1. comic. 2. unusual. 3. impertinent. 4. alarming.

GENERALLY: 1. universally. 2. often.

JUST: 1. equitable. 2. very recently. 3. wholly. 4. good.

LEFT: 1. sinistral. 2. residual. 3. departed. 4. went away without.

ORDER: 1. rank in a sequence. 2. tidiness. 3. readiness. 4. command. 5. reservation, request. 6. religious denomination. 7. secular organisation.

ONLY (see p 277).

PRACTICALLY: 1. empirically. 2. almost. 3. competently.

PRETTY: 1. pleasing. 2. somewhat. 3. very. 4. almost.

QUITE: 1. somewhat. 2. wholly. 3. I agree.

RATHER: 1. somewhat. 2. preferably.

RIGHT: 1. dextral. 2. correct. 3. privilege.

SENSIBLE: 1. detectable by the sense organs. 2. equipped in the sense organs. 3. intelligent. 4. judicious.

SO: 1. that *or* it. 2. as. 3. very. 4. in this way. 5. true. 6. . . . . that = in order that. 7. SO Q THAT = so Q that.

SOME: 1. one sort of. 2. several. 3. even a few. 4. even a little.

STILL: 1. motionless. 2. soundless. 3. till now *or* till then. 4. despite that.

TOO: 1. also. 2. excessively.

TRY: 1. attempt. 2. judge. 3. vex.

no other sense. On the other hand, it may happen that a common word has two (or more) meanings for which no other familiar alternatives are available. Of several different meanings we attach to BACK, the word is essential as an adverb conveying, after such verbs as *come* and *go*, the notion of motion towards the source, whence more generally an equivalent to restitution of the *status quo*, e.g. *give back*. As a noun, BACK may mean (*inter alia*) the dorsal aspect of the body and, as an adjective, may be equivalent to *rear* or *posterior*. In the anatomical sense, it is well-nigh indispensable if we wish to sidestep the charge (=*accusation*) of pedantry. Fortunately, dictionary entries (*adv.*) and (*n.*) against equivalents cited simplify the choice of the correct one. The reader may find it instructive to investigate the semantic credentials of the highly multivalent word *charge* in the last sentence but one.

For the Anglo-American beginner, it would do much to sweeten the pill of learning a foreign language, if one could here say that construction of an abridged code, i.e. vocabulary of recall, for self-expression calls only for:

(a) a lay-out of the minimum number of vocables (as in Ogden's *Basic English* project) essential for self-expression in the Mother Tongue;
(b) a specification of the separate meanings of each item;
(c) an entry from a bilingual dictionary against each such meaning.

For several reasons, each of which is instructive, this would be an over-simplification of the undertaking:

1. Words enter into so-called idioms, i.e. combinations of which the meaning is not deducible from that of the constituents, e.g. in Basic *get along with, put up with*, etc.

2. In particular, particles which have a clear-cut territory of meaning in many situations also enter into such combinations with no intelligible justification, e.g. *to* in *to err is human* or *similar to that; at* in *laugh at; from* in *different from; upon* in *look upon*.

3. Languages differ greatly with respect to the extent to which they provide class-words in which Anglo-American abounds, e.g. *container* (*vessel, box, packet, carboy, can*, etc.); *boat* (*ship, frigate, catamaran, canoe* and at least thirty other terms); *cook* (*fry, roast, boil, poach, grill*, etc.).

4. Languages also differ greatly with respect to which concepts they break down into more general components, e.g. *go up* for *rise, ascend, climb, mount; go away* for *depart, leave; go away without* for *leave, forsake; go down* for *fall, descend*, etc.

5. Languages also differ with respect to the *obligatory* use of overburdened words, e.g. *whither, hither, thither* and *whence, hence, thence* in Tudor English after a verb of motion (*come, go*, etc.) instead of *where, here, there*, as in Anglo-American.

6. Grammatical etiquette may prescribe different word forms with the same semantic content for different situations, e.g. *my* before a noun, *mine* if not; cf. also remarks elsewhere on *during, while, meanwhile* (p. 177).

7. More or less arbitrary peculiarities of the table manners of a language may

dictate restrictions on use of words whose semantic content is not easily distinguishable. Thus Anglo-American permits us to speak with propriety of a mountain
as *high*, of a man as *tall*, and a tree as either in the same sense.

On different assumptions, with reference to what we should rightly regard as
indispensable, there have been several attempts* to prescribe the minimum number
of words (exclusive of technical jargon, now largely international) essential to self-
expression in Anglo-American; but the writer knows of no similar coverage for any
of the sister languages. One cannot yet therefore provide a foolproof recipe for
construction of a minimum vocabulary of recall suitable to the requirements of the
aspirant to self-expression in any one of them. The best one can do is to proffer a plan
which can progressively reduce reliance on a dictionary at the minimum expenditure of time. We can do this if we recall a distinction already made between the
source of words we use or meet most often in a given context, e.g. a page of printed
matter, and the source of words which make up most of the entries in a dictionary.
Of Anglo-American, as we have seen, it is true to say that the former are all native
and that certain definable categories of words are almost exclusively so. Of those
we meet on a printed page, more than 30 per cent. fall into the following traditional
categories for which little more than 150 entries in our prospective abridged code-
book suffice:

(a) auxiliary verbs;
(b) personal pronouns and numerals;
(c) demonstrative, relative and interrogative pronouns and adjectives;
(d) demonstrative, interrogative and conjunctive adverbs;
(e) other particles variously classified as prepositions, conjunctions and adverbs.

Before proceeding to discuss the best way of building up our abridged code-book
for self-expression with minimum tax on the memory, it will be well to dispose of a
possible source of misunderstanding. When one states the requirements in figures,
the outcome will depend on whether one believes that it is really economical to use
one word for several different meanings or to list only words which have a unique
meaning. Since the writer rejects the first assumption, he also rejects both the *Basic*
of Ogden (850 words) and the *New Method* of West (1,500 words); but if one prefers
the alternative, one has to face the fact that far too few Anglo-American words
(not more than 1,500) satisfy one's criterion of eligibility. This means that one must
either place a restriction on the admissible semantic territory of many words cited
or list separate meanings of the same item more than once. As regards the foregoing
groups of about 150 words in all, we rarely have at our disposal single words which

---

* Ogden's *Basic English*, West's *New Method English Dictionary*, Hogben's *Essential World English*.

have only one meaning. One must either list them as two or more items (cf. FOR, p. 289) separately or have recourse to two or more long-winded constructions, as will be sufficiently clear, if it is not already, below.

At a later stage, we shall find it convenient to subdivide the groups mentioned on p. 283. Henceforth we may appropriately refer to their items as the *cement words* of our language. Since they subsume the words which we use most often, it goes without saying that they include words most liable to semantic erosion and words most liable to participate in idiomatic constructions. Hence, by definition of the latter, we are likely to meet them in situations in which their semantic credentials are void. However, their meaning is not the only consideration relevant to our task. The choice of many of them involves other issues which belong to the table manners of language rather than issues relevant to meaning as such. We therefore need to scrutinise scrupulously the eligibility of candidates to our essential recall list of 150-odd cement words both from a semantic viewpoint and with due regard to considerations of acceptable local usage with as little relevance to meaning as the local propriety of using a toothpick at meals.

Having assembled with due clarification of meaning and usage our list of cement words, the next most profitable target in our quest for self-expression with the minimum load on the memory is to list essential adjectives. This class need not include more than 250 items, and we then have at our disposal at least 55 per cent. of the words we should meet on a printed page of prose in Anglo-American or its sister languages. Appropriate choice of these involves a few issues of linguistic table-manners, e.g. *big—great, tall—high, fat—thick, thorough—intense*. What is more important is that Anglo-American adjectives are peculiarly liable to semantic erosion by metaphorical extension, especially from the physical to the mental, emotional or abstract domains. For illustrations of this, the reader may refer to the entries against *clear* and *bright* in the list on p. 281. We may here dispose our essential requirements under this heading.

To say that our essential list of now no more than 400 words accounts for about 55 per cent. of words we meet on a printed page of prose or use in a letter to a pen-friend does not mean that we have now assembled 55 per cent. of a word list to meet the minimum requirements of recall, i.e. that we need no more than about 750 words when we have added to it essential nouns and verbs. If we stick to the rule that each word should have a unique meaning, a person learning the use of Anglo-American will need at least twice as many as the figure last cited. From our viewpoint in this context, Anglo-American is, moreover, highly economical compared with any of its sister languages. *Inter alia*, it scores heavily over all of them because of the enormous class of verbs whose dictionary form is identical either with that of an adjective (e.g. *clean, blind, open, dry*) or with that of a noun (e.g. *love, praise, hate, purchase*). The number of nouns of this type is on the increase (cf. *earth, park*, etc.)

and includes two very large groups. Names of most instruments stand for their uses as verbs (e.g. *brush, comb, saw, hammer, drill, fiddle*), and names of substances or products used for covering surfaces are very commonly employable as verbs for the act of doing so (e.g. *powder, grease, carpet, tile, butter, dress*).

The foregoing remarks draw attention to a difference between Anglo-American and all its sister languages. Another way in which Anglo-American makes parsimonious demands for a vocabulary of recall is especially relevant only to the study of a Latin language. It is highly characteristic of the latter both to overload its verbs with meaning and to prohibit their breakdown into simple components. Many Anglo-American verbs of French or Latin origin, especially the class conveying the notion of movement, illustrate this forcibly. For instance, compare the following couplets of which the first component is of Romance, the second of native, origin: *depart—go away, enter—come in* or *go in, mount—go up*. On this account, one may well need for complete self-expression in French to list at least four times the 500 or even fewer verbs which suffice for use if one is learning a Teutonic language.

As regards abstract nouns, it is a salutary discipline to cut down one's requirements by relying on the use of adjectives. One Anglo-American abstraction designated TIME calls for comment because it embraces three different notions which another language may distinguish: (a) a clock reckoning, e.g. *the time was three fifteen p.m.*; (b) an interval, e.g. *during the time of Erasmus*; (c) an occasion, e.g. *at times when she had migraine*. It is fruitless to draw up a recipe for *common* nouns, i.e. names for tangible entities, because our needs are individual with respect both to what we know and to what we wish to convey. For instance, a town dweller may never need to know the difference between a *vole*, a *pine marten* and a *hogget* (yearling sheep); nor need one ever have occasion to convey the meaning of these words in writing to a resident in Melbourne. Similarly, a confirmed bachelor may be content to remain happily ignorant of names for female underwear familiar to all the ladies whose attention he successfully evades.

(i) Of the classes of words which one here designates as cement words, our first group to consider will be the auxiliaries. We define an auxiliary by one or both of two criteria: (a) it can precede the dictionary (so-called *infinitive*) form of another verb without the intervention of TO; (b) in questions and negations it does not require the DO constructions mentioned on p. 217. So defined, those of Anglo-American are as follows, but not all of them are essential.

1. BE. 2. HAVE. 3. DO. 4. CAN—COULD. 5. MUST. 6. WILL—WOULD. 7. SHALL—SHOULD. 8. USED TO. 9. OUGHT TO. 10. MAY—MIGHT. 11. LET (=PERMIT).

We have already noted (p. 217) that the use of DO as a helper in negative and interrogative constructions is peculiarly Anglo-American. It is essential to our word list, therefore, only as a synonym for *perform*. Similarly, LET is essential only in the sense that it is interchangeable with *permit*. Items 1, 2, 4, 5 and 8 call for little comment. The imperfect tense form of the Latin languages provides for USED TO. Likewise, the future or conditional tense forms of Latin languages provide for corresponding uses of WILL and SHALL. When WILL and SHALL revert to their original meanings, BE WILLING and MUST (or OUGHT TO) respectively cover their meanings. The trickiest item is 10, with two different meanings for which the sister languages may prescribe different equivalents. Thus *X may do Y* may mean:

(a) *it is possible that X will do Y;*
(b) *it is permissible for X to do Y.*

The most important qualifications to make about the mixed bag BE are that (a) German and Scandinavian languages do not employ it in the passive construction (e.g. *to be bored*); (b) Latin sister languages rely largely on reflexive and impersonal constructions in such situations.

(ii) Our next group of cement words is the pronouns and numerals. The latter, being unequivocal, call for no comment, and any grammatical primer will list them along with the former, whose semantic vagaries (p. 174) we have already touched on. In the same context, we have discussed the use of the Anglo-American pronoun ONE and its relation both to the numeral (*unity*) and to the so-called indefinite article, correct use of which is the province of grammar. In Teutonic sister-languages MAN is an alternative to EN, EIN, etc., used as a pronoun equivalent to *people*, as when one says in Anglo-American: *man wants but little here below*. To this group, side by side with the numerals, we may consign the so-called indefinite article A or AN and the negative article NO used as in *no orchids for Miss Blandish*.

(iii) As a third group of cement words, we here list the following:

1. EACH—EVERY—ALL. 2. THE WHOLE=ALL THE. 3. THE SAME. 4. OTHER. 5. ANY. 6. SOME. 7. ONLY. 8. EVEN. 9. A LITTLE (=*a small quantity*). 10. SMALL—SMALLER—SMALLEST. 11. FEW—FEWER— FEWEST. 12. MUCH—MORE—MOST. 13. MANY—MORE—MOST. 14. NEAR—NEARER—NEAREST *or* NEXT. 15. SEVERAL=A FEW (=NOT VERY MANY).

Since we have already (pp. 278, 280-281) discussed 5, 6 and 7 there is no need to say more about them. EVEN appears in the same *galère*, because we need it to distinguish between one meaning which is peculiar to ANY (=EVEN ONE) and one meaning which it shares with SOME (=EVEN A LITTLE). It is noteworthy that MUCH and MANY, unlike SMALL and FEW, have the same comparative and superlative forms. This is not true of their equivalents in Scandinavian languages.

Item 15 may cover one of the situations in which SOME conveys a nuance of meaning, if any. Often, SOME is an empty word as in: *there were (SOME) people at the bar.* We lose nothing here by liquidating it, and need seek no substitute for the unnecessary in another tongue. Since ANY and SOME offer so many pitfalls to a translator, it goes without saying that we need not list *anywhere* and *somewhere* as essential words. Why say *it may be anywhere?* It is more definite to say *I (we) do not know where it is.*

(iv) After listing FEW, MUCH, etc., it is appropriate to add without comment as *quantifying* particles:

1. TOO (*=exclusively*). 2. TOO MUCH. 3. ALSO (*=too*). 4. WHOLLY (*=quite*). 5. VERY. 6. VERY MUCH. 7. ALMOST (*=nearly*). 8. THOROUGHLY (*=well*). 9. SOMEWHAT (*=rather, quite*). 10. PREFERABLY (*=rather*).

The paranyms cited in parentheses make explicit the precise meaning of ambiguous items in this list. The need to list separately TOO and TOO MUCH, VERY and VERY MUCH is in deference to the etiquette of language, e.g. in Welsh TOO = *rhy*, TOO MUCH = *gormod*, in French VERY = *très*, VERY MUCH = *beaucoup*.

(v) We now come to a group which we can describe as simple *demonstratives*:

1. THE. 2. THIS—THESE. 3. HERE (*=in this place*). 4. THERE (*=at that place*). 5. NOW (*=at this time*). 6. THEN (*=at that time*). 7. THEREFORE (*=for that reason*). 8. THUS (*=in that way*). 9. YET (*=till now, till then*). 10. ELSEWHERE (*=in another place*). 11. LIKEWISE (*=in the same way, to the same extent*).

These raise no semantic issues not yet mentioned in connexion (p. 212) with the origin and use of 1 and 2; but they do raise issues of grammatical etiquette. Thus we may require separate forms for 2, listed in the dictionary as *pron.* or *adj.*, in accordance with whether they stand alone (cf. MINE) or precede a noun (cf. MY). Also (with verbs of motion) we may require to translate as one word:

FROM HERE (*=hence*)   TO HERE (*=hither*)
FROM THERE (*=thence*)   TO THERE (*=thither*)

It is also important to note that Anglo-American THERE enters into a large number of idiomatic constructions, such as *there is, there must be, there have been.* To render these correctly we must rely on textbooks of grammar. All that remains to say about them is that the journey is not always necessary. If we state that there are no snakes in Iceland (or Ireland), all that we convey is that snakes are not viable in Iceland (or Ireland).

(vi) It may puzzle the reader to notice the absence of THAT—THOSE in our last list. The reason is that our next group is a more mixed bag which includes forms which we need to cross-classify in traditional terms more or less definitely from a semantic viewpoint or merely in terms of the toothpick rules of discourse, as demonstrative, relative, interrogative and conjunctive pronouns or adverbs. Thus we need to consider separately their several uses both in terms of meaning, if so distinguishable, and otherwise as an issue of acceptable usage.

1. THAT (—THOSE). 2. WHO—WHOM—WHOSE—WHICH. 3. WHAT. 4. ELSEWHERE. 5. WHY. 6. HOW. 7. WHERE. 8. WHEN. 9. WHILE. 10. WHETHER.

When dealing with these items, it is by no means clear if we are or are not dealing with a semantic issue when we make allowance for more than one equivalent prescribed by the usage of a language other than as above. For instance, consider the sentence: *How do you know what word to use?* We can reconstruct it as: *What word should one use? How do you know?* Now we can here say that WHAT is clearly an interrogative pronoun, and in traditional terms, subject of *should use.* Alternatively, one may express the same meaning by: *How do you know the word which one should use?*; and here the traditionalist will say that the equivalent of WHAT is clearly a relative pronoun. Though such distinctions are trivial from a semantic viewpoint, they may be immensely important in terms of the table-manners of language; and a good bilingual dictionary will then classify the appropriate situations for use of a particular equivalent by the parenthetical abbreviations *rel. pr., interrog. pr.,* etc.

THAT is especially tricky. We have noticed that it can be: (a) demonstrative; (b) a relative pronoun on all fours with *who, whom* and *which*; (c) a conjunction introducing a so-called noun clause, as in *I know that my redeemer liveth.* So we need to provide a niche in our essential word list for at least three uses. Nor is this all. As a demonstrative it may stand alone (*who said that?*) or accompany a noun (*it's that man again*). This distinction (cf. *my* and *mine*) is important, if one wants to write or speak French correctly. As regards WHO, WHOM, WHOSE, we need to anticipate the possible need for two uses, as interrogative and as relative pronouns. We do not use WHO or WHOM before a noun, but we use WHICH interrogatively either alone or before a noun, as in *which word do you mean?* Thus grammatical etiquette may call for three entries against WHICH, two being interrogative and one being relative. WHAT can be interrogative or relative, but we may again require three equivalents, because (like WHETHER) it can introduce a so-called noun clause, as in: *you know what I mean.* When providing for WHETHER, one should bear in mind the all-too-frequent and deplorable use of IF as a substitute. We list this below only as a particle to introduce a condition. Each of the interrogative adverbs HOW,

WHY, WHERE and WHEN can also introduce a so-called noun clause, being respectively equivalent to *the way in which, the reason for which, the place in which, the time at which*. For use in this way we may have to make special provision in our abridged code for recall. WHERE, WHEN and WHILE are equivalent to relative pronouns with an accompanying preposition when replaceable by *in which, on which, at which* or *during which*, and we may play safe by translating them as such, e.g. *this is the house WHERE* (=*in which*) *Jack lived throughout that severe winter WHEN* (=*during which*) *all the pipes in the village burst*. It is important to allow for the need for separate entries to accommodate the use of WHEN, WHERE and WHILE as conjunctions introducing a so-called adverbial clause or phrase, e.g. *when in Rome, be romantic*.

(vii) The following are simple or compound prepositions, some of which, with more than one meaning, are indispensable without recourse to periphrasis. Below we list their meanings separately:

1. ABOUT (=*concerning*). 2. ABOVE. 3. ACROSS. 4. AGAINST (= *in opposition to*). 5. AGAINST (=*leaning towards*). 6. AMONG. 7. AROUND. 8. AT. 9. BECAUSE OF. 10. BEHIND. 11. BESIDE. 12. BETWEEN. 13. BEYOND. 14. BY (=*the author being*). 15. BY (=*the means being*). 16. DESPITE (=*in spite of*). 17. DURING. 18. EXCEPT. 19. FOR (=*on behalf of*). 20. FOR (=*with a view to*). 21. FOR (=*as a means of*). 22. FOR (=*in favour of*). 23. FROM. 24. INSTEAD OF. 25. INTO. 26. OF. 27. ON (=*in contact with*). 28. ON (=*upon*). 29. OUT OF (=*outside*). 30. THROUGH. 31. TO (two entries). 32. TOWARDS. 33. UNDER. 34. WITH (=*by means of*). 35. WITH (=*in the company of*). 36. WITH (=*at the home of*). 37. WITHOUT.

We here cite ABOVE in preference to *over* because one sometimes uses the latter loosely when the *mot juste* is ACROSS. Similarly, one loosely uses *by* for BESIDE. Items 19-22 do not cover all the protean uses of FOR, for which in some situations the preferred word would be 9 (*all for the love of a lady*) or 24 (*what do we use for money?*). The insertion of a third value (36) of WITH in the preceding list is to accommodate French *chez* and Scandinavian *hos*, as when one says: *staying with Fru Dahlberg*. The two entries for TO are to provide for: (a) TO as a vector opposite to FROM; (b) the empty particle coupled with the dictionary (so-called *infinitive*) form of the verb, e.g. *to make*. One German word *zu* covers both uses, but Scandinavian requires for (a) *till* (Swed.) or *til* (Dan., Norw.) and for (b) *att* (Swed.) *at* (Dan.) or *å* (Norw.). TO and WITH have idiomatic uses which are too diverse to cite. This is also true of AT and ON. The reader should note that neither specification of ON as preposition is equivalent to its adverbial use in the expression *go on* = *go onward*, but no definition of ON or of AT as applied to position on a map or a clock-reading explains why it is usual to say ON *Friday* in contradistinction to AT *Easter*. Nor does any definition of IN (e.g. *enclosed by*) in contradistinction to DURING justify the expression IN *April*. The reader who has any familiarity with French will recall that one says *à Paris* but *en Angleterre*. In Swedish one translates *in the street* by *på gatan*. A literal translation into Anglo-American (i.e. *on the street*) might be libellous if referable to a lady.

(viii) Our next items are simple conjunctions:

1. AND.   2. AS (=*in the way that*).   3. AS (*or* SO) . . . AS.   4. BECAUSE.   5. BUT (=*yet*).   6. IF (=*on condition that*).   7. OR.   8. SO. . . THAT (e.g. *so big that*).   9. THOUGH.

Of these THOUGH (=*despite the fact that*) stands in the same relation to DESPITE as WHILE (=*during the time that*) to DURING. In completing our abridged code we should carefully distinguish between *conditional* IF and *if* used where WHETHER would be the *mot juste*.

(ix) The following twenty-four items are (with one exception, 9) simple adverbial particles:

1. ABROAD.   2. AGAIN.   3. ALSO.   4. AWAY (=*off*).   5. BACK.   6. BACK-WARD.   7. FORWARD.   8. HOME (=*to one's home*).   9. AT HOME.   10. NEARLY.   11. NEVER.   12. NOT.   13. OUT.   14. PREFERABLY (=*rather*).   15. RECENTLY (=*just*).   16. SOMEWHAT.   17. SOON.   18. TO-DAY.   19. TOGETHER.   20. TO-MORROW.   21. TO-NIGHT.   22. TOO.   23. WHOLLY.   24. YESTERDAY.

Item 13 merits comment inasmuch as Scandinavian dialects prescribe different forms in accordance with whether the verb partner implies or does not imply motion.

(x) The following may require separate entries as prepositions and adverbs:

1. DOWN.   2. IN.   3. UP.

(xi) Similarly, the following may require separate entries as prepositions and conjunctions:

1. AFTER.   2. BEFORE.   3. EITHER . . . OR.   4. NEITHER . . . NOR.   5. SINCE.   6. THAN.   7. TILL (=*until*).

Of these one can use 1, 2 and 5 adverbially as respectively equivalent to *thereafter*, *previously* and *thenceforth*. SINCE is indispensable only in a *temporal* sense. Otherwise the appropriate equivalent is BECAUSE.

(xii) The last group of cement words we shall cite is labels of orientation and units of time:

1. SECOND.   2. MINUTE.   3. HOUR.   4. DAY.   5. NIGHT.   6. WEEK.
7. MONTH.   8. YEAR.   9. TOP.   10. BOTTOM.   11. MIDDLE.   12. SIDE.
13. REAR.   14. END.   15. EDGE.

16. EAST.   17. NORTH.   18. SOUTH.   19. WEST.   20. LEFT.   21. RIGHT.

22. SIDEWAYS.   23. TO AND FRO.

In making up an abridged code for recall, one should allow for the need for different adjectival (e.g. *weekly, yearly*) and noun forms of 1–21. Items 16–21 may each require separate entries as *noun, adjective* and *adverb*.

The foregoing discussion and word-list touches merely the fringe of a complete recipe for design of a minimal vocabulary of self-expression in a speech alien to one's own. It should, however, help the beginner to proceed with such a programme, and the effort should be doubly rewarding. Only by critical examination of the uses of words, each in its most unique sense if any, can one hope to acquire a lucid and economical use of one's own language as a means of communicating factual data and their formal interpretation in terms of scientific hypotheses. Only by so doing can we also prevent what is today the most widespread available instrument of inter-communication between different speech communities on all the five continents from disintegrating into a welter of dialects as different as Roumanian and French among the descendants of Imperial Latin.

QUIZ CORNER 8

Quiz 1

Bad Language

Code as below a more explicit word for the one italicised:

1. You look *so* tired. ......
2. Several *factors* intervened. ......
3. That is *just* enough. ......
4. I would *rather* go there. .18.
5. He *generally* takes sugar. .18.
6. This is *quite* nice. ......
7. *Some* people think otherwise. ......
8. He did so *for* payment. ......
9. *So* you really must come. ......
10. Prime numbers have no *factors*. ......
11. I have *just* come. ......
12. He is *always* pleasant. ......
13. I am *practically* certain. .7.
14. She is *rather* foolish. ......
15. *Apparently* she is not coming. ......
16. The theorem of Pythagoras is *generally* true of right-angled triangles. ......
17. Have you *some* tape? ......
18. It is *quite* full. .3.
19. I am not *so* tired as I look. .4.
20. Theoretically and *practically*. ......
21. Another *factor* of the situation. ......
22. I am not *particular* about such things. .29.
23. She uses it *for* trimming. ......
24. He brings his fiddle *always*. ......
25. I told you *so*. ......
26. *Apparently* to all present. ......
27. The *just* man made perfect. ......
28. Heat is a *factor* promoting expansion. ......
29. He was acting *for* his partner. ......
30. He stood *by* the bed. .27.

31. *Just* you wait.   . . . . . .
32. There is a *particular* reason.   . . . .

1. therefore	2. it	3. very
4. as	5. feature	6. recently
7. circumstances	8. exactly	9. divisors
10. at all times	11. agency	12. righteous
13. every time	14. somewhat	15. preferably
16. (empty word)	17. almost	18. commonly
19. seemingly	20. universally	21. completely
22. evidently	23. empirically	24. certain
25. as a means of	26. special	27. beside
28. with a view to	29. fussy	30. any
31. on behalf of		

Quiz 2

Preposition, Conjunction or Adverb?

Label each of the following twelve sentences as either P, C or A, to indicate the use in the sentence of the word in italics.

1a. *While* she was working, he sat and watched.   . . . .
  b. He sat and thought; *meanwhile* his task grew harder.   . . . .
  c. *During* the day, the sun grew hotter.   . . . .
2a. *Since* last summer we have had much rain.   . . . .
  b. I thought it was a dreadful play, and I have not changed my mind *since*. . . . .
  c. *Since* he hurt his arm, he has been unable to write.   . . . .
3a. *Before*, he was happy; now, he is very sad.   . . . .
  b. *Before* he had read many pages, he grew bored.   . . . .
  c. He hopes to do much *before* next summer.   . . . .
4a. Before the war he was carefree. *After*, he had completely changed. . . . .
  b. *After* the train had started, a man ran along the platform, waving his
     newspaper.   . . . .
  c. *After* one song, even the dog had had as much as he could bear.   . . . .

Now make up sentences containing: 5. *since* used as a preposition; 6. *after* used as a conjunction; 7. *before* used as an adverb.

5. ....

6. ....

7. ....